NEW HOPE FOR BINGE EATERS

NEW HOPE FOR BINGE EATERS

ADVANCES IN THE UNDERSTANDING AND TREATMENT OF BULIMIA

Harrison G. Pope, Jr., M.D.

AND

James I. Hudson, M.D.

HARPER COLOPHON BOOKS

Harper & Row, Publishers, New York
Grand Rapids, Philadelphia, St. Louis, San Francisco
London, Singapore, Sydney, Tokyo, Toronto

Grateful acknowledgment is made for permission to reprint the following:

Table on page 141 and description on page 142 from "Treatment of bulimia with antidepressants." Reprinted from *Psychopharmacology* (1982) 78: 176-179, by permission of Springer-Verlag.

Table on page 143 from "Treatment of bulimia with monoamine oxidase inhibitors" by Dr. Timothy Walsh and others. Reprinted from the December 1982 issue of *American Journal of Psychiatry* by permission of Dr. Timothy Walsh and the American Journal of Psychiatry.

Graphs on page 151 and table on pages 152–3 from the May 1983 issue of *American Journal of Psychiatry*. Reprinted by permission.

A hardcover edition of this book is published by Harper & Row, Publishers, Inc.

First HARPER COLOPHON edition published in 1985.

Designer: Helene Berinsky

Library of Congress Cataloging in Publication Data

Pope, Harrison
    New hope for binge eaters.

    1. Bulimarexia. I. Hudson, James I. II. Title.
RC552.B84P66 1984   616.85'2   83-48120
ISBN 0-06-015233-8
ISBN 0-06-091239-1 (pbk)

90 91 92 MPC 20 19 18 17 16 15 14 13 12 11 10 9 8 7 6

For Mary and Margo

Contents

Acknowledgments

More than all others, two people have supported us at every stage of our work: Dr. Jeffrey Jonas, our associate in most of our studies, and Debbye Yurgelun-Todd, our research assistant. Both have borne the frenzied pace and conflicting schedules of our multiple research projects—often running deep into evenings and weekends—throughout the past two years.

Many individuals—research scientists, therapists of many orientations, leaders of self-help groups, and others—have read and commented on our manuscript. We particularly thank Dr. Shervert Frazier, Dr. Joseph Lipinski, Dr. Margo Hudson, George Smith, Patricia Warner, Dana Atchley, Bobbie Atchley, Dr. Michael Poliakoff, and Dr. John Atchley for their advice. Each brought a unique perspective to the book and helped us to balance its views.

Our typist, Dave Lavender, tirelessly coped with our impossible deadlines and last-minute changes, as new scientific studies appeared and we incorporated them into the manuscript.

Most of all, we thank our patients with bulimia and anorexia nervosa, many of whom read the book with care and offered us detailed suggestions. Confidentiality prevents us from listing their many names, but we extend to all of them our deepest thanks for everything that we have learned.

Foreword

by Shervert H. Frazier, M.D., Professor of Psychiatry, Harvard Medical School, and Psychiatrist in Chief, McLean Hospital, Belmont, Massachusetts

Bulimia, the syndrome of compulsive binge eating and purging, together with its sister disorder, anorexia nervosa, has leaped into national awareness in the last few years. Newspaper reports, television talk shows, and magazine articles—some involving celebrities with self-professed cases of bulimia—have suddenly alerted the public to the remarkable frequency of this strange and often covert psychiatric illness. Countless authorities and commentators have offered speculations on the causes and consequences of the seeming epidemic, although few have quoted medical research to support their theories.

Bulimia is in fact hardly new; we have been aware of its presence for decades, particularly when it appeared in conjunction with anorexia nervosa. However, for many years, little was learned about its causes or treatment, as attested by the long-standing dearth of scientific studies in the field. The treatment of bulimia continued to be empirical, primarily with various sorts of psychotherapy. Occasionally these seemed to produce success, but often they achieved no consistent relief of the symptoms. And so, until recently, we have had little with which to respond to the public's increasing demand for reliable medical information.

In recent years, however, a new vista has opened in the field of eating disorders: A growing body of scientific evidence suggests that many cases of bulimia, and perhaps of anorexia nervosa as well, may be closely related to depressive illness, or to that family of disorders now referred to in psychiatry as "major affective disorder." To those of us in academic psychiatry, this has great theoretical interest; much is known from research in major affective disorder, and those research findings and techniques can now be directed at the eating disorders as well. But to those who suffer from bulimia, there is a much more immediate benefit— the possibility that their symptoms may be treated, using the medications we have been using for many years in the treatment of depression.

Drs. Harrison Pope and James Hudson have established themselves as major contributors to this exciting research. Their initial studies, together with others presented in this book, strongly suggest that we may at last be at the beginning of a major advance in the understanding and treatment of bulimia.

But the findings of this research, though rapidly spreading through scientific circles, are still largely unknown to the general public. As our scientific knowledge of bulimia has grown, the need for an authoritative account, understandable to the non-medical reader, has become obvious.

New Hope for Binge Eaters answers that need. It covers practically all of the medical findings on the subject available to date, and contains a particularly detailed description of the new studies which suggest that many cases of bulimia may now be effectively treated. As a handbook for the professional involved in the treatment of bulimic patients and their families, it should prove an invaluable source of information. But most important, for many individuals who suffer from bulimia, and for those who are close to them, this book may bring hope, and represent the first step on the path to recovery.

Preface

Bulimia has come to concern many people—not only those who suffer from the disorder, but their families and friends, therapists of many orientations who are engaged in treatment, and research scientists investigating different aspects of the problem. It is hard to speak to all of these individuals in a single book. As a result, our account is at times narrative and anecdotal, at times somewhat scientific and technical. We have begun by describing the experience of bulimia, the evidence of its surprising prevalence, and the many syndromes associated with it, all illustrated with personal accounts from our experience with patients. Starting with Chapter 5, the discussion grows more scientific: We review practically every major study of bulimia published to date, together with a fair number of the studies of anorexia nervosa as well. This review may be more detailed and exhaustive than many readers need, but others will find it essential.

Now, in the paperback edition of the book, we have had an opportunity to update the scientific findings. In the fourteen months since our book originally went to press, several new placebo-controlled double-blind studies of antidepressant medications have emerged. All have produced positive results—further reinforcing the scientific foundation upon which our book is based. In a word, antidepressant treatment of bulimia, considerd "preliminary" or "experimental" only two years ago, has now become firmly established in the medical literature. We have provided an update, at the end of Chapter 8, to describe these new studies. We have also added updates to chapters 5, 7, and 9 describing important new studies of family patterns, psychotherapy, and group therapy in anorexia nervosa and bulimia. Finally, we have added an extra question and answer at the end of Chapter 10, responding to a question frequently asked by readers of the original edition of this book.

Throughout most of chapters 9 and 10, we return to the more anecdotal format used in the beginning of the book. Only by writing a popular book that was at times technical did we feel that we could answer the requests of such a varied group of readers.

At its heart, though, this book is written for the women and men who have suffered from bulimia, for people like those whom we have seen in our offices, who have taught us more about the illness than technical studies could. If you are one of them, and even if you haven't the slightest scientific education, don't be dismayed by the technical material in the middle chapters. It is there if you want it, but you do not need it to understand that much has now been learned about bulimia, and that a new treatment is now available.

Harrison G. Pope, Jr., M.D.
James I. Hudson, M.D.

Belmont, Massachusetts
June 15, 1983

SALLY'S STORY

Even her closest friends and associates would have been unable to guess why Sally left work early one April afternoon and drove to our offices at McLean Hospital, in Belmont, Massachusetts, for her initial appointment. To the casual observer, she was a poised, attractive, rather slim, tastefully dressed woman, in her late twenties or early thirties.

Once she entered the office a different picture of her emerged. She began quickly: "I've been hearing all kinds of things about your research, but frankly, I'm afraid I may be a hopeless case. I've had this problem for almost nine years now. I've tried everything—all kinds of treatment—but nothing has helped."

Her story was familiar. As far back as her sophomore year, while a student at a prestigious women's college in Massachusetts, she had already noticed that she seemed unusually preoccupied with food. In the cafeteria line, she often stopped to study the labels on bottles of salad dressing, cans of juice, and containers of yogurt, to see how many calories each contained, often calculating and recalculating the total number of calories that she had consumed during the day. She was not at all overweight then—although at times, in the privacy of her room, she critically examined herself in the mirror and wished that she had the self-discipline to be thinner. But these feelings seemed little different from those of her friends. Perhaps, during those early years, she had been a bit more depressed than average—particularly so, she remembered, during the days just prior to her men-strual periods—but on the whole her life in the dormitory, her dates with the boys from a nearby college, her grades, her sum-mers in Maine with her family, seemed much the same as those of everyone else.

It was in her senior year that the eating binges began. During the early fall of that year, she felt despondent and unhappy with herself. With this depression came a rise in her preoccupation with food and her thoughts about wanting to lose weight. She paid more attention to her diet. But then one night, alone in her room, she suddenly found herself compulsively devouring choc-olate cookies until the entire package of sixty cookies was gone. But the craving for food continued. She rushed to the corner store to buy more supplies. Minutes later, back in her room with an entire gallon of chocolate chip ice cream, abandoning any last pretense of restraint, Sally began eating it with a tablespoon, straight from the carton. Incredibly, it was gone in twenty min-utes. Feeling sick, sedated, and disgusted with herself, she col-lapsed into her bed and slept for twelve hours.

The next morning she discovered to her horror that she had gained seven pounds. Only a strict diet, if not an outright fast, could erase what she had done. Slowly, painstakingly, over the next eight days she lost all of the dreadful weight. But toward the end of that time a strange, uneasy feeling built up inside her—and on the eighth night, it all happened again.

The second binge started a new cycle of fasting, but this time, before she had quite lost all the weight she had gained, a third binge erupted. Soon the binges settled down into a regular pat-tern, occurring every fourth or fifth night, with rigorous diets in between. Sally quickly learned to recognize the vague tension that heralded the approach of the next episode; she found her-self making elaborate plans to be alone on that evening, to stock-pile the food in advance in her room, and to guard against any possible interruption.

The cycle of binging and fasting developed its own inexorable momentum. Whatever her attempts to control it, whatever schemes she tried to interrupt it, it continued. She did not dare to confide in other girls at the school or in her boyfriend, al-though she was convinced that he must have guessed her secret from watching her sharp fluctuations of weight. When he broke up with her that winter, it seemed to confirm that he knew.

Her depression mounted. Within six months she had gained

thirteen pounds; each new binge left guilt and hopelessness in its wake. She recalled a dark morning in February, when she awakened in her room after a binge the previous night, overcome with shame and loneliness, and thought seriously, for the first time, of suicide. She even fumbled through the medicines on her bureau—aspirin, decongestants, cough medicine—wondering if enough of them could be painlessly fatal. The feeling dissipated within a few hours, but it was to return many times in the following years.

That spring came a blessing and a curse: Sally discovered how to use laxatives. At first they were an immense relief; she could purge some of the food that she ate, and no longer was forced to fast between binges. She even managed to lose ten pounds before her graduation. But before long, she had to take twenty, then fifty, and sometimes even a hundred times the usual dose to achieve an effect—and felt wasted and drained for the next twenty-four hours.

After graduating, she began her first job as a public relations consultant for a firm in Boston, and found an apartment of her own in a quiet suburb west of the city. Even though her job proved rewarding, the work atmosphere inviting, and her associates friendly, her work offered only scant relief from the tyranny of her chronic preoccupation with food. The binges occurred almost nightly, as soon as she got home from work. Soon she found herself spending eighty to a hundred dollars a week on food, and another twenty or thirty on laxatives. Her social life dissolved. She no longer had a boyfriend, but it didn't matter; food seemed to occupy all of her thoughts. She developed a repertoire of excuses to extricate herself from evening social obligations so as to be free to go home and binge. Arriving at her local supermarket, she often felt compelled to explain as she was checking out that she was throwing a party, in order to justify a shopping cart filled with ice cream, cookies, and other carbohydrate-rich foods. Then she usually drove several miles to a large pharmacy in a neighboring town; the clerk in the local drugstore had noticed her too many times buying laxatives.

"There was no one to whom I could talk about it," she said. "I didn't know anyone else who ever had these experiences, or at least admitted to them. I thought I must just be weird; I'd never heard the word *bulimia*. There wasn't any publicity about it in those days."

From time to time, Sally resolved to fight her affliction, forcing herself to go without binging. But within two or three days, intolerable tension and anxiety would begin to build, her resolve would collapse, and the cycle would begin again.

After countless attempts, Sally eventually learned to make herself vomit. Vomiting was difficult at first, but it liberated her from her dependence on laxatives, and made it easier for her to lose weight. In fact, she soon lost another fifteen pounds, to the point where she dipped several pounds below the lowest weight she had attained in college. Even then, she still found herself wondering, many times a day, if she looked fat. Often she would forgo breakfast and eat only sparingly at lunch—but this only increased the ferocity of the nightly binges. Recognizing this, she tried deliberately to eat more during the day, but could not bring herself to do so; the thought of consuming even a few hundred calories, without the option of vomiting, aroused too much anxiety.

Despite this, she managed to advance at work, fulfill her few social obligations, and maintain an unblemished exterior. She even began dating, but her sexual drive, she recalled, was almost nil; ninety-nine percent of her thoughts revolved around food.

It was nearly five years after the onset of the bulimic symptoms that Sally finally sought out counseling.

"I would have seen someone sooner," she said, "but I didn't know where I could find someone who could possibly understand my problem. Then I learned the name of a psychologist who had seen a friend of mine at work, and I decided to give it a try.

"At first, I was embarrassed even to describe my problem to him. But he proved to be a very warm and understanding person, and he quickly put me at ease. After I had seen him only a few times, I learned a number of things about myself—that I had constantly tried to be perfect in my family, in my schoolwork, and in my appearance. It seemed to make a lot of sense. But I still binged. The therapist tried hard to work with me, but I was never able to gain much control. I felt like a failure."

Sally continued seeing him once a week, sometimes twice, for more than a year. Finally she stopped, not because she questioned the value of the sessions, but because the expense seemed too great for her to manage. Little did she realize the new expense that awaited her: a dentist discovered that the enamel on her teeth was seriously eroded as a result of her vomiting. He estimated that the work required would cost a minimum of two thousand dollars. The news stunned her, but it did not stop the binges.

A few months later, she experienced a period of new and unfamiliar symptoms: strange attacks of anxiety began to strike her, seemingly at random, several times a week. She described one such episode that occurred while she was riding to work on the train: A sudden feeling of dread came over her; her heart raced, her hands tingled, and she gasped for air. Something horrible seemed about to happen—as if she were about to have a heart attack, or suddenly go crazy. Her only thought was to find some escape, someplace to hide. The attack faded over the course of half an hour; she hastily got off the train in Boston, shaken but able to get to work. For months afterward she drove her car to work, fearing that another trip on the train might trigger a similar experience. But the attacks continued; more and more she sought the safety of her apartment when not at work. Finally, she decided to consult a psychiatrist.

"I never got the feeling that he really understood my problems. After only two sessions, he prescribed some large orange pills that made me feel like a zombie even when I took only half the prescribed amount. He called them 'major tranquilizers.' I could barely get out of bed in the morning, and I walked around feeling dazed and uninterested in everything going on around me.

"The pills did nothing for the anxiety attacks, and they seemed to make the eating binges worse. I complained to the doctor, but he felt that I should continue to take them, even though I could not understand his explanation of what they were supposed to do. I finally stopped taking them on my own, and stopped seeing him soon afterward."

Sally's medication had probably been one of the phenothiazines—a family of drugs designed to treat psychotic symptoms such as delusions and hallucinations. Although Sally had displayed none of these symptoms, it was not surprising to hear that someone had prescribed a phenothiazine for her; these powerful drugs, with numerous side effects, are sometimes prescribed for syndromes in which they are valueless, based on the questionable assumption that they are effective for ordinary anxiety or depression.

But after her unfortunate encounter with the psychiatrist

something good finally happened. Sally heard of a self-help organization dedicated to the problem of eating disorders. She found the organization filled with women who told stories very much like her own. Soon she joined a group workshop. Talking with the other group members gave her immense relief and new resolve, for the first time in years. Her self-esteem improved; no longer did she feel quite so ashamed. In a bold move, she even described the binges—at least in part—to her boyfriend. He seemed to understand, and, contrary to her fears, did not seem alienated by her confession. In fact, they grew closer, and six months later they became engaged.

But despite her release from shame and isolation, Sally found that the binges stubbornly persisted—and the morning depressions that followed them remained devastating. Most of the other women in her group admitted that they still binged as well; only one seemed to have freed herself from the symptoms. Like Sally, some wondered aloud if they would ever be liberated from their compulsion; they spoke of successive experiences with three, four, or five different courses of treatment, with many different sorts of therapists. Several of the group members described positive and rewarding experiences in therapy—but they were still binging.

Sally concluded her story:

"I've got to keep trying. Cliff and I plan to get married in September. It's been nine years now, and I'm still binging three or four times a week—never less than once a week even during the best periods. I can't stand it anymore; I'm tired of spending my life constantly obsessed with food; I'm tired of making myself throw up; I'm tired of wrecking my body."

With each passing month, more and more patients like Sally come to our offices, and to the offices of other professionals around the country. They tell stories of years of uncontrollable binge eating—sometimes unknown to even their closest friends—accompanied by depression, anxiety, and suicidal feelings. Often their occupational, social, and sexual lives have been eroded as a result of their all-consuming preoccupation with food. With growing desperation, as one treatment after another has failed, they come, as Sally did, torn between hope and skepticism, afraid to believe that any treatment could possibly be successful. Some are well informed about bulimia; others are the victims of fanciful ideas or frank misinformation. Many never reach the offices at all. For every Sally who seeks professional help, there may be five, ten, or even twenty others who covertly suffer from uncontrollable eating binges—perhaps not even knowing that their syndrome is a recognized illness, for which effective treatments are now being developed. It appears that bulimia is reaching epidemic proportions in this country, and probably around the world. But it is a secret epidemic, and we in our offices see only a tiny portion of those who suffer from it.

Fortunately, new research suggests that bulimia, unlike some other epidemic illnesses, can now often be treated rapidly. Thus, it becomes all the more tragic that so many people—numbering into the millions in the United States alone—may suffer unnecessarily, unaware that improved treatment is available. This book attempts to reach some of these people—and the many others who know and care about them.

WHAT IS BULIMIA?

Sally's story may sound familiar—you or someone you know may have experienced similar symptoms. But what constitutes mere heavy eating and what constitutes true bulimia? When does a bad habit become an actual psychiatric disorder? Of course, there is no definitive answer to this question, but we have designed a small quiz, based on our experience with actual bulimic patients, which may give you some idea of where you lie on the scale of eating patterns. If you are uncertain about how to answer some of the questions, make your best guess: Most of the phenomena described in the questions will be explained in detail later in this chapter.

BINGE EATING QUIZ

	Frequently	Occasionally	Rarely or Never
1. Do you experience eating binges in which you consume large quantities of calorie-rich foods, usually in the space of less than 2 hours? (If you answer "rarely or never," skip to question 7; score questions 2 to 6 as zero.)	☐	☐	☐
2. Do you tend to binge on high-calorie, easily ingested foods that require no preparation, such as candy, ice cream, etc.?	☐	☐	☐

3. Do you try to be inconspicuous during binges, so that others will not notice your eating? ☐ ☐ ☐

4. Do the eating binges ever go on without stopping until your stomach hurts too much to eat any more? ☐ ☐ ☐

5. Do you ever feel depressed or down on yourself after an eating binge? ☐ ☐ ☐

6. Have you ever had suicidal thoughts after an eating binge? ☐ ☐ ☐

7. Do you ever feel that you've lost control and cannot stop once you've started eating? ☐ ☐ ☐

8. Do you ever eat foods without preparing them in the usual way—such as eating dough without baking it, or eating canned frosting or maple syrup directly from the container—because you cannot delay the satisfaction of eating them? ☐ ☐ ☐

9. Have you ever felt that your eating pattern was abnormal? ☐ ☐ ☐

10. Do you find yourself thinking continuously about food for the entire day? ☐ ☐ ☐

11. Do you find yourself continuously preoccupied with your weight throughout the day? ☐ ☐ ☐

12. Have you ever experienced rapid weight fluctuations of greater than 10 pounds as a result of alternating binge eating and fasting? ☐ ☐ ☐

13. Have you ever used pills such as diet pills or diuretics (water pills) in an attempt to control your weight? ☐ ☐ ☐

14. Have you ever used large amounts of laxatives to lose weight after eating? ☐ ☐ ☐

15. Have you ever deliberately made yourself vomit after eating in order to lose weight? ☐ ☐ ☐

SCORING

Allow 2 points for each response of "frequently," 1 point for each response of "occasionally," and 0 for a response of "rarely or never."

Score of 0–7: The odds are low that you have a serious eating disorder. Your behavior is probably within the normal range for Americans.

8–15: Your eating patterns are probably abnormal, and there is a definite possibility that you have bulimia. You should read the next several chapters in detail in order to decide whether you should consult a psychiatrist or try one of the treatments described in this book.

16–23: Your eating patterns are definitely abnormal, and you probably do have bulimia. There is a good chance that your eating symptoms can be successfully treated with antidepressant medications by a psychiatrist, as described in this book.

24–30: You almost unquestionably suffer from bulimia. You should definitely consult a psychiatrist and seriously consider treatment with one of the medications described in this book.

Now that you have a rough approximation of what constitutes bulimia, let us go through the symptoms in more detail, using as our starting point the diagnostic criteria proposed by the American Psychiatric Association in 1980.

The American Psychiatric Association Recognizes Bulimia

Although bulimia probably has existed for thousands of years— as illustrated, perhaps, by the binge eating and vomiting of the Romans—it was not until 1903 (as best as we have been able to discover) that it was first described in modern medical terms. The French psychiatrist Pierre Janet, in his famous book *Les Obsessions et la Psychasthénie*,[1] described a young woman, Nadia, who developed compulsive eating binges, many of them in secret. We will tell Nadia's story, and others, in detail in Chapter 5; suffice it to say that for nearly eighty years afterward, bulimia was not formally recognized as a psychiatric syndrome in itself, although it was described in increasing numbers of patients. It was not until 1980, when the American Psychiatric Association published the new third edition of its *Diagnostic and Statistical Manual of Mental Disorders*,[2] that bulimia was at last formally listed as a psychiatric diagnosis.

One of the great advantages of *DSM*-III (as the manual is called for short) is that it provides explicit criteria for diagnosing each of the psychiatric disorders. Some have argued that such explicit criteria are dehumanizing, that they ignore the actual feelings and depth of experience described by those who suffer from psychiatric syndromes. But although this, of course, is true to some extent, the *DSM*-III criteria have proved a blessing to psychiatric researchers, since they help to ensure that we all mean the same thing when we talk to one another about a given psychiatric condition. For example, researchers in California who publish a paper on "20 patients meeting *DSM*-III criteria for bulimia" can be reasonably sure that they are studying the same sort of patients as researchers in Massachusetts who are using *DSM*-III to define their patient groups. So although explicit diagnostic criteria cannot help but miss many of the human aspects of the story, they provide us with an invaluable base from which to start our research. Here, then, are the *DSM*-III criteria for bulimia:

A. Recurrent episodes of binge eating (rapid consumption of a large amount of food in a discrete period of time, usually less than two hours).
B. At least three of the following:
   1. consumption of high-caloric, easily ingested food during a binge
   2. inconspicuous eating during a binge
   3. termination of such eating episodes by abdominal pain, sleep, social interruption, or self-induced vomiting
   4. repeated attempts to lose weight by severely restrictive diets, self-induced vomiting, or use of cathartics or diuretics
   5. frequent weight fluctuations greater than ten pounds due to alternating binges and fasts
C. Awareness that the eating pattern is abnormal and fear of not being able to stop eating voluntarily.
D. Depressed mood and self-deprecating thoughts following eating binges.
E. The bulimic episodes are not due to Anorexia Nervosa or any known physical disorder.

These criteria have some limitations; for example, they do not specify how frequently the binges must occur to qualify for the diagnosis of bulimia. Also, they do not permit bulimia to be diagnosed in the presence of anorexia nervosa, although both disorders frequently coexist. But in general, we have found the criteria accurately descriptive. In fact, when we have shown the criteria to some of our patients, they have exclaimed, "Why, that's an exact description of me. How did they know?" Many are shocked and relieved to discover that they are not alone.

Some illustrations will convey what these symptoms can be like.

What Is a Binge?

A binge, according to *DSM*-III, is "rapid consumption of a large amount of food in a discrete period of time." A correct description, certainly. But only a personal story can begin to portray the severity that real binges may achieve. One of our patients, a twenty-one-year-old college student named Susan, vividly described the experience:

It would start to build in the late morning. By noon, I'd know I had to binge. I would go out, almost driven like a machine, to the supermarket down the block and buy a gallon, or maybe even two gallons, of maple-walnut ice cream and a couple of packages of fudge brownie mix—enough to make seventy-two brownies, at least according to the package. I would always be convinced that I was just getting the mix to make brownies for my roommates, and I always swore to myself that I would eat only one or two brownies myself.

On the way home, the urge to binge would get stronger and stronger. I could hardly drive my car because I couldn't think about anything except food. There was a doughnut shop that I passed on the way home. Almost always I'd stop the car, buy a dozen doughnuts, and start munching on them even before I was walking out the door. On the way home I invariably finished all twelve doughnuts.

I'd hurry up the apartment stairs with the urge for more binging growing stronger by the minute. Still, I'd keep myself under the illusion that I was making brownies for my roommates. I'd hastily mix up the brownie mix and get the brownies in the oven, usually managing to eat a fair amount of the mix myself as I was going along. Then, while they were cooking, I'd hit the ice cream. Only by constantly eating ice cream could I bear the delay until the brownies came out of the oven. Sometimes I'd finish the whole gallon even before the brownies were done, and I'd take the brownies out of the oven while they were still baking. At any rate, I'd start eating brownies, even though by this time I was feeling sick, intending to stop after two or three. Then it would be five or six. Pretty soon, I'd have put away fifteen or twenty of the brownies, and then I'd be overcome with embarrassment. What if one of my roommates were to get home and see that I had eaten *twenty* brownies! The only way to disguise it, obviously, was to finish the other fifty-two brownies myself, wash the pan, and clean everything up so that no one would know what had happened.

Seventy-two brownies later, the depression would begin to hit. I'd go to the bathroom, stick my finger down my throat, and make myself throw up. I was so good at it that it was almost automatic—no effort necessary, just instant vomiting, over and over until there was nothing coming out of my stomach except clear pale-green fluid.

And then it would be over. I'd be sitting alone in the apartment. The sun would have set and there'd be darkness outside. No one to talk to, no one to turn to. I'd sit there and think, You idiot, you disgusting idiot, why did you do that? And I'd swear I'd not do it again. But I knew in my heart that the cycle would repeat itself the next day, and the next, and the next.

Many binge eaters, like Susan, describe an almost clocklike daily cycle in which the urge to binge rises to a peak at the same time every afternoon or evening. This type of daily cycle may be a form of what is called *diurnal variation*. Many biological events in the body, such as body temperature and the secretion of hormones by various glands, run on such a twenty-four-hour cycle. And interestingly enough, in some psychiatric illnesses, such as manic-depressive illness, diurnal variation may be a dramatic feature, the symptoms rising and falling in a daily rhythm. In fact, the diurnal cycle in bulimia was one of the observations that suggested to us that bulimia might be a biological illness; psychological factors alone were unlikely to produce symptoms that occurred with such regularity.

Although evenings are the most common times for binges, some patients have described binges occurring primarily in the dead of the night. As one described it:

I'd go to bed, having successfully made it through the day without binging. But it would be hard to fall asleep. Usually I'd have a couple of drinks, maybe three. Finally I'd fall asleep for a few hours. Then the awakening would come at 2 or 3 A.M., and there would be nothing in my mind but food. I'd stumble downstairs and eat anything and everything I could find. Sometimes there wouldn't be enough in the refrigerator and I'd invade the freezer. I'd put frozen pastry dough under hot water to try to thaw it, and gobble it down half-thawed. Only when I was completely bloated would I be capable of going back to bed. I'd sleep the rest of the night as soundly as if I'd been drugged.

Can't Eat Just One

As the above accounts reveal, there is a strikingly compulsive, automatic quality to the binges: Once under way, they are unstoppable. We all know the feeling of "not being able to eat just one," be it with potato chips, peanuts, doughnuts, crackers—whatever our special weakness. But after a certain point, the normal individual is able to stop—reluctantly, perhaps, knowing that too many such morsels are fattening, or because it's too long a trip from the TV set to fetch a new supply. Even the most controlled eaters will occasionally permit themselves a jumbo banana split with whipped cream, nuts, and cherries. But this "binge" ends voluntarily. There is little compulsion to order another banana split, and another, and another, or to rush off to the nearest supermarket for more high-calorie, easily ingested foods.

In bulimia, the normal shutoff mechanisms fail, almost as if some piece of circuitry had been miswired in the brain. And so the binge continues unchecked until it is terminated by some external force, such as (in *DSM*-III's words) abdominal pain, sleep, social interruption, or self-induced vomiting. Before the binge is over, the total food consumption may be staggering. Drs. James Mitchell, Richard Pyle, and Elke Eckert, working at the University of Minnesota, calculated that an average binge goes on for 1.18 hours and adds up to 3,415 calories before it has run its course.[3] Among the forty patients they studied, some described binges lasting as long as eight hours and reaching 11,500 calories in a single sitting. And since most of the patients resorted to self-induced vomiting, they were able—and often felt compelled—to binge more than once in the same day. A few described consumption of 50,000 calories per day (ten binges of 5,000 calories each), the equivalent of what some people eat in an entire month.

Such habits can become expensive. We have seen patients who spent more than $100 a day on food, and who found themselves stealing food from supermarkets because the need to binge outstripped their incomes. "It was unimaginable to me that I was becoming a common thief," one of our patients said. "I had a religious upbringing in an upper-class home in a lovely neighborhood. No one in my family had gotten more than a parking ticket. And yet there I was, risking jail, like an addict needing to get heroin. I couldn't stop."

People who don't have bulimia themselves, and have not closely observed or lived with someone who has the syndrome, have trouble believing that it can be so uncontrollable. Often they exhort the binge eater to learn some control or to make more of an effort to stop, and they become angry and frustrated when the symptoms refuse to go away. A young woman, Jennifer, hospitalized for treatment of her bulimia, described the pain of dealing with people who did not understand her inability to control her compulsion:

I was on a ward where they had never seen any other patients with bulimia. Of the other forty patients on the ward, most had depressions, or schizophrenia, or other things like that. I tried to explain to the nurses that they had to keep me out of the kitchen. They just said, "Well, if we deliberately keep you out of the kitchen, you'll never learn to control it by yourself, will you?" I told them that I'd tried to control it by myself for seven years, in every way I knew how, but that didn't convince them.

Before I was in the hospital, I used to buy laxatives and take between fifty and a hundred of them right after a binge so I wouldn't gain weight. But in the hospital I wasn't able to get laxatives, so when I got into the kitchen and binged, I had no way to get rid of the weight. I was 104 pounds when I came into the hospital, and after three weeks I was up to 128.

I got desperate. I begged them to watch me and keep me out of the kitchen. They made a token effort to watch me, but, of course, when the urge came on, I just found myself becoming more and more sneaky in order to elude them. "Come and tell us when you feel the urge to binge," they said. "The only way you'll learn to control it is if you talk about the feelings when they come on." I tried, but it was impossible. When you get the urge to binge, the last thing you're going to do is to go talk to somebody, knowing that that will cut off your chances to get to the food.

Then a new patient was admitted and they had to rearrange the rooms. They moved me to the room right across from the kitchen! I begged them to move me to any other room, anywhere, so that it wouldn't be so easy for me to sneak in there. I told them it was like opening up a bar across the corridor from an alcoholic.

"You're being manipulative again, Jennifer," they told me. My doctor came and told me that I was deliberately making an issue over this in order to "split" the hospital staff so that I could get them fighting with each other over whether to move my room or not.

I must have spent half the day crying. I don't think I was being paranoid, but it seemed that they all hated me, especially the female staff members, most of whom were overweight. They blamed me for not getting better, claimed that I was putting no effort into my treatment program, and gave up any attempt to keep me out of the kitchen.

The shock came in the sixth week, when I got on the scale and found I weighed 143. I had resolved once that I would commit suicide if I ever went over 140. I went into my room and cried with desperation. Then one of the nurses—one of the nice ones—came in and wondered why I was crying. "You're not overweight," she said comfortingly. "You look fine at 143." She had no idea what that figure on the scale did to me, how terrifying it was to me to be 143. Sure, I knew it was irrational to be so afraid, but that made no difference. It would be like taking somebody with terrible claustrophobia, locking them in an elevator with the lights turned off, and then lecturing them that they shouldn't be so nervous and should just start making an effort to control the fear.

That night I escaped from the hospital. It was in the middle of winter and I had no coat and only about four dollars on me. I had just binged, so I ran to the drugstore on the corner next to the hospital, spent the entire four dollars on laxatives, and took them all.

Then I saw one of the aides who worked on my ward. I knew if he saw me he'd know I'd escaped, since I wasn't supposed to be off the ward. I darted out of the drugstore and leaped into the back seat of a car stopped at a traffic light with a young woman driving it. "There's a drunk man chasing me!" I yelled. The woman gasped and promptly drove us away. She took me to her apartment.

I called the hospital, but I didn't tell them where I was. I couldn't go back. They would have interpreted my escape as the ultimate manipulation, as final proof that I was "not invested in my treatment program," as they would put it.

Finally I remembered that I had heard about a self-help organization for people with binge eating and anorexia nervosa and other problems like that. I called their number and miraculously someone was there. She was a very kindly older woman and she drove into the city and picked me up. At first she tried very hard to persuade me to go back to the hospital, but as I told her my story, I could see that she began to relent. She had a daughter who had been hospitalized for bulimia and depression and I could tell that she knew what I was feeling. It was such a relief to have someone who knew, who could understand that it was beyond my control, who could understand that I was trying as hard as I could.

The next day I called up the hospital again, and they agreed to discharge me "AMA," as they called it—"against medical advice." And so there I was, free after two months, with forty pounds to lose, feeling worse than when I began.

Such stories are distressingly common among the patients we have seen. Like Jennifer, many have remarked that being misunderstood is almost worse than the disease itself; they have endured years of exhortations, from well-meaning parents, friends, counselors, psychiatrists, to "learn control" over their uncontrollable symptoms, and faced mounting impatience and anger when they protested that they were trying their hardest, to no avail. "Only one thing ever worked for me," said one of our patients. "I was living with my boyfriend, and when I'd start binging and I got halfway into it, I'd finally force myself to yell, 'Chuck, Chuck, help me! Stop me!' And then Chuck would come barreling in, rip the food out of my hands, lock my arms to my sides, and drag me out of the kitchen."

This lack of control is a hallmark of bulimia. Indeed, it is even more severe than is admitted by many bulimic patients themselves. We have seen a number of patients who claimed, with great pride, that they had conquered their illness, mastered their urge to binge—and an equal number of patients who blamed themselves entirely for their relapses, crediting the symptoms to their immaturity, or failure to handle life stresses, or perfectionism, or need for love. After hearing many such stories, it appeared that what we were seeing was usually the spontaneous process of exacerbation and remission of the illness itself. But for our patients, it was difficult to admit that the changes—for better or for worse—were merely spontaneous. After all, none of us wants to believe that we are pawns of Nature, subject to her whims, with symptoms that rise and fall beyond our control. It is only human to concoct explanations for why we are feeling better or feeling worse. The explanations, however plausible and attractive they may be, may do little to counteract the symptoms, but they're comforting, at least.

Such is the case with bulimia, as with countless other psychiatric and medical conditions. In talking to our bulimic patients, when we tried to factor out this very human, but fallible, need to explain the fluctuations of the symptoms, the actual lack of voluntary control, the autonomy of the symptoms, became even more graphically clear.

It was this autonomy, like the phenomenon of diurnal variation mentioned earlier, that again made us suspect that bulimia must be based on some biological abnormality, and not purely on psychological factors. But we will return to that later.

Bulimia and Weight

If binges are so hard to control, do bulimic patients get fat? Many people are surprised to learn that most of our patients are close to normal weight—although they experience very abnormal *fluctuations* of weight from their cycle of binging and purging, often as much as ten pounds in a few days or even hours.

However, a sizable minority of bulimic patients are well below normal weight; at some point in their lives, many of these patients lost more than 25% of their original weight, and thus qualified for a diagnosis of anorexia nervosa. Depending on the population studied, anywhere between 10% and 50% of bulimic individuals will have a past or current history of anorexia nervosa. We will discuss the close relationship between bulimia and anorexia nervosa in Chapter 4.

What about the other extreme—binge eaters who become obese? We have seen few such patients, and little is known about them. This is particularly surprising, given that early accounts of binge eating often associated it with weight gain; in fact, the first contemporary American description of bulimia, in 1959, was offered by Dr. Albert Stunkard,[4] one of the world's foremost authorities on obesity. Perhaps one reason for our lack of knowledge in the area is that obese individuals with bulimia may tend to appear at the offices of professionals specializing in obesity, and thus are less often seen by other mental health professionals.

We do have a few pieces of data, however. Researchers at Duke University found that 31% of obese subjects reported eating binges.[5] A study at the University of Maryland found that 55% of obese subjects reported moderate binge eating; an additional 23% reported severe problems with binge eating.[6] However, it is difficult to be certain how these figures compare with those obtained in normal-weight subjects. For example, in our survey of three student populations, presented in the next chapter, we found that more than a third of students reported eating binges. However, only a fraction of this group met the *DSM*-III criteria for bulimia. By analogy, then, it seems likely that many of the obese individuals studied at Duke or Maryland did not have true bulimia.

In short, we suspect that only a minority of obese individuals have bulimia and, conversely, that only a minority of bulimic individuals are obese. However, this is certainly an area requiring further study, particularly to ensure that obese individuals with bulimia are correctly diagnosed and treated.

Binging and Sex

Bulimia would be enough of a problem if it affected only eating and weight. But it may have sweeping effects on many other aspects of life, particularly on such daily rhythms as sleep, energy, and mood. And of all the functions of the body and the brain, one of those that is most exquisitely vulnerable to disruption is the sex drive. We began routinely to ask our patients about this, and almost always got the same answer: "My sex drive? What sex drive? Sex has just gone by the wayside. I'm thinking about food all the time. I don't have time to think about sex. I haven't gone out with anyone in ages. There's really no opportunity. Besides, I feel so unlovable, I hate myself the way I am and just don't want to be involved with anyone else now. It's a physical thing, too. I never fantasize about sex the way I used to. My hormones must be out of balance, because I only get my periods occasionally and I was always regular before."

Bulimia is usually coupled with a drastic decrease in sexual desire, or libido. While psychological factors may contribute to this, we believe it may be primarily a physiological effect. This is because patients with depressive illness experience the same kind of decrease in libido, and, as you will read in subsequent chapters, many of the physiological abnormalities found in depressive illness are also found in bulimia. Further evidence of a physiological role in the decreased libido of bulimic patients is the fact that they often have irregular menstrual cycles, pointing to disruption of the pattern of sex-hormone secretion.[7]

Of course, there are also definite psychological factors in bulimia that affect sexual functioning. The obsession with food leaves little time to think about other aspects of life, as illustrated in the account above. And the person with bulimia characteristically feels demoralized and down on him/herself—not so much incapable of giving love, but unlovable. More than one of our patients has remarked, "How could anyone love me the way I am, with this horrible compulsion?" They feel worthless and flawed, and often fear lest anyone become closely involved with them and learn their terrible secret.

Then there are the social aspects of sexual functioning. In order to be sexually active, one must enjoy being with others in social situations. But, as described in Sally's story, and again in Chapter 4, a number of people with bulimia often develop a fear of social situations, and occasionally even fear leaving their homes. More commonly, less and less time is spent with others as the compulsion to binge eat becomes more and more dominant.

It is this domination, this tyranny of food and weight obsessions, that becomes the central feature of bulimia—particularly in those patients who have severe cases.

The Tyranny of Obsessions

Psychiatric disorders may or may not cause distress to the patient. We have names for this: An *ego-syntonic* disorder is something we don't mind having (although society may mind it very much); an *ego-dystonic* disorder is one that causes us distress—we would like to be rid of it.

Many forms of drug abuse, sexual perversion, and antisocial personality disorder, to give some examples, can be ego-syntonic. Such patients rarely appear at the psychiatrist's doorstep demanding to be changed; indeed, they often become rather annoyed with anybody who proposes to overhaul their characters. Even psychotic symptoms may be ego-syntonic. The patient who believes he is Jesus Christ will become quite irritated when we approach him with large orange pills to quell his delusions; after all, being the Messiah is more fun than taking antipsychotic drugs. On the other hand, such disorders as depression, phobias, and panic attacks are almost invariably ego-dystonic; few patients would pass up the chance to be relieved of them.

On this scale, severe bulimia must rank as one of the most profoundly ego-dystonic disorders that we have witnessed in all psychiatry. We have seen few other patients with such manifest suffering and with such a desperate desire to be freed from their illness. For many, perhaps the most unpleasant aspect of their syndrome is not the binges themselves but the chronic obsessions about food and weight that accompany them. As one woman put it, "I'd say that about ninety-eight percent of all the thoughts in my head, from the moment I wake up until the moment I go to bed, are about food, binging, or about my weight. On a good day, when I'm feeling really happy and things in my life are going really well, it might drop to ninety-five percent."

Like the binges themselves, the obsessions cannot be shut off. The patient recognizes that they are unreasonable, acknowledges that they are grossly exaggerated, but feels them as an uncontrollable force. "When I try to turn them off, and deliberately make myself think of something else," said one patient, "anxiety starts to build up until I capitulate, and my mind falls back into the groove of thinking about food again."

The tyranny of the obsessions may be incapacitating. We have seen patients who weighed themselves forty times a day. Between weighings, they obsessed about whether there might be some slight error in the scale, or perhaps some anomaly of the humidity, which might cause it to register a shade lower than the true weight, or some angle of the light that caused them to slightly misread the dial.

Calories may become an unremitting preoccupation. One patient described frequent fears that a few grains of sugar might be clinging to an unwashed spoon. Another patient, hospitalized for treatment of her bulimia, worried herself sick over the possibility that someone had inadvertently put ordinary salad dressing in the diet-salad-dressing bottle. When we performed a placebo-controlled study of the medication imipramine for treatment of bulimia (to be described later), two of our subjects began to obsess about the fact that the placebo pills were filled with lactose; they could not rid themselves of the fear that they would receive placebos, and that this minute amount of sugar might cause them to put on weight.

Arguing with the obsessions is futile. The patient feels them as profoundly ego-dystonic, knows that they are absurdly irrational, but cannot make them go away. Reassurance from a doctor or a friend may banish them momentarily, but they are back in a minute or two, as soon as the reassuring voice has stopped.

With this background, one can begin to imagine the misery of an illness that can cause someone to gain ten or twelve pounds in the space of an hour. Many of our patients could hardly find the words to describe their horror when they experienced their first binges and then stepped on the scale. Few of them knew how to use laxatives or self-induced vomiting when they started binging; the only way to lose the fearsome weight was by the most rigorous dieting or outright fasts. As described in the criteria of *DSM*-III, rapid weight fluctuations of more than ten pounds are common in the experience of most bulimic patients. Many individuals, particularly those who do not purge after their binges, develop a cycle of three to seven days: They binge, gaining anywhere from six to fifteen pounds, then virtually starve themselves for several days in order to make the dreaded pounds go away. As they begin to approach their base-line weight level, their mounting uneasiness, anxiety, and craving for food becomes intolerable; another binge is triggered, and the cycle begins again. Often, feelings of depression rise and fall in synchrony with the binges, with depression peaking during the twelve to twenty-four hours after the binge, gradually falling to a tolerable level over the ensuing days, and then peaking again.

Discovering how to purge—with huge doses of laxatives, by self-induced vomiting, or, more rarely, with diuretics—often comes as a transient relief. Said one of our patients:

> I knew that other girls vomited, but I never could seem to do it myself. I'd stick my finger down my throat, do everything I could, but it never seemed to work. Finally, one night, after a particularly heavy binge, I felt sick to my stomach and I was able to get it started. It was disgusting, but at the same time it was a wonderful relief; I was instantly liberated from all the awful food I'd stuffed in my stomach, and I knew I wouldn't have to starve myself the next day. Gradually, I got so good at vomiting that I didn't even have to think about it. It became so automatic that I'd sometimes vomit after ordinary meals when I didn't even want to.

Laxatives, particularly phenolphthaleins (such as Ex-Lax and Correctol) or even castor oil, become the mainstay of many of those who cannot make themselves vomit. "It says on the package that you're supposed to take one of those little chocolate squares to get an effect," explained one patient. "I used to take fifteen or twenty of them at first, but then I started getting immune to them and I'd have to take at least a hundred. My laxative bill reached fifty dollars a week. I would walk miles to go to different drugstores so that no one druggist would realize how many boxes of laxatives I was buying."

Purging is a relief, but rarely a lasting one. Often it simply enables one to binge more frequently; more hours of time, and far more money, are poured into constant binging and purging rituals throughout the week. Heavy vomiting and laxative abuse may rapidly cause electrolyte imbalances and other medical complications (discussed below), leading to chronic fatigue, malaise, and other symptoms. And however effective the vomiting or laxatives may be, however nicely they help the individual to maintain his or her weight, they do nothing to purge the endless food and weight obsessions, or to ease the depression that follows on the heels of the binges.

These are the tribulations that are not revealed by any set of diagnostic criteria or by dry scientific treatises; they can be appreciated only from direct experience with those who have themselves suffered from the syndrome. As we talked to our first patients, we were astonished at how many of them had become so depressed that they had tried to commit suicide. As our research continued, we discovered that forty-seven of our first 136 subjects had made at least one major suicide attempt during their lifetimes.

With greater experience, these figures no longer seem astonishing; indeed, we have found ourselves wondering how many others may have made successful suicide attempts, and never reached our offices. We have even questioned how many unexplained suicides—particularly in young, attractive, apparently successful women—might represent undiagnosed, untreated, "closet" cases of bulimia. Afflicted with a bizarre disorder, tyrannized by chronic obsessions and cycling depression, unable or afraid to reveal their symptoms to others, they may have seen suicide as the only remaining exit from their prison.

One of our patients, a poised and sophisticated young woman and a brilliant student at a prestigious university near Boston, was among those who came to the brink of a successful suicide in a bleak moment during a nighttime binge:

It was always the same. I'd be unable to fall asleep; I'd toss and turn as thoughts of food and binging danced through my mind. I'd think, This time I won't let it happen! But at the thought of preventing myself from binging, I'd be gripped with anxiety, and I'd know I'd have to give in.

That particular night, as usual, I waited until I was sure my two roommates were asleep, then stole down to the kitchen to see what I could find. A box of cereal—that was gone in a few minutes—a loaf and a half of bread, then some pound-cake mix, a few stray pieces of candy and more cereal, until there was nothing left that I could find. And then, almost mechanically, I went to the bathroom and threw up about six times. As I knelt there with my face still over the toilet bowl, waves of depression swept over me. I was worthless. All my efforts to control the binging were a complete failure. I could never escape from a nightmare no ordinary person could imagine. I was going to be trapped there forever.

It was then that I went, almost without emotion, to the medicine cabinet and started systematically counting out how many pills were there. Forty Valiums, twenty or thirty Darvons, half a bottle of Fiornal, a few Percodans, a bottle of aspirin, some other painkiller . . . That, superimposed on half a quart of vodka, ought to do the job. I went to the kitchen and methodically poured myself a sixteen-ounce glass of pure one-hundred-proof vodka and started gulping it like soda pop. But it began to burn a lot and I had to drink more slowly so that I could keep it down. By the time I had nursed down the last of the vodka, the room was reeling. I got up and staggered toward the bathroom, but as I went I hit the table and sent dishes and glassware to the floor with a crash. Jan and Kim came rushing in, saw me clutching the counter for support, and dragged me to my bed.

The next morning I had one hell of a hangover, but I felt strangely glad to be alive.

This particular story and others in this chapter, illustrate vividly some of the experiences of patients with bulimia. Obviously only a minority of cases are as severe or as dramatic as these, but only through such graphic accounts can one step beyond the diagnostic criteria to witness the anguish, the isolation, and the imprisonment that the syndrome can cause.

Warning: Binging May Be Dangerous to Your Health

The accounts so far in this chapter illustrate the severe psychological problems that may accompany bulimia. But this is not all: Bulimia can lead to serious medical complications as well. Bulimia-associated medical complications fall into four groups: problems due to (1) self-induced vomiting, (2) laxative abuse, (3) use of diuretics ("water pills"), and (4) binge eating per se.

Self-induced vomiting can cause some of the worst problems, particularly as a result of the harmful effects of stomach acid.[8] One of the functions of the stomach is to make hydrochloric acid, which combines with food to initiate one of the first steps in digestion, or food breakdown. The stomach wall is well protected against the effects of acid, but other parts of the digestive tract, including the mouth and the esophagus, are not. Even though stomach acid is not particularly strong, repeated exposure can cause damage. Even in nonbulimic people, the lining of the esophagus sustains an occasional hydrochloric-acid burn, producing symptoms we all know as "heartburn." Bulimic vomiters suffer vastly more acid burns than ordinary people, and research has shown that patients who suffer long-standing heartburn have a higher risk of developing cancer of the esophagus. So far we have no hard proof that bulimic individuals run a greater risk of this deadly form of cancer, but it is a frightening possibility.

There are other, more immediate effects of stomach acid. One is to corrode the enamel protecting the teeth. In fact, it is often the dentist who first recognizes the problem of bulimia from the telltale erosion of the enamel. Not uncommonly, patients with bulimia need thousands of dollars' worth of dental work done, and some damage their teeth so badly that they have to have them removed entirely and replaced with dentures.

Another very common problem is swelling of the salivary glands—the small glands, located in the cheek and under the jaw, that produce saliva. Again, this problem seems to develop mainly in bulimic vomiters. We don't know for sure why these glands become swollen, but one theory is that the culprit again is stomach acid, trickling from the mouth back into the glands, and causing a chemical burn in the tiny salivary ducts. The delicate tissues become inflamed and swollen, the gland cannot drain properly, and swelling and further inflammation ensues. Some patients have swelling so severe that a casual observer might take it for mumps. In the short term, this is not a dangerous condition, but it can be painful and unsightly. As for long-term dangers, we just don't know.

The burning effect of stomach acid is only one problem; the loss of that acid from the body is another. One of the basic principles of all living things, first described by the great French physiologist Claude Bernard, is that body cells need a certain *"milieu intérieur"*—internal environment—to function properly. That is, they need a constant temperature, the right amounts of various minerals, the right balance of acids and bases, and so forth. The body has elaborate mechanisms to guard the *milieu intérieur* against any changes from the outside: We sweat when it is hot; become thirsty when the body needs more water; crave salt when the body requires sodium. But massive vomiting can defeat even the body's best efforts to maintain chemical equilibrium. As stomach acid is lost, the body's pH increases; there is too much base in the body. This is called "alkalosis," a condition that, in its mild form, can lead to weakness and fatigue; as it grows more severe, it can cause pounding headaches, inability to keep warm, and strange feelings of anxiety. And since acid in the urine protects against urinary infections, the more alkaline the urine becomes, the more susceptible the urinary system is to recurrent infections, which are not only painful but sometimes can damage the kidneys.

Stomach juices contain not only acid but also essential minerals, called electrolytes, including sodium, potassium, magnesium, calcium, and others. When these minerals are lost by frequent vomiting, other problems can occur: muscle cramps and weakness, fatigue, and abnormalities of the heartbeat. There may even be damaging long-term effects on the solidity of the bones. In pregnant women, electrolyte deficiencies may have harmful effects on the unborn child.

As if this were not enough, these metabolic problems are further accentuated in those who starve themselves between binges and in those who have developed severe weight loss (anorexia nervosa) in conjunction with their binging. Under conditions of low weight and/or long periods of abstaining from food, electrolyte disturbances can mount to the point where they may have

fatal consequences. These are most commonly due to inter-
ference in the functioning of heart muscle, which can either start
to pump irregularly (arrhythmia) or stop beating altogether (cardiac arrest).

To give one striking example, three years ago the medical
world was shocked to learn that a volunteer research participant
died in the course of what seemed a harmless experiment—
studying the effect of a rather benign medication on the sleep of
normal individuals.[9] Upon investigation, it emerged that this
"normal" volunteer was far from normal. She had a severe problem with bulimia and would alternate episodes of binging and
vomiting with periods of abstinence from food. She had been
hospitalized in the past for anorexia nervosa. Although basically
of normal weight, she had severe metabolic abnormalities. It is
likely that deficiencies of potassium and magnesium made her
heart extraordinarily vulnerable to the effects of the test medication and that she died because of a fatal arrhythmia that led to
cardiac arrest. She had been carefully screened medically, but
had told no one of her secret illness. Indeed, as will be described
in a later chapter, bulimia in conjunction with anorexia nervosa
carries probably the highest risk of death of any psychiatric condition, greater even than manic-depressive illness or schizophrenia.

A second group of problems develops in bulimic individuals
who use laxatives to purge.[10] Most laxatives act by irritating the
lining of the intestine; the irritated organ contracts more vig-
orously, and food is moved along more quickly. When vast
amounts of laxatives are used, the food does not stay in the
intestines long enough to be absorbed—this is, after all, the desired effect of purging—and once again, electrolytes and nu-
trients are lost, leading to consequences similar to those
experienced with vomiting. One difference, however, is that
base is lost instead of acid, causing the body's pH to drop. When
the concentration of acid in the body rises abnormally, it causes
nausea and, over the long term, erosion of bones.

Even more serious than the loss of electrolytes is the damaging
effect of laxatives on the functioning of the intestines themselves. Because laxatives stimulate contraction, the intestines can
gradually lose their ability to contract on their own, causing the
so-called lazy bowel syndrome. The intestines become abnormally enlarged, may begin to perform their digestive function

poorly, and become impaired in their ability to absorb protein and fats. Malabsorption of protein diminishes one's capacity to fight infections or to build new muscle fiber. Malabsorption of fat can cause deficiencies of vitamins A, D, E, and K, which in turn may lead to bone destruction, kidney damage, poor skin, hair loss, poor night vision, and problems with blood clotting. At least some bulimic individuals may develop these complications, as was learned in a recent study.[11]

A third group of complications comes from the use of diuretics, sometimes called water pills, which cause the kidneys to put out more water in the urine. Diuretics are not a very effective method of losing weight since there is only a fixed amount of fluid that can be lost in this way (two or three pounds), but they are commonly used. Complications include dehydration and the loss of both potassium and acid, the consequences of which we have already mentioned.

Fourth, even in individuals who do not use any of the various methods of purging, there are problems caused by the binging alone. Most commonly, for example, the stomach may become stretched and less able to perform its function of mixing food together with stomach acid by its powerful rhythmic contractions, and also less able to propel the food properly down into the small intestine.

Are there complications that develop simply from the abnormal eating pattern and the high amount of carbohydrates eaten in binges? Once again, we can only guess. We can say, however, that if the food eaten during binges is not supplemented by other, balanced meals, deficiencies of vitamins and minerals will develop. Also, it is hypothesized that some individuals can develop reactive hypoglycemia—low blood sugar—from large amounts of carbohydrates. This happens because a massive load of carbohydrates can rapidly increase the blood sugar level, stimulating the release of a sudden surge of insulin to cope with the load; but since simple sugars can be absorbed very quickly, by the time the peak levels of insulin are achieved, there may not be much carbohydrate left coming into the bloodstream. Thus, the insulin response is "too much, too late": The insulin drives too much sugar into body cells, leading to hypoglycemia—which can cause dizziness, fatigue, and depression. Again, we have no hard evidence of how often this occurs in bulimic patients, but it is a possibility.

Needless to say, all these problems can become even more serious in an individual who already has some medical condition, such as heart disease or kidney disease.

The presence of bulimia with diabetes can be particularly hazardous. Diabetic patients lack insulin, the hormone that regulates the body's carbohydrate metabolism. In order to avoid the serious medical complications of high blood sugar, patients with diabetes must keep to a strict, balanced diet with few sweets, and many must give themselves regular insulin injections. Bulimia can create a terrible problem for such patients, causing them to binge on the very foods that should be avoided at all costs! We and others have reported several cases of patients with both diabetes and bulimia in whom life-threatening complications developed.[12]

Even though some of the medical consequences are not fully known, it should be obvious that bulimia—particularly when it occurs in conjunction with anorexia nervosa—presents a constant psychological and medical threat to those who experience severe cases of the disorder. Clearly there is a desperate need to find some safe, rapid, and effective treatment for the symptoms. But before we go on to this, let us set aside the accounts of individual patients and step back to look at the big picture. How great a problem is bulimia on a national scale? Is this psychological and medical suffering confined only to a few seriously ill individuals, or must we rank bulimia as a significant public-health problem in the United States?

Even if you think you've guessed the answer, the statistics will astonish you.

3

THE 1980s:
BULIMIA COMES OUT
OF THE CLOSET

The Early Rumblings

Just how common is bulimia? Certainly millions of us have gone on an eating binge now and then, but how many people develop cases of true bulimia, such as those just described? As recently as a few years ago, almost everyone—even the experts—would have guessed that bulimia was an uncommon disorder, certainly not a national public-health problem. But what people failed to take into account is that bulimia is usually "in the closet"—the bulimic man or woman is not visibly different from anyone else in external appearance or behavior. Indeed, the typical bulimic patient is a thin, attractive, perfectly normal-appearing woman in her twenties or thirties, usually successful in her social and occupational life. It would be practically impossible for the keenest observer to detect anything wrong with her at all. Her illness may be so secret that her closest friends, and sometimes even her husband and children, may know nothing of it.

How many people, across America and around the world, have secretly lived with this strange problem? There was virtually no information available on this question until the middle of the 1970s, when a few bits of evidence began to surface in the scientific literature, suggesting that a massive problem might lie hidden from view. In 1977, a group of scientists in California decided to perform a study to see whether the anticonvulsant drug phenytoin, better known as Dilantin, might curtail eating binges.[1] In order to recruit twenty subjects for the study, they placed small advertisements in two local newspapers—the *San Jose Mercury*, with a circulation of about 207,000, and the *Palo Alto Times*, with a circulation of 44,000. In eleven days they received telephone calls from no less than 242 people wanting to participate! Of course, many of these respondents did not meet the researchers' criteria for true bulimia, but the numbers are still remarkable; one can only guess at the much larger number of individuals, in these two communities alone, who never saw the advertisement, or who saw it but were reluctant to participate in a study.

Two years later, in England, Dr. Gerard Russell published one of the world's first major papers on bulimia.[2] He noted that not only did bulimia appear to be a common disorder but that the number of referrals he received had risen steadily from 1972 to 1977. Of course, part of this might have been due to Dr. Russell's expanding reputation, and it might also have been that bulimic individuals were increasingly willing to identify themselves and seek treatment. But perhaps bulimia had itself been on the rise during these years.

In any case, by the end of the 1970s, people were beginning to take notice. Magazines devoted articles to bulimia and its sister disorder, anorexia nervosa.[3] Television documentaries on bulimia appeared across the country. Movie stars, rock singers, and other celebrities publicly confessed that they had suffered from bulimia. Commentators offered theories about the causes of bulimia—be it because our society rewards thinness, or because our society victimizes women, or because we have bad diets. Now bulimia has become almost fashionable, "the psychiatric disorder of the Eighties," as one of our associates dubbed it.

Is all this publicity justified? Are we making a big production over a small number of individuals, or is it really true, as the commentators would have us believe, that bulimia is sweeping the country, afflicting hundreds of thousands—even millions—of women and men?

The Prevalence of Bulimia: The Facts

To answer this question properly, one would have to do a formal study, giving confidential questionnaires to a random sample of people. This seems simple enough, but apparently no such studies were published in major scientific journals before 1980. Why?

It's hard to say, but we recall in this connection an interesting anecdote told by Dr. Joseph Lipinski, a psychiatric researcher at Harvard Medical School who is best known for his studies of psychotic disorders such as schizophrenia and manic-depressive illness. Sixteen years ago, in 1968, during morning rounds at McLean Hospital, Dr. Lipinski was discussing a hospital patient who displayed bulimic symptoms. Several student nurses at the meeting, each from a different school in the area, all began to giggle. On questioning, they told him that binging and self-induced vomiting were common at their respective schools. Later, he queried several women college students and got the same response.

Although this was not his usual field of research, Lipinski was so intrigued that he decided to conduct a confidential questionnaire study at several local colleges to assess the prevalence of bulimia. He sent letters to the appropriate administrative officials, explaining that the study would be conducted in the strictest confidence and that no college or university would be named or recognizably identified in any publications arising from the study.

To his amazement, they all turned him down cold.

"We're fascinated by your study," one dean told him. "We know that binge eating and vomiting is a terribly common problem at our school. But you can't do your study here, because if it ever leaked out that we have such a widespread problem with this, our alumni would be shocked and outraged. It would be a scandal; we'd lose contributions. Don't get me wrong—I really wish you the best of luck with your study; I only hope that someone else gives you permission to do it in some other school. And, by the way, is there any way that we could see the results when you get them? We'd be extremely interested."

Lipinski visited officials at the other institutions and received almost exactly the same explanation. And so his pioneering idea for a study could not be executed, and the scientific world lost what might have been a striking observation, years before bulimia hit the popular press.

But the "cover-up" could not last forever, and now the facts are beginning to flow in. In 1980, Drs. Ronnie Stangler and Adolf Printz reported on 500 students who applied for psychiatric treatment at a large university health service.[4] They found that 5.3% of the 318 women and 1.1% of the 182 men met all the

DSM-III criteria for bulimia. And these figures omit a number of other students, who did not mention their bulimia at first but revealed it in subsequent meetings with their therapists. Of course, the study does not allow us to extrapolate back to calculate the prevalence of bulimia in the university as a whole, since we cannot know what percentage of bulimic students actually went to the health service. As the reader will see in the data below, the percentage of bulimic students who actually consult mental-health professionals might represent only the very tip of the iceberg.

The Student Surveys

In 1981, a new study appeared, providing more direct answers to the prevalence question. Dr. Katherine Halmi, one of America's best-known researchers on eating disorders, together with two other investigators, conducted a questionnaire study of 355 summer students on one of the campuses of the State University of New York.[5] This was a diverse sample, ranging in age from fourteen to sixty-seven, of whom 59.8% were women and 33.4% were men, with another 6.7% not indicating their sex. An astonishing 13% of these people proved to meet the full *DSM*-III criteria for bulimia. On the basis of these unexpected results, Dr. Halmi and her colleagues suggested that bulimia might represent a much more serious public-health problem than previously thought.

Looking at the summer-school students, is there any reason to suppose that they would be more likely to suffer from bulimia than a random sample drawn from the U.S. population as a whole? The sample contained more women than men; we have to correct for this, since bulimia is more common in women. And the sample contained a larger percentage of individuals in their teens, twenties, and thirties (the mean age was 25.6 ± 10.7 years) than we would find in a completely random sample of the U.S. population. Finally, the summer-school population might be skewed somewhat in favor of the upper social classes, and bulimia may be more common in the upper classes (although this hypothesis is untested). Even if we divide the 13% figure by 6 to correct—generously—for these three statistical anomalies, and assume that the prevalence of bulimia in the population as a whole is only 2.2%, this would still mean that *5 million people* in the United States have bulimia at some time in their lives.

Could these figures possibly be correct? Recently, one study at a college in North Dakota and another study, conducted by our group, at two colleges and a secondary school in New England, have produced figures that seem to support the New York results.

In the first study, Dr. Richard Pyle and his associates administered a confidential questionnaire to the freshman class at the University of North Dakota.[6] More than 98% of the freshmen filled out the questionnaire—a remarkably high rate of return. Of the 780 men, 1.4% met the *DSM*-III criteria for bulimia; 0.4% of them met the narrower criterion of bulimia with binges occurring once per week or more. Of the 575 women, 7.8% had *DSM*-III bulimia, and 4.5% binged once a week or more.

Admittedly, these figures are lower than those found in the New York summer students, but it must be remembered that the freshmen probably averaged nineteen years of age, as opposed to nearly twenty-six years for the summer students. If we were to follow the freshmen for seven more years, until they had attained an average age of twenty-six, perhaps many more of them would have developed bulimia at some point during that interval, thus bringing the prevalence rate up toward that found among the summer students. One way to test this conjecture would be to examine several more groups of students, of other age ranges.

Our own study did just that. Using a confidential questionnaire, we looked at two samples of college seniors—with an average age of twenty-two—and at the students in a secondary school, with an age range of thirteen to eighteen.[7]

In college A—a prestigious rural college for women—12.6% of the 287 questionnaire respondents had met the *DSM*-III criteria for bulimia at some time in their lives; an additional 2.1% reported a history of both bulimia and anorexia nervosa, for a total rate of 14.7%. The portion reporting once-a-week binging was 10.0%. Thus, in this sample, intermediate in age between the North Dakota sample and the New York sample, we found prevalence rates about halfway between those reported in the other two studies—consistent with the hypothesis that additional cases of bulimia appear in a population as its members grow older.

Even more striking findings emerged from college B, an urban coeducational university. Of 102 women respondents, 18.6% had met the *DSM*-III criteria for bulimia at some time, and another 1.0% reported a history of both bulimia and anorexia nervosa. In this group, 12.9% reported binging once a week or more. None of the forty-seven men respondents reported bulimia—but then forty-seven is not a very large sample for statistical purposes.

The 19.6% figure among women actually exceeds the New York results—but there is one major precaution. Since we had to rely on the mail to distribute our questionnaire in college B, we had a response rate of only 52%, much less than that obtained by direct distribution of the questionnaires in the North Dakota study. It could be argued that women with bulimia might be particularly likely to fill out and return the questionnaire, whereas those with normal eating patterns might throw it away, thus biasing the results toward a high prevalence figure. Of course, one could also argue, in reverse, that women with bulimia might be embarrassed to fill out and return the questionnaire, biasing the results in the opposite direction. But even if we make the most conservative assumption, namely that every woman who failed to return the questionnaire had normal eating, we would still have a prevalence rate of over 10% in college B. A similar most-conservative calculation for college A would yield 9.3%.

In the secondary school, with the youngest population, one might predict the lowest rates. Consistent with this, we found that 6.5% of 155 girls reported past or present bulimia, and another 1.9% reported bulimia and anorexia nervosa. We found no cases of bulimia among the 105 boys. The 8.4% figure among girls was particularly striking in view of the fact that most of them had not even reached the age of eighteen. And in the secondary school sample, the figure could not be seriously questioned on the grounds of a poor response rate, since the response rate among the girls approached 90%.

In summary, the results of these five student samples, drawn from differing institutions in different areas, agree with one another fairly well when one corrects for the differing mean ages of the samples. Among the girls in the two youngest samples, we find a prevalence of bulimia of about 8%; among the two samples of women who were college seniors the rates are

14.6% to 19.6% (although these figures may have to be corrected downward a bit to compensate for the effects of response rate); and among women in the oldest sample the rate is 19%. The figures suggest that in older samples, virtually all of the individuals liable to develop bulimia have already developed it; in younger samples, there are still cases due to occur at a later age.

One objection to these figures is that the *DSM*-III criteria for bulimia are quite broad; technically, one could have only a few major binges a year and still meet the definition of bulimia. But even if we restrict our definition to the subgroup of women reporting weekly binges, the prevalence rates still range from 4.5% (in the North Dakota freshmen) to 12.9% (in college B).

We must distinguish between current and lifetime prevalence rates for bulimia. About a third of the women in our two college groups, for example, reported bulimia in the past but had apparently recovered by the time they answered the questionnaire. In the secondary school, the recovered group was slightly smaller—about one-fourth. Therefore, to obtain the number of individuals with *active* bulimia in each of our samples, one should reduce the prevalence rates by one-quarter to one-third. In the New York and North Dakota studies, however, the prevalence figures appear to represent cases of active bulimia.

Parenthetically, our study found an even higher rate of recovery from the related disorder, anorexia nervosa. Of the 544 women in all three groups combined, nineteen reported a history of anorexia nervosa meeting *DSM*-III criteria (with or without a history of bulimia), but only one had anorexia nervosa at the time of answering the questionnaire. Of course, one can argue that these figures were not representative: Some other students with active and severe anorexia nervosa might not be in school at the time; some might even be in the hospital. Nevertheless, the presence of eighteen remitted cases argues that the spontaneous remission rate for anorexia nervosa must be quite high—perhaps higher than that of bulimia.

Returning to the bulimia data: Even allowing for spontaneous remission in some cases, narrowing the criteria to include only women with more serious cases of the disorder, and correcting for the low response rate in some of the samples, we are still left with substantial prevalence rates in all five of the varying groups of students. The accumulating evidence depicts a problem of sweeping proportions.

The Shopping Mall Study

Despite the close correspondence between our student survey results and those of other researchers, we still could not help but be skeptical of the data. If we were to take our findings at face value, even allowing for such factors as age, sex, response rate, and severity of illness, they would imply that the number of Americans with bulimia reaches well into the millions. To us, this seemed implausible: We suspected that the student survey results were somehow producing inflated estimates of the true prevalence of bulimia in the population at large. We noted, for example, that the student samples were biased toward the upper socioeconomic classes, and we conjectured that many of the students reporting bulimia might have only transiently experimented with it as a result of peer pressure in the dormitory. These and many other factors might cause students to be nonrepresentative of the American population. Therefore, in search of a more random sample, we took our study to a middle-class suburban shopping mall.[8]

We stood in the middle of the mall and offered every woman shopper a dollar to fill out the same confidential questionnaire and deposit it in a sealed box. Although we were careful to reveal nothing about the subject matter of the questionnaire in advance, only four of the 304 women who accepted a questionnaire refused to complete it when they discovered its purpose.

When we opened the box and scored the results, we were stunned. No less than 10.3% of the shoppers met the *DSM*-III criteria for bulimia at some time in their lives; among the women aged thirteen to twenty, the figure was 17.7%. Even when we narrowed our criteria to women with what we called "narrowly defined bulimia"—those reporting binges once a week or more *and* a history of self-induced vomiting or laxative abuse—the prevalence rate was 3.0% of the total sample and 5.1% of the group aged thirteen to twenty.

Since we possessed the ages of all respondents, we were able to adjust for the difference between the age distribution of the sample of shoppers and the age distribution of the American female population. With this adjustment, we obtained an estimate of 7.6 million American women with a history of *DSM*-III bulimia and 2.2 million with "narrowly defined bulimia."

About half of these individuals would be expected to have currently active bulimic symptoms. And these figures, large as they are, neglect the many women still too young to have developed bulimia, an unknown number of men, and an even larger "gray zone" of individuals with significant eating disorders, but not quite meeting the *DSM*-III criteria for bulimia.

It is difficult to dismiss these figures as a statistical aberration. The mall contained no large grocery stores or supermarkets; there seems no reason that bulimic women would be more likely to shop there. Since no one knew the subject of the questionnaire in advance, there could not have been any selection in favor of bulimic respondents. Finally, we tested the validity of the questionnaire itself, using a separate sample of known bulimic and nonbulimic individuals. The questionnaire did not produce a false diagnosis of bulimia in any of the 85 nonbulimic individuals tested.

Finally, very similar results have just been reported from a population study in England.[9] Of 369 women attending a family planning clinic, 20.9% reported an eating binge within the past two months; 6.8% reported weekly binging; 4.9% reported recent abuse of laxatives; and 2.9% reported self-induced vomiting.

In summary, five student surveys and two general-population surveys have all produced the same answer: both in America and elsewhere, literally millions of individuals suffer from bulimia at some time in their lives. Admittedly, most of these cases are not as severe as those described in this book, and probably many remit without the need for treatment. But the number of Americans who develop serious cases, with at least weekly binging and purging, is probably between 1 and 3 million. Furthermore, our shopping mall data suggest that these numbers may be gradually increasing, since younger shoppers more often reported a history of bulimia than did older ones.

If this is true, we may be seeing nothing less than a national, if not international, epidemic.

Why Women?

Throughout this discussion, we have bypassed one glaring fact: Bulimia is clearly many times more common in women than in men. Why should this be true?

If you hear any "definite" answer to that question, don't believe it. Countless psychiatric and medical diseases are more common in one sex than in the other, for reasons that in some cases are entirely unknown. The preponderance of bulimia in women may be due to social factors, as suggested by the popular theory that it stems from our society's demand that women be thin. Or it may be due to environmental factors: In most cultures, women are more involved than men with the purchase and preparation of food, and might perhaps be more likely to experiment with binging. Psychological factors may play a role: Food, weight, and the body image may be more important to women than to men. Or the difference might be biological: Perhaps the hypothalamus, or some other part of the central nervous system concerned with eating behavior, is more easily affected in women than in men.

We would offer another way of looking at this question: Could it be that bulimia is just one of several possible syndromes that may be caused by a larger underlying psychiatric disorder? Perhaps bulimia is one of the characteristic "female" expressions of this underlying disorder, whereas a male with the same underlying disorder would be more likely to develop a different syndrome—say, alcohol abuse. Analogous situations exist in internal medicine. For example, the large illness category called collagen vascular disease may be present in many forms: one form, systemic lupus erythematosus (lupus) is far more common in women; whereas another, ankylosing spondylitis, occurs almost entirely in men. Might bulimia, similarly, be but one syndrome in a larger family of psychiatric illnesses?

Our research suggests that this may be the case. In order to examine this possibility in detail, let us take a look at a number of syndromes that appear to be closely allied to bulimia.

4

EIGHT BULIMIA-ASSOCIATED DISORDERS

If you have had eating binges, you may have experienced other types of psychiatric difficulties as well, since a number of syndromes seem to occur more often in bulimic patients than would be expected by chance alone. So let us start off with another quiz—a longer one this time—covering eight of the disorders that we and others have frequently observed in association with bulimia. Many of the questions in this quiz are derived from *DSM*-III—the diagnostic manual mentioned in the previous chapter—and from the National Institute of Mental Health Diagnostic Interview Schedule, an interview designed by Dr. John Helzer and his associates at Washington University in St. Louis.[1]

BULIMIA-ASSOCIATED DISORDERS QUIZ

	YES	NO
I. 1. Have you ever thought that you were too fat, or likely to become too fat, even when other people such as friends or family members said you were too thin?	☐	☐
2. Have you ever developed an intense fear of becoming fat, which was not relieved even when you had lost a good deal of weight?	☐	☐
3a. (if over 18) Have you ever lost more than 25% of your original body weight by dieting (i.e., *not* because of a physical illness or because of having a baby)?	☐	☐

YES　NO

3b. (if under 18) Have you ever weighed more than 25% below what would be normal for an individual of your age and height (again, *not* because of a physical illness)?　☐　☐

4. Have you ever been extremely thin, yet refused to maintain your body weight over a normal minimum for your age and height?　☐　☐

5. (women only) Did your periods stop shortly before or during the time that you were losing weight?　☐　☐

6. Have you ever consulted a doctor because of having deliberately lost too much weight?　☐　☐

II. 1. Have you ever had a period of *two weeks or longer* during which you persistently felt depressed, sad, or blue, and when you lost interest in things—even things you usually enjoyed? (If you're sure the answer is "no," skip to III.)　☐　☐

2a. During such a period, did you ever have a change in your appetite, to the point where you *either* lost *or* gained at least 10 pounds within a few weeks without deliberately trying to do so?　☐　☐

2b. During such a period, did you have a consistent change in your sleep pattern, so that you *either* had trouble falling asleep for a long time, trouble waking up very early in the morning and not being able to get back to sleep, *or* had the reverse problem of sleeping too much—say, 10 or 12 hours a day?　☐　☐

2c. During such a period, did you have a change in your powers of concentration, so that you couldn't read a newspaper article, or couldn't do housework, or felt that your thinking was mixed up?　☐　☐

2d. During such a period, did your sex drive decrease to the point where you were hardly interested in sex for a period of at least several weeks?　☐　☐

2e. During such a period, did you experience a drop in your energy level or feel continuously fatigued for two weeks or more?　☐　☐

2f. During such a period, did you consistently experience *either* that you were talking or moving more slowly than is normal for you, *or* that you were agitated and had to be moving all the time, so that you were constantly wringing your hands or pacing up and down?　☐　☐

2g. During such a period, did you feel continuously worthless, or sinful, or guilty?　☐　☐

YES NO

2h. During such a period, did you think constantly about death or suicide, or did you actually make a suicide attempt? ☐ ☐

3. Did such a period occur only at a time when you were suffering from some medical condition such as a prolonged illness? ☐ ☐

4. Did such a period occur only at a time when someone close to you had just died? ☐ ☐

5a. During such a period, did you ever become paranoid— such as thinking that people were talking about you or were out to get you? ☐ ☐

5b. During such a period, did you ever get the feeling that people on the radio or TV might be talking about you? ☐ ☐

5c. During such a period, did you ever hear voices when there was no one there? ☐ ☐

III. 1. Have you ever had a period *of one week or longer* during which you became so happy, or excited, or irritable that you got into trouble, or your family and friends worried about it, or you were taken to see a doctor? (If you're sure the answer is "no," skip to IV.) ☐ ☐

2a. During such a period, did you sleep much less than is usual for you, night after night for a week or more, and still not feel tired or sleepy? ☐ ☐

2b. During such a period, did you become "hyper"— running around and doing too many things at once, such as cleaning your house at two in the morning, or starting too many projects at work, or becoming much more sexually active than is normal for you? ☐ ☐

2c. During such a period, did you continuously talk so much that you developed "motor mouth" or "verbal diarrhea"—so that people just couldn't interrupt you? ☐ ☐

2d. During such a period, did you experience a week or more during which thoughts raced through your mind so fast that you could not keep track of them? ☐ ☐

2e. During such a period, did you get an exaggerated idea of your importance or your abilities, such as thinking you had special powers, or writing letters to the President about how to run the country, or believing you had some great religious insight? ☐ ☐

2f. During such a period, did you become unusually distractible, so that any little interruption could get you off the track of what you were doing? ☐ ☐

YES   NO

2g. During such a period, did you get involved in risky or ill-advised activities such as spending sprees with money you didn't have, indiscreet sexual activity, foolish investments, driving far above the speed limit, etc.? ☐ ☐

3. Did such a period occur only at a time when you were suffering from some medical condition or because you were taking drugs? ☐ ☐

4a. During such a period, did you ever become paranoid— such as thinking that people were talking about you or were out to get you? ☐ ☐

4b. During such a period, did you ever get the feeling that people on the radio or TV were talking about you? ☐ ☐

4c. During such a period, did you ever get the feeling that other people could read your thoughts or that thoughts that were not your own were being somehow inserted into your mind? ☐ ☐

4d. During such a period, did you ever get the feeling that your thoughts, your feelings, or your actions were being controlled by some outside force? ☐ ☐

4e. During such a period, did you ever hear voices when there was no one there, or see a vision of something or somebody that was not there? ☐ ☐

IV. 1. Have you ever consumed enough alcohol to get drunk? (If the answer is "no," skip to V.) ☐ ☐

2a. Have you ever drunk as much as a fifth of hard liquor in a day, or three bottles of wine, or three six-packs of beer in a day? ☐ ☐

2b. Has there ever been a period of *two weeks or more* when you were drinking at least seven beers, or seven four-ounce glasses of wine, or six 1½-ounce drinks *every day?* ☐ ☐

2c. Has there been a period of at least *two months* when you drank that much—seven beers, seven four-ounce glasses of wine, or six 1½-ounce drinks—*at least once a week?* ☐ ☐

3a. Have you ever thought that you were drinking too heavily? ☐ ☐

3b. Have your family or friends ever objected because you were drinking too much? ☐ ☐

3c. Have you ever intended to stop drinking but couldn't? ☐ ☐

3d. Have you ever had to have a drink in the morning after you had gotten out of bed? ☐ ☐

YES   NO

3e. Have you ever had troubles at your job (or at school) □ □
because of drinking, such as missing a day of work, or have
you ever had periods of drinking on the job (or at school)?

3f. Did you have a car accident because of drinking, or get □ □
arrested for driving while intoxicated?

3g. Have you ever been held at the police station because □ □
of drinking or gotten into physical fights while drinking?

3h. Have you ever gone on a "bender" where you kept □ □
drinking for two days or more without sobering up?

3i. Have you ever had blackouts because of drinking—in □ □
other words, had a period where you drank so much that
you couldn't remember what you had done the previous
night?

4a. Have you ever developed a substantial tolerance for □ □
alcohol; that is, a need to drink a *much* larger quantity of
alcohol in order to get the same effect you used to get
from a small amount?

4b. Have you ever had "the shakes," or a fit, or seizures, or □ □
the DT's after stopping or cutting down on drinking?

4c. Have you ever had hallucinations—seen or heard □ □
things when there was nothing there—after stopping or
cutting down on drinking?

V. 1. Have you ever had a spell or an attack when you □ □
suddenly began to feel terribly anxious and afraid, even
though there was no overt reason to feel anxious? (If "no,"
skip to VI.)

2. Did the attack often seem to come "out of the blue," □ □
when you were not doing anything in particular?

3. Did the attack seem to rise to a peak over a few minutes □ □
or so, then gradually dissipate?

4. Have you ever had as many as three such attacks in a □ □
three-week period?

5. At the peak of the attack, did you experience any of the □ □
following symptoms?

   a. Shortness of breath or hyperventilating? □ □
   b. A feeling that you were choking or smothering? □ □
   c. Tingling in your hands and feet? □ □
   d. Heart palpitations? □ □
   e. Pain in your chest? □ □
   f. Dizziness or light-headedness? □ □

YES   NO

g. Feeling faint? ☐ ☐

h. Hot or cold flashes? ☐ ☐

i. Breaking out in a sweat? ☐ ☐

j. Trembling or shaking? ☐ ☐

k. Feelings of unreality, as though you weren't really there and were just watching a movie? ☐ ☐

l. Feeling that you were going to die? ☐ ☐

m. Feeling that you were suddenly going to go crazy or go out of control in some way? ☐ ☐

6. Were the attacks due to any medical disorder that you know of? ☐ ☐

VI. 1. Have you ever suffered from marked fears of being outside in public places, such as on a bus, in a movie theater, in crowds, or some other place from which it might be hard to escape in a hurry? (If "no," skip to VII.) ☐ ☐

2. Have these fears been severe enough to actually affect your daily activities, so that you customarily didn't ride buses, did not attend movies, or avoided bridges and tunnels, or the like? ☐ ☐

3. Have these fears ever become so severe that you have not even wanted to leave your house or apartment, and have stayed inside for more than two days at a time? ☐ ☐

VII. 1a. Have you ever been bothered by persistent unpleasant thoughts that you couldn't get out of your head, such as a persistent fear that you might harm or kill someone you loved, even though you would never really want to? ☐ ☐

1b. Have you ever had persistent thoughts such as the idea that your hands were dirty and had germs on them, no matter how much you washed them? ☐ ☐

2. If you have had such persistent thoughts, have they been about subjects *other* than just food, calories, or your weight? ☐ ☐

3. If you have had such obsessions or persistent thoughts, have they lasted as long as several weeks, no matter how ridiculous you knew they were and no matter how hard you tried to get rid of them? ☐ ☐

4a. Have you ever felt you had to perform the same act over and over again, such as washing your hands repeatedly or checking again and again to see if you set the alarm clock or turned off the stove? ☐ ☐

	YES	NO

4b. Have you ever had times when you had to do something in a certain order, such as getting dressed, or getting ready for bed, and had to start the sequence all over again if the order was wrong? ☐ ☐

4c. Have you ever had a compulsion to count things, such as the number of tiles on the floor, or to tap your foot a certain number of times before going to bed, or any other little "rituals" like that? ☐ ☐

5. If you have had such compulsions or rituals, have they been about subjects *other* than food, calories, or your weight? ☐ ☐

6. If you have had such compulsions or rituals, have they continued for as long as several weeks, no matter how ridiculous you knew they were and no matter how hard you tried to stop them? ☐ ☐

VIII. 1. Have you ever had irresistible impulses to steal items from stores, even when the items were not of great value and you could have afforded to buy them? ☐ ☐

2. Have you actually stolen such items? ☐ ☐

3. If so, did you steal items *other* than food or laxatives? ☐ ☐

4. If so, was the theft impulsive—i.e., something you had not planned well in advance and were not doing in collaboration with others? ☐ ☐

5. If so, was there a sense of buildup of tension before the act, and a feeling of pleasure or release after you had done it? ☐ ☐

6. If so, are these thefts different from your usual behavior, in that you are otherwise a law-abiding person who would not normally do something illegal? ☐ ☐

7. Have you ever felt guilty afterward, to the point where you have actually tried to return the item to the store when no one was watching? ☐ ☐

8. Just out of curiosity: Did you steal this book? ☐ ☐

SCORING

Score each of the eight sections separately.

I. If you said "yes" on 1, 2, 3a *or* b, 4, and 5 (if applicable), you have probably had *anorexia nervosa*. Perhaps only one-third of anorexic individuals have seen a doctor for their symptoms, however (question 6).

II. If you said "yes" on 1, "yes" on *four or more* of the items in 2a–h, and "no" on 3 and 4, you have probably had *major depression.* Some people with episodes of major depression also experience psychotic symptoms (questions 5a–c), but whether or not these occur does not affect the diagnosis. The *depressed phase of manic-depressive illness* is one type of major depression.

III. If you said "yes" on 1, "yes" on *three or more* of the items in 2a–g, and "no" on 3, you have probably had a *manic episode.* This is known in *DSM*-III as *bipolar disorder,* and is also called *manic-depressive illness, manic phase.* Psychotic symptoms (questions 4a–e) often accompany manic episodes, but this does not affect the diagnosis.

IV. If you said "yes" on 1, "yes" on at least one item in 2a–c, and "yes" on at least one item in 3a–i, you may have had *alcohol abuse.* If you said "yes" on *three or more* of the items in 3a–i, then you almost certainly have had alcohol abuse. If, in addition, you said "yes" on at least one item in 4a–c, then you have probably had *alcohol dependence*—in other words, some degree of actual addiction to alcohol.

V. If you said "yes" on 1–4, "yes" to *four or more* of the items in 5a–m, and "no" on 6, you have probably had *panic disorder,* the syndrome of panic attacks.

VI. If you said "yes" on 1 and 2, you have had at least mild *agoraphobia.* If you said "yes" on 3 as well, you probably have had severe agoraphobia. Agoraphobia may or may not be accompanied by panic attacks (V, above).

VII. If you said "yes" on 1a *or* b, 2, and 3 (questions about obsessions), or "yes" on 4a, b, *or* c, 5, and 6 (questions about compulsions), you probably have had *obsessive-compulsive* disorder.

VIII. If you said "yes" on 1–6, you probably have had *kleptomania,* the syndrome of compulsive shoplifting. Many people with kleptomania feel guilty about their behavior but cannot stop it (question 7). As for question 8—if you answered "yes," our publisher is going to get very upset!

The above quiz is of course no substitute for a formal clinical interview, but it provides some rough guidelines. Many people are surprised to learn that they meet the criteria of one or more of the psychiatric disorders listed. Studies suggest, however, that much more than one-third of the adult population would meet the criteria for at least one of these psychiatric syndromes. Major depression alone strikes 18% to 23% of women and 8% to 11% of men in this country, according to *DSM*-III. Other recent studies—such as those by Drs. Myrna Weissman and Jerome Myers at Yale,[2] and by Drs. Sally Vernon and Robert Roberts in Texas,[3]—have reported that major affective disorder (major depression or bipolar disorder) afflicts 6% to 26% of Americans. (The 26% figures were for Caucasian and Mexican-American women, with black women and men of all groups showing lower rates.) When one adds the large segment of the population with alcohol abuse or dependence, plus the various other disorders whose prevalence is not even known (such as agoraphobia or kleptomania), the numbers grow even larger. In other words, if the quiz suggests that you have one or more of these disorders, you have plenty of company.

Among individuals with bulimia, these eight other psychiatric disorders appear to be even more common than they are in the population at large. In a recent study, we performed very detailed diagnostic evaluations of seventy-four patients with bulimia.[4] More than 80% of them had at least one, and many had several, of the eight psychiatric disorders covered in this quiz. The exact prevalence rates are given in Table 1.

What are these various disorders, and why are they apparently so common in people with bulimia? Are all of these psychiatric syndromes—bulimia included—possibly interrelated in some way? Needless to say, this was one of our questions when we initiated our studies of bulimia, and it was from our observations that we were able to develop medical treatments for bulimia. But before we get too far ahead of our story, let us present a brief description of what we will call, for short, the "bulimia-associated disorders."

TABLE 1
Lifetime Prevalence of Other Psychiatric Disorders
in 73 Bulimic Patients

Disorder	Number of cases	Percent
Anorexia Nervosa	25	34
Major Depression	49	66
Bipolar Disorder	10	14
Alcohol Abuse	20	27
Panic Disorder	30	41
Agoraphobia	11	15
Obsessive-Compulsive Disorder	23	31
Kleptomania	23	31
All Other Forms of Drug Abuse	10	14
Personality Disorders of All Types	11	15
Schizophrenia	0	0

NOTE: Disorders occurring simultaneously in a given patient are scored separately. Normally in *DSM*-III, panic disorder, agoraphobia, and obsessive-compulsive disorder are not diagnosed if they occur simultaneously with major depression. However, this convention was not used for the above table, hence prevalence rates for these three disorders are higher than would be obtained by standard *DSM*-III criteria.

Bulimia and Anorexia Nervosa

Although bulimia is about four times as common as anorexia nervosa[5], the latter is better known to the general public, probably because of its highly visible symptoms.[6] Anorexic patients—usually young women—develop an inexplicable fear of growing fat and begin to diet compulsively. Even as they become emaciated, they still see themselves as too fat and cannot be convinced to stop losing weight. Parents, friends, and therapists exhort them to resume eating, argue with them, punish them, analyze them—but often to no avail; they remain terrified of eating, and resolute in their dieting. Most anorexic patients do acknowledge that they have an illness, and many say that they would like to be rid of it, but they feel incapable of changing their behavior. This, as the reader may remember, is quite similar to the way bulimic patients feel about their binges. In general, however, anorexia nervosa often seems more ego-syntonic than bulimia; compared with bulimic patients, anorexic patients are usually not as eager to give up their symptoms.

Individuals with anorexia are often admitted to psychiatric hospitals, where a treatment team will try to help them gain weight. Treatment programs often include reward and punishment—e.g., the patient is not allowed freedom or hospital privileges until he or she has gained a specific amount of weight. If this fails, the patient is often fed liquid nutriment through a nasogastric tube—a thin tube that is fed through the nose, down the esophagus, and into the stomach. This may sound barbaric, but, interestingly, many anorexic patients have told us that they preferred the NG (nasogastric) feedings to having to eat themselves. "I don't have to feel as guilty about having gained weight, because it was someone else's fault," one girl put it.

It comes as a shock to most lay people to hear that a fair number of anorexic individuals—as many as 5% to 10% in some studies—literally starve themselves to death. Modern medical treatment has probably reduced this rate below 5% today, but even in hospitals with the best of medical supervision, deaths may occur. One of our anorexic patients, a young girl who had failed to get better after several intensive psychotherapy and behavior-therapy programs, described a close call during one of her previous hospitalizations:

I had gotten myself down to sixty-one pounds. The nurses on the ward didn't know that I had gotten that low, because I kept several rolls of pennies in my pockets when they weighed me each morning. I still thought I was too fat, so I was exercising—pacing back and forth in my room—when I suddenly passed out. When I came to, there was a team of doctors standing around me. They told me that my heart had stopped for almost three minutes.

Another patient who had dieted down to the 60-pound range, despite being 5'4" tall, described how she suddenly came down with a lung infection called klebsiella pneumonia as a result of her impaired resistance to infection: "My temperature shot up to 106° and they rushed me to the intensive-care unit. I was on huge doses of antibiotics for weeks. Sometimes I lost consciousness or was completely delirious from the fever, but after six and a half weeks in the ICU, I finally turned the corner and recovered."

Amazingly enough, both of these patients continued their compulsive dieting, compulsive exercise, and other anorexic behavior. Neither of them wanted to die—they just couldn't stop their dieting. This illustrates, again, the striking lack of voluntary control in anorexia nervosa, a phenomenon closely resembling the lack of voluntary control described by bulimic patients.

It seems that anorexia nervosa and bulimia must be linked to similar mechanisms in the brain, since the two disorders often occur simultaneously or sequentially in the same patients. A very common evolutionary sequence was described by one of our patients who came to us with symptoms of both anorexia nervosa and bulimia. She was binging at least every day, but by vomiting she kept her weight down to only 82 pounds, despite her height of 5'4". Although once obviously a very beautiful woman, she had dieted to the point where she looked like a concentration-camp victim: Her face looked like a skull, and her eyes bulged from the deep pockets created by loss of the normal periorbital fat that surrounds them. She told her story as follows:

It began on Christmas three years ago. I got very depressed that winter. I always got depressed around the holidays, but this was more than ever before. Around that time I started becoming concerned about my weight. I was a little overweight then, but not much. After Christmas I started dieting more and more. But after I'd reached my goal of losing around twenty pounds or so, I began to develop a terrible craving for sweet things—especially the dough-nuts at the office in the morning and other things like that.

Early that spring we had an office party for someone who was going away. I let myself have a piece of carrot cake, and suddenly I couldn't stop. I ate countless pieces of cake and then went out and bought more food and ate that. The next morning I was horrified to find that I had gained nine pounds! I forced myself to eat only 200 calories a day for the next several days, and eventually I lost the weight.

But the next week, I had another binge, this time when I was alone in my own apartment. It took me ten days of almost complete fasting to lose the weight. After that, I got onto a regular cycle of binging and fasting.

I don't remember exactly how I hit upon the idea of vomiting. I guess it was when someone told me about using ipecac to induce vomiting in children who had eaten poisons. I bought some ipecac and it worked. You can't imagine how relieved I was—I woke up the next morning with no weight gain. Soon after that, I learned to vomit by myself, without the ipecac.

That's when the anorexia nervosa really started. Now that I had a wonderful new ability to binge without gaining weight, I could lose all the weight I wanted. My weight plummeted. I lost over thirty pounds in less than two months. People at the office began telling me I looked too thin, but it had no effect on me. I was determined to lose more weight and nothing could deter me.

I guess I was down to about ninety pounds or so when I collapsed on a flight of stairs and my boss insisted that I see a doctor. The doctor quickly figured out that I had anorexia nervosa and sent me to a psychiatrist. But in spite of the psychiatric help, I still haven't changed very much, I'm afraid.

This sequence from depression to anorexia nervosa to anorexia nervosa plus bulimia is one of the most common progressions we have observed. But we have also seen many patients who were pure anorexics at one time, pure bulimics at another, and displayed symptoms of both disorders at another. We vividly remember one patient—one of the first eating-disorder patients we treated, many years ago—who had tripled in size, from a low of 76 pounds when she was at the peak of her anorexia nervosa to nearly 250 pounds when she was binge eating daily (but not vomiting or using laxatives). One can hardly imagine this girl's emotional turmoil as she helplessly watched these astounding fluctuations in her weight, and endured endless shame and embarrassment before fellow students and her very few friends.

Further evidence of the close link between bulimia and anorexia nervosa comes from studies of family trees. A number of our bulimic patients had anorexic relatives, and a number of our anorexic patients had bulimic relatives. In some instances, the relatives were not even aware of each other's illness; we discovered it only through personal interviews of family members.

Do such findings indicate that anorexia nervosa and bulimia are both caused in part by some hereditary abnormality? We suspect so, for reasons that will become clear below. But the observation that bulimia and anorexia nervosa run in families does not *prove* that they are hereditary; they might both be caused by some idiosyncrasy of the family environment.

Regardless of the relative contributions of heredity and environment, however, the fact that the two disorders run together in families clearly suggests that they are related disorders—and that a treatment successful for one might also be successful for the other. We will get back to this in Chapter 6.

Bulimia and Major Depression

Table 1 (p. 48) shows that major depression is the single most common psychiatric disorder we have observed in bulimic patients. Given the accounts of depression and even suicidal feelings of the bulimic patients quoted in the previous chapters, this should come as no surprise. We have found depression almost ubiquitous in bulimia, and most other researchers studying bulimia have reached the same conclusion. Dr. Gerard Russell, one of England's best-known experts on bulimia, reported that 43% of his bulimic patients had experienced one or more of the following: "complaints of severe and persistent gloom with suicidal ideas, minor suicidal acts, marked irritability, severe impairment of concentration." An additional 43% had experienced one or more of the following: "severe depressive symptoms leading to inability to work or cope with daily activities, a previous course of electroconvulsive therapy, a serious suicidal act."[7] Dr. Richard Pyle and his colleagues in Minnesota, studying thirty-four patients with bulimia, similarly noted a high prevalence of depression, and found that scores for depression were significantly elevated on the Minnesota Multiphasic Personality Inventory, a personality test.[8] In Japan, two scientists at a medical school in Tokyo described depression in 75% of their sixteen cases.[9] Recently, in a systematic study by Dr. Timothy Walsh and colleagues, using detailed interviews, a history of major depression was found in 72% of thirty-nine bulimic subjects—a figure that agrees closely with our own results.[10] Dr. David Herzog and his associates at Massachusetts General Hospital, examining a population of ninety-nine bulimic patients, reported a similarly high prevalence of depressive disorders.[11]

Everyone seems to agree, then, that there is a close link between bulimia and depression. But what is the direction of causality? Does bulimia cause the depression, does an underlying depressive illness cause bulimia, or are both depression and bulimia caused by some third factor?

In the past, many researchers have assumed the first of these possibilities—namely, that depression was largely a reaction to the eating binges. After all, it would be only natural to feel depressed and self-critical after having lost control, eaten thousands of calories, and gained many pounds. The accounts of many of our patients would certainly seem to support such a theory.

Plausible though this theory may be, it does not explain all the facts. Many studies suggest that the reverse is more likely to be true: Depressive illness may be the underlying factor, with bulimia being merely one of its symptoms. There are several lines of evidence to support this view.

First, in a large number of bulimics—48% in the study quoted earlier in this chapter—the depressive illness began more than a year *before* the bulimia started. An example of this would be the patient quoted earlier, who began with a depressive episode in the winter, then experienced her first eating binge several months later, in the spring. In such cases, one cannot reasonably argue that the bulimia caused the depression.

Second, major depressive illness, and its cousin, manic-depressive illness (now known as bipolar disorder), tend to run in the families of individuals with bulimia. In fact, in one study, we found that 53% of bulimic patients had at least one first-degree relative (parent, sibling, child) with bipolar disorder or major depression.[12] If one were to look also at second-degree relatives (grandparents, aunts, and uncles), the number of our patients with such a positive family history would be even higher. Other researchers have come up with similar findings. Again, if bulimia were the cause of depressive illness, it would be difficult to explain why so many family members of bulimic patients would also display depressive illness but *not* bulimia.

Third—and this is the most crucial point—the depressions we have observed in bulimia are usually not reactive depressions, but instead appear to be endogenous depressions. A reactive depression, in simple terms, is depression that develops in reaction to something, for purely psychological or situational reasons: You get fired from your job, you lose a close friend, you fail at some pursuit, and you become depressed. This type of depression presumably has little to do with a chemical imbalance in the brain; it is rarely associated with prolonged changes in sleep, appetite, or other physical functions; and antidepressant medications are usually ineffective for it.

Endogenous depression, on the other hand, is believed to arise from a biochemical abnormality in the brain.[13] Unlike reactive depression, endogenous depression often appears out of the blue; it does not seem to be a reaction to anything in particular. Also unlike reactive depression, endogenous depression usually causes sustained changes in sleep patterns, appetite, weight, energy level, concentration, sex drive, and other biological functions. If you look back at questions 2a–h in Part II of the quiz at the beginning of this chapter, you will see that the questions are aimed at these symptoms, which typically accompany endogenous ("biochemical" or "major") depression. We are not certain of the exact biochemical abnormality in the brain that produces major depression—although there are several promising theories—but we know that major depression is hereditary, that it is closely related to manic-depressive illness, and that it can usually be successfully treated with antidepressant drugs.

You'll hear more about this in later chapters. Suffice it to say for the present that more than two-thirds of the bulimic patients we have interviewed have experienced at least one episode of what appears to be endogenous, or major, depression. Most recall that the periods of depression felt "different" from ordinary day-to-day depressions. One patient, a twenty-three-year-old man with bulimia, described his symptoms as follows:

As I look back, there have been two distinctive periods. The first depression came on, apropos of nothing, during my junior year of college. There was no reason for me to feel depressed—everything was going along fine—but I gradually began to find that I just couldn't experience pleasure like I used to. Things didn't seem to turn me on anymore. I started sleeping a lot—twelve or thirteen hours a day—and even when I got out of bed, I still didn't feel as though I'd had enough sleep. It got really hard to do my work. Normally, physics problems and stuff like that were routine for me, but it got so that even simple stuff was incredibly difficult. I fell so far behind that I finally had to drop one course.

Then, in the fall of my senior year, the whole thing cleared, for no apparent reason. It simply evaporated over the course of a few weeks. All my powers of concentration came back, my energy came back, and my sex drive came back. During the depression, I almost forgot about sex. But by the next fall, I was going out with girls again and feeling completely normal.

The normal period lasted more than a year. And then the tired feeling and the trouble working started to creep back again. By that point, I was working at a firm out on Route 128, and it would take me an hour to write a computer program that would ordinarily have taken me five minutes. I was really scared, because I had some idea what was happening to me this time, and there was nothing I could do to make it go away.

I still have it now. It's always worst in the morning. I have to drag myself out of bed, and I have a sickening feeling of anxiety in my gut. Those are the times I even think of suicide. The anxiety continues through the morning, and then by later in the day the feeling seems to dissipate. By late evening, I feel half-decent, and I'm even reluctant to go to bed, because I know the sequence will repeat itself the following morning.

It was right in the middle of this, about six months ago, that the eating binges started.

One feature of this story, which we hear often, is the *diurnal variation* of the depression—a daily cycle with a peak at the same time each day (in this case, the early morning)—much like the diurnal variation we have described in bulimia itself. In fact, the presence of diurnal variation is often one of the best indicators that someone is suffering from major depression as opposed to the milder, reactive type. If one is suffering merely from a depressing situation or psychological difficulties that lead to depression, the symptoms of depression will usually occur throughout the day, with peaks and valleys coming at varying times or in response to specific stimuli. Endogenous depression, on the other hand, may distinguish itself because of its daily rhythm, with the worst period typically occurring at the same time every day, apparently because it is controlled by some inner biological clock rather than by external events.

Does the same biological clock, the same apparent cycling chemical abnormality, contribute to eating binges in some way? Given the close relationship between bulimia and major depression in so many patients, one might be tempted to think so. (More about this in Chapter 6.)

Bulimia and Manic-Depressive Illness

Manic-depressive illness, now called bipolar disorder, is closely related to major depression.[14] But instead of having purely depressed phases—"lows"—bipolar patients also have manic phases or "highs," hence the name *bi*polar. Manic episodes are usually just the opposite of depressed ones, with euphoria, irritability, hyperactivity, decreased need for sleep, racing thoughts, "pressured" speech, and other symptoms, such as those listed in question 2 of Part III in the quiz. Mania may also display diurnal variation, with the symptoms peaking more often in the evening. Often, a manic patient will look like someone who has taken too much amphetamine or "speed"—he or she simply can't slow down.

Frequently manic patients show psychotic symptoms, such as delusions (beliefs in things that are not actually happening) or hallucinations (seeing or hearing something that is not there). Manic patients may believe that the announcer on the radio is talking about them, that the words on advertising signs contain special hidden messages, that the CIA is out to get them, or that mysterious influences from outer space are controlling their thoughts. They may hear voices talking about them, calling them names, or instructing them to do various things. To make matters worse, most manic patients are not aware that there is anything wrong with them; they may be picked up by the police and taken, screaming and kicking, to a nearby psychiatric hospital, where they often refuse medications and demand their freedom, insisting that they are perfectly normal.

As recently as ten years ago many psychiatrists thought that such psychotic symptoms occurred only in schizophrenia. As a result, manic patients (and some patients with major depression who also had psychotic symptoms) were frequently misdiagnosed as schizophrenic. In recent years, however, psychiatry has come to recognize that delusions and hallucinations occur commonly in manic-depressive illness, and that great care should be taken to *not* misdiagnose such patients as having schizophrenia.

Looking back at Table 1, you will find that about 14% of our bulimic patients had displayed manic-depressive illness (bipolar disorder) at some time. However, more than half of them had previously been misdiagnosed as schizophrenic.

The point is this: If you or someone in your family has ever been diagnosed as schizophrenic, the diagnosis may well be wrong. Look back at sections II and III in the quiz and see if the symptoms are consistent with bipolar disorder, or perhaps major depression with accompanying psychotic features. We believe, on the basis of our research, that there is no significant link between bulimia and schizophrenia. But bulimia, major depression, and manic-depressive illness appear closely linked both in individuals and in family trees.

Bulimia and Alcohol Abuse

About one-fourth of our bulimic patients have suffered from alcohol abuse or alcohol dependence (addiction) at some point in their lives. Alcohol abuse is analogous to bulimia in many ways: The individual has impulses to consume alcohol; the impulses typically override voluntary control; and the disorder becomes gradually more severe and frequently chronic.[15] In the same manner that a taste of food can set off a binge in bulimia, a drink can set off a binge in the alcoholic. But there is one important difference: We don't have to drink to live. Therefore, complete abstinence from alcohol may solve the problem of alcoholism, but abstinence from food is not an option in bulimia.

As a matter of fact, we have seen a number of patients who

were alcoholics for several years; then managed to break their habits through Alcoholics Anonymous, professional counseling, or sheer self-discipline; and almost immediately found themselves victims of a new affliction: compulsive binge eating. "It was as if my body could not survive without an addiction to something," said one woman. "I guess I'm just an addictive personality."

It is difficult to be sure whether there really is such a thing as an "addictive personality." But listening to patients' accounts, it seems possible that alcohol abuse and food abuse are triggered by a similar mechanism.

Bulimia and Panic Disorder

Panic disorder—the syndrome of spontaneous panic attacks—is another of the syndromes which we have often observed in association with bulimia (although this particular association was not noted in the New York study[10]). Yet, like bulimia itself, it often goes undiagnosed, because many people (including professionals) are unaware that it is now a well-recognized illness.[16] Many of our bulimic patients, when asked the questions in Part V of the quiz, have been surprised and relieved to discover that their strange spontaneous attacks of fear and anxiety represented a common syndrome. Many had thought that the attacks were "neurotic," or due to some personality weakness or a dietary problem. Often they had devised elaborate measures to try to deal with the attacks or to avoid them, such as refusing to visit places where attacks had occurred, or carrying tranquilizers in their pockets to take at the moment of an attack. Some described attacks so severe that they rushed to the local emergency room, thinking that they were having a heart attack. Almost all described remarkably similar symptoms: palpitations, sweating, hyperventilating, light-headedness, and a characteristic feeling of doom that descended on them out of the blue. One of our patients, himself a physician, gave us the most vivid description we can remember:

You can never really know how bad a panic attack is unless you've actually had one, but perhaps I can give you some idea. I used to do a lot of work in intensive-care units, dealing with cardiac emergencies, strokes, and other life-threatening situations. I've seen many patients who were having massive myocardial infarctions [heart attacks], with severe crushing chest pain that would suddenly stop. When they reached that final moment when the pain stopped, they somehow knew that they were about to die, that it was a terminal event. I've looked into their eyes at that moment and seen the unspeakable terror there as they knew that death had arrived. That look, that feeling—that is what it is like at the peak of a panic attack.

Fortunately, this horrible syndrome is now quite easily treated, using the same medications we are now using to treat bulimia. If you or someone you know has panic disorder and it has never been treated, you can quickly receive help from any experienced psychopharmacologist.

Bulimia and Agoraphobia

Agoraphobia—the fear of being in crowds, or even out of doors, away from one's home—is often the final outcome of panic disorder.[16] Dominated by the constant fear of an attack, the individual may come to restrict his or her life more and more, eventually reaching the point where even a brief foray away from home is terrifying. Some people develop agoraphobia without experiencing panic attacks. They usually describe a pattern of gradually increasing anxiety in public situations, particularly in places from which there is no quick escape, such as a bridge, an elevator, a theater, or a bus. One woman with bulimia and agoraphobia made a concerted effort to drive twenty miles from her home northeast of Boston to our offices west of the city. She made it as far as the bridge over the Mystic River, then was struck by the fear of being on the bridge and unable to get off quickly. An hour later she called from home and sheepishly explained what had happened. It took her two more tries before she finally made it, but now she is doing much better with the antidepressant medication phenelzine.

Interestingly, the first case of bulimia ever described in detail in the medical literature—Pierre Janet's "Nadia"—was a woman who suffered from severe agoraphobia in conjunction with bulimia. We will tell Nadia's story in detail in the next chapter.

Bulimia and Obsessive-Compulsive Disorder

Everyone has had an occasional obsession or compulsion: We go back to recheck that the door is locked, even though we know perfectly well that we have just locked it, or we have to arrange things on the desk or in the kitchen in a certain way, and become slightly irritated if anyone tries to arrange them differently. Such symptoms are usually harmless and even amusing. But true obsessive-compulsive disorder, in which such symptoms become grossly exaggerated, can become a miserable and disabling condition;[17] uncontrollable obsessions and compulsions are among the most frequent complaints of our patients with bulimia.

We have already described the chronic obsessions about food and weight that plague many bulimic patients. But in about 30% of patients, these obsessions spill over into other areas of life, and the individual becomes dominated by constant obsessive thoughts and compulsive rituals that persist through practically every moment of the day. Here are examples from four of our patients:

> For ten years since I've had bulimia, I've had to check all the closets in my house to be sure no one is hiding in them. Sometimes I check every closet, sit down, and then have to get up and check them all again fifteen minutes later, because I begin to doubt whether I've checked them completely or not.

> I have to count things. Every morning when I go to the bathroom, I have to count all the tiles that run around the periphery of the room where the wall meets the ceiling. I know it's stupid, but I can't stop myself from doing it. At times when I try to stop myself from doing it, I get extremely anxious, and then I break down and start again.

> You know how I worry as to whether there are any stray calories on a spoon that was not washed completely. Well, in addition to that, I now have started worrying about dirt on my hands. I'm washing my hands twenty or thirty times a day now, and they're getting chapped and sore, with a couple of large cuts as a result of the chapping. But I can't stop it. Just looking at my hands right now, I'm fearing that they might have germs on them from that doorknob there.

> When I set the table for myself and my roommates, I have to set everything in a certain way—first the plates, then the glasses, then

the napkins, and the silverware last, starting with the spoons and ending with dull knives, like butter knives, and finally sharp knives, like steak knives. If anyone else sets the table, or does even part of it, I get very upset, and sometimes I have to take everything off the table and start the whole process again, even though I know there is no point to what I am doing.

Obsessions and compulsions, then, are analogous to eating binges. They are ego-dystonic—the patient does not enjoy them, would like to be rid of them, but cannot shut them off. As with binges, it is as if some crucial circuitry in the brain, the circuit that "shuts off" useless impulses, is not working properly; the obsessions and compulsions cycle over and over, unchecked.

Bulimia, Kleptomania, and Other Disorders of Impulse Control

Finally, we come to the most exotic of the bulimia-associated syndromes: compulsive shoplifting. People are invariably shocked when we report that about one-third of our bulimic patients—many of them affluent, law-abiding people with sterling reputations in their communities—regularly engage in thousands of dollars' worth of compulsive shoplifting.

Nor are we alone in the finding. Dr. Richard Pyle and his colleagues in Minnesota, in their report on thirty-four bulimic patients mentioned earlier,[8] found "stealing behavior" in no less than twenty-two of the cases—almost two-thirds of the sample. A number of the patients stole exclusively food, but three stole clothing, three stole cosmetics or jewelry, and one stole alcohol.

Other researchers studying patients with both anorexia nervosa and bulimia have recorded a similar association. Dr. Regina Casper and her colleagues found kleptomania in 24% of their forty-nine cases,[18] and Dr. Paul Garfinkel and colleagues found it in 12% of their sixty-eight cases.[19]

What are we to make of this? First, the kleptomania of bulimic patients is not ordinary stealing for gain. They rarely steal things (except perhaps food or laxatives) because they cannot afford to buy them or for their monetary value. One of our bulimic patients, for example, was the wife of a very successful trial lawyer who probably earned several hundred thousand dollars a year, yet she found herself routinely stealing clothes costing ten or twenty dollars from a local discount store. No one—neither her husband nor her closest friends—was aware of her kleptomania, since she had never been caught. When we asked her, in the initial interview, if she had ever shoplifted, she was stunned. "How could you possibly have guessed?" she asked. When we told her that one-third of our other patients shared her disorder, she was amazed and visibly relieved.

Second, virtually none of our kleptomaniac patients had ever committed any other crimes. Few had police records beyond a parking ticket. Unlike true criminals—so-called sociopaths, or individuals with "antisocial personality disorder"—our patients hardly ever planned their stealing in advance; they rarely calculated the risks or selected the most valuable objects to steal; they never used an accomplice. A number of them felt so guilty after stealing that they would attempt to surreptitiously return the stolen item to the store the next day, at considerable risk—only to find themselves compulsively stealing something else an hour later. Surely this is not the behavior of criminals.

Third, kleptomania, unlike ordinary criminal behavior, but like most of the other syndromes described in this chapter, is largely *not under voluntary control*. The individual walks into a store with little or no intention to steal, and then is seized with an irresistible impulse, just like the irresistible impulse to binge, which cannot be refused. The tension mounts and mounts until the act is completed and a feeling of release is achieved. One bulimic woman, a happily married mother of two in an affluent suburb on Boston's North Shore, describes the phenomenon:

You're not going to believe this, but I'd estimate that I must have stolen between thirty and forty thousand dollars' worth of cosmetics. I didn't have trouble with items in some stores, but I'd find myself on the first floor of Filene's, in Boston, and I'd feel the urge coming over me that I just absolutely *had* to steal some makeup or perfume. I had the money in my purse to buy it, but that never seemed to make any difference. I'd sit there, wrestling with the feeling, telling myself that I was taking a ridiculous chance to do such a stupid thing, but I'd know that I was helpless. The feeling just took over. I'd start trembling, look around to see if anybody was watching, and then lunge for some object and stuff it in my purse.

I shudder to think of some of the risks I took. I just can't imagine the pain and humiliation I would have suffered if I'd ever been caught. Often, the minute I was out of the store, I would impulsively throw the object away—fifty-dollar bottles of perfume and the like— because I was afraid someone would apprehend me, and because I didn't even want the thing anyway. It was just incredible, but I couldn't stop it.

Readers who have not actually experienced kleptomania, and have never talked to someone who has it, may doubt that such acts could truly be beyond voluntary control. After all, for thousands of years it has been a fundamental tenet of Judeo-Christian philosophy that man has the capacity to choose between right and wrong. An *illness* that literally compels one to repetitively commit what one knows perfectly well to be crimes defies our whole notion of free will as opposed to determinism.

And yet, upon hearing many such accounts, it becomes obvious that shoplifting, like binging, is caused by a breakdown of the voluntary control mechanisms. Practically all of us have experienced the urge to binge eat or to steal things from a store, but most of us never do so, because we quickly "turn off" the urge before it becomes overwhelming. Probably during a day we turn off dozens of such urges to do harmful or inappropriate things; the process is so rapid and automatic that we are hardly aware of it—we take our voluntary impulse control for granted.

It is easy to understand that one's liver or kidneys could fall ill and malfunction. It is more difficult to acknowledge that something like impulse control could fall ill too, and that patients with severe bulimia or kleptomania could be no more capable of turning off their urges than patients with pneumonia could stop coughing, or epileptic patients could turn off a seizure. Seduced by the illusion of a mind-body duality, we forget that voluntary impulse control, however lofty it may seem, has its seat in a network of ordinary nerve cells somewhere in the brain, and that these are as vulnerable to illness as any other organ of the body.

Indeed, it seems possible that many other disorders of impulse control, such as pathological gambling, fire-setting (pyromania), and temper outbursts (intermittent explosive disorder)—all of which, incidentally, we have observed in the family trees of bulimic patients—may stem from the same, possibly hereditary, abnormality in the impulse-control "circuitry."[20] These disorders share the features of bulimia and of many of the other bulimia-associated disorders described above: Patients are usually aware that the symptoms are abnormal or destructive, and often they want to be rid of them, but exhorting such patients to change, admonishing them to exercise more control, and decrying their failure to improve usually accomplish absolutely nothing. In fact, this sort of "therapy" may even heighten their agony.

TABLE 2
Bulimia-Associated Disorders

APPARENTLY CLOSELY RELATED TO BULIMIA
    Anorexia nervosa
    Major affective disorder
      Major depression
      Bipolar disorder (manic-depressive illness)

SOME RELATIONSHIP TO BULIMIA
    Anxiety disorders
      Panic disorder
      Agoraphobia
      Obsessive-compulsive disorder
    Kleptomania
    Some substance-use disorders (especially alcohol and stimulants)

POSSIBLE BUT UNTESTED RELATIONSHIP TO BULIMIA
    Other impulse-control disorders (pathological gambling,
      pyromania, etc.)
    Histrionic personality disorder
    Borderline personality disorder

PROBABLY UNRELATED TO BULIMIA
    Most organic mental disorders
    Most substance-use disorders (except some cases of alcohol and
      stimulant use)
    Schizophrenic disorders
    Paranoid disorders
    Other psychotic disorders (with exception of major affective
      disorder; see above)
    Somatoform disorders (i.e., hypochondriasis)
    Dissociative disorders (i.e., multiple personality)
    Most psychosexual disorders
    Adjustment disorders
    Most personality disorders (except histrionic and borderline
      personality; see above)

The Family of Bulimia-Associated Disorders

By now it should be clear that bulimia does not stand alone as an isolated psychiatric disorder, but is often closely interrelated with other syndromes. These are listed in Table 2, which also enumerates those syndromes apparently *not* related to bulimia.

The disorders listed in the first two categories of the table—anorexia nervosa, major affective disorder, anxiety disorders, kleptomania, and certain cases of substance abuse—appear related not only to bulimia but to each other. Many of them seem to run together in family trees, and individuals with one disorder seem to have a higher than average chance of developing one or more of the others during their lifetime.

Although the exact mechanism of this relationship is unknown, it is conceivable that the bulimia-associated disorders share some underlying biological abnormality. In some individuals, this hypothetical abnormality may produce, or predispose to, major affective disorder—bipolar disorder or major depression. In others, the same abnormality may predispose to bulimia, or anorexia nervosa, or one of the anxiety disorders. In some patients, several different syndromes might develop: One patient might first develop major depression and panic disorder, then as a result of the panic attacks, go on to develop agoraphobia and perhaps alcohol dependence. Another might begin by abusing alcohol as a young adult; after managing to give up alcohol, he or she might develop bulimia; and finally, perhaps many years later, an episode of major depression or even bipolar disorder might occur.

Of course, such conjectures are speculative; we have no proof of any single underlying abnormality. And we certainly must not assume that *all* cases of alcoholism, or of obsessive-compulsive disorder, or of bulimia itself, are necessarily part of the same family. But given the hereditary and symptomatic interrelationship of many cases of these disorders, it seems at least possible that we can eventually trace many of them back to a common biochemical "mistake" somewhere in the brain, and perhaps even unlock their secret. Of course, we would have to be lucky to have it all come out so simply; the true answer is probably much more complicated. Another decade or two of research will help to tell. But in the meantime, the interrelationship of bulimia and its associated disorders is of far more than academic interest, because it provides us with many clues about how to treat bulimia and related syndromes right now, without waiting for the next twenty years of research results to become available. We will discuss this in detail in Chapters 6 and 8.

5

WHAT CAUSES BULIMIA?

What causes the syndrome of compulsive eating binges? What could account for the accompanying depression and self-depreciation, the uncontrollable obsessions with food, and, particularly, the striking autonomy of the binges themselves? Though most patients are disgusted with their constant binging, desperate to be rid of their symptoms, why are they unable to shut them off? Surely a powerful mechanism acts to perpetuate such an unpleasant illness. And this mechanism, whatever it is, must also be linked in some way to the many bulimia-associated disorders described in the previous chapter. In other words, any proposed theory of the cause of bulimia must of necessity explain why such disorders as anorexia nervosa, major depression, panic disorder, agoraphobia, and so forth appear so commonly in bulimic patients.

For more than a century, these questions have baffled some of the best-known thinkers in the history of psychiatry, as a review of their writings will show.

The Wandering Uterus and "Canine Hunger"

It is hard to know when in history a physician first saw a case of true bulimia; prior to 1903, case descriptions in the medical literature are all somewhat equivocal. To be sure, many physicians throughout the ages have commented on the phenomenon of self-induced vomiting. But were these ancient purgers some-times covert bingers as well? It seems possible, even likely, but there is no way to be certain.

As far back as the time of the pharaohs, Egyptian physicians had developed colorful theories on the causes of self-induced vomiting.[1] They thought that the uterus—the womb—could be-come detached from its natural position in the base of the pelvis and wander freely about the body, causing various symptoms as it came to rest at different locations. If it migrated to the region near the heart, its pressure could cause vomiting. The Greeks inherited this theory: The modern word *hysteria* evolved from the Greek word for uterus.

Later, Roman physicians, such as Galen, described individuals who deliberately vomited after devouring large quantities of food without satisfaction. Seneca may also have been describing bulimia when he wrote: *"vomunt ut edant, edunt ut vomant"* ("they vomit in order to eat; they eat in order to vomit"). In the follow-ing centuries, subsequent scholars used several names to de-scribe the syndrome, including "bulimia" (Greek for "hunger of an ox") and "kynorexia" or "fames canina" (Greek and Latin for "hunger of a dog"). Here is one example from Dr. Robert Whytt, an English neurologist writing in 1767: "Doctor Lomer has ob-served that hypochondriac and hysteric people are often trou-bled with an uncommon hunger or *fames canina;* and while this lasts, they are almost free of other complaints; but that their usual ailments return with their natural appetite."[2]

Is *fames canina* what we now call bulimia? Unfortunately, Whytt gives no further information beyond this brief note.

Nearly a century later, in 1859, the famous French psychiatrist Dr. Pierre Briquet wrote his classic *Traité de l'Hystérie (Treatise on Hysteria)*, one of the most comprehensive descriptions of hysteria ever written.[3] Briquet devotes an entire section of this work to hysterical stomach ailments. Among many other cases, he de-scribes a young woman who consistently vomited everything she ate, but never lost her appetite. The poor girl spent her entire day alternately eating and vomiting.

Again, it is hard to know whether Briquet's patient was truly bulimic or was eating normally between episodes of vomiting. Like Whytt, Briquet simply categorized this condition under the umbrella of hysteria. It seems likely that most physicians prior to 1900, confronted with a bulimic patient, would make the diagnosis of hysteria for a woman or hypochondriasis for a man.

Nadia: The First Modern Case of True Bulimia

Not until 1903 do we find the first detailed modern case report of bulimia. She is described by Pierre Janet, another of France's famous early psychiatrists and a meticulous observer of human behavior.[4] He calls her Nadia.

Nadia is the gifted and intelligent daughter of a wealthy and very distinguished French family. A voracious reader, she speaks fluent French, English, German, and Russian, and can read Italian and Spanish as well. Her encyclopedic knowledge of the world's literature is complemented by remarkable artistic talents; she draws well, plays the piano brilliantly, and composes music that impresses even sophisticated musicians. Surely she would seem destined to a distinguished place in the upper echelons of Parisian society. And yet at the time that Janet writes, she is twenty-eight years old and has confined herself for the last five years in semidarkness in a tiny apartment from which she almost never departs, seeing no one except her housekeeper and her doctor, and spending the bulk of her time obsessing about food, her weight, and her body.

How did she become this way? Janet begins by noting a family history of obsessive-compulsive disorder in her mother and probably in other relatives. Nadia's sisters also display agoraphobic and obsessive tendencies, albeit to a lesser degree. None of them has ever married.

Nadia had experienced clearly recognizable obsessions since the age of four. As she grew older, she became preoccupied with the ugliness of various parts of her body: her hands, her feet, her thighs, her head. The arrival of puberty triggered a surge of obsessive-compulsive behavior patterns: If she touched the same note on the piano exactly four times during the course of a given piece, she felt as though she were tacitly consenting to grow fat and never be loved by anyone again. She swore to herself to say the same prayer five times, or ten times, to jump five times on the same foot. Then, realizing that this was ridiculous, she swore not to perform these acts, only to be plunged into endless obsessive doubtings as to which of the two courses—to act or not to act— was superior.

By the age of fifteen or sixteen, anorexia nervosa set in. Her diet, in Janet's words, was *"fantastique"*: Two bowls of clear bouillon, one egg yolk, a large spoonful of vinegar, and a cup of extremely strong tea with the juice of an entire lemon in it—that was her quota for the day.

Several times she was hospitalized, force-fed for six months, and then released, only to resume her frantic dieting immediately. But her hunger remained very much alive; she was chronically hungry, ravenously hungry, and soon eating binges began. Periodically, Janet writes, she would "gluttonously" devour everything she could find. It is not clear whether she vomited afterward, but her binges were followed by *"remords horribles"*—terrible remorse. Nevertheless, she soon binged again.

Her obsessions with food were monstrous. "Sometimes I spend entire hours thinking of food, because I'm so hungry," she confides. "I swallow my saliva, I chew on my handkerchief, I roll on the ground, so desperate am I to eat. I search in books for descriptions of great banquets, and try to trick my hunger by imagining that I, too, am tasting all of those wonderful things."

By age twenty-eight, Nadia leaves her dark little apartment only at times of dire necessity, and then only at night. Horrible scenes ensue when she is required to go outside; she must marshal all her courage merely to jettison herself from her doorway into the darkness of a waiting enclosed carriage. The rest of her time she spends in the sanctuary of her rooms, tyrannized by endless obsessions and compulsions. "It would unquestionably take her eight days to decide on a course of action that you or I could decide in two minutes," writes Janet. "It would take her months to adjust, and even then imperfectly, to the tiniest change." As a bright woman, Nadia is painfully aware that her obsessions and eating patterns are abnormal, even ridiculous, but she is powerless to change them.

In Nadia's miserable existence, we see practically all the elements described eighty years later in bulimia: her preoccupation with food; her secret binges, followed by shame and self-depreciation; and her recognition that the eating pattern was abnormal, but beyond voluntary control. Nadia also suffered severely from at least three bulimia-associated syndromes: anorexia nervosa, agoraphobia, and obsessive-compulsive disorders. She probably had a history of major depression as well, but it is difficult to be certain.

Alas, we never learn what happens to Nadia; she is presented by Janet merely as a case example in his treatise on obsessional disorders. He does not offer a specific theory of the origin of her symptoms, but he makes a number of important observations. First, he emphasizes the hereditary component in the disorder, which is clear upon analysis of Nadia's family. Also, he recognizes that bulimia is but one of a complex of related disorders, anticipating much of what we have discussed. Finally, he goes to considerable lengths to point out that Nadia does *not* suffer from hysteria. Even upon very careful inspection, he says, there are no signs of hysteria at any point in Nadia's history. In a departure from the ideas of centuries past, he is convinced that her symptoms represent some quite different disorder.

In all of these impressions, Janet was far ahead of his time—indeed, ahead of many mental-health professionals today. Even in the 1980s, many do not recognize the magnitude of the hereditary component in bulimia and its associated disorders. Some remain unaware of the close links between bulimia and a wide range of other psychiatric syndromes. And a majority of professionals, we suspect, still continue to classify bulimia as a "hysterical" disorder. In modern diagnostic terminology, they would diagnose bulimic patients as having "histrionic personality disorder" or "borderline personality disorder," not acknowledging, as Janet did, that bulimia is perhaps a quite different illness.

The Celebrated Case of Ellen West

One of psychiatry's most famous cases of bulimia, interestingly enough, was never actually diagnosed as bulimia at the time. The patient is given the name Ellen West, and she is the subject of an extensive case report written in 1943 by the famous Swiss psychiatrist Ludwig Binswanger.[5]

Like Nadia, Ellen is the attractive, intelligent daughter of a wealthy family. As a child and in her teens, she travels all over Europe and even to America, writing poems and copious notes in her diary to chronicle her experiences. All seems well until the age of twenty, when, on a trip to Sicily, she first notices an increased concern with being fat and, with it, the onset of a depressive episode. "Everything is so uniform to me, so utterly indifferent," she writes in her diary. "I know no feeling of joy and none of fear."

Fortunately, the depression remits after a few months. But a second episode follows two years later, and now the dread of becoming fat is accompanied by an exaggerated longing for food, especially sweets. She tries harder to lose weight. By the age of twenty-four, she "does everything to get just as thin as possible, takes long hikes, and daily swallows thirty-six to forty-eight thyroid tablets! . . . She arrives [at her parents' house] completely emaciated, with trembling limbs, and drags herself through the summer in physical torment, but remains spiritually satisfied because she is thin." The following year she spends a month in the hospital because of her depression.

By age twenty-six, she is no longer thin; her weight has risen to 160 pounds. She gets married, and experiences some enjoyable intervals during the next several years, but continues to be plagued by periodic depressions. By age thirty-one, the symptoms of both anorexia nervosa and bulimia erupt with increased severity. She becomes preoccupied with calorie charts and recipes. Foods with low caloric content, such as shellfish and clams, she devours "with great greed and haste." True binges begin: "On her way home she eats up things she has bought for the household and then upbraids herself severely for it." She begins to abuse laxatives with alarming frequency: "Every morning she takes sixty to seventy tablets of a vegetable laxative, with the result that she suffers tortured vomiting at night and violent diarrhea by day, often accompanied by a weakness of the heart."

The next year she starts her first psychoanalysis with a "young and sensitive analyst." But it does little good. She begins to leave out entire meals, only "to throw herself indiscriminately with all the greater greed upon any foods which may happen to be at hand. Each day she consumes several pounds of tomatoes and twenty oranges." She stops the analysis after six months.

Soon she starts a second psychoanalysis, but with no better success than the first. Within two months she has made two suicide attempts. The desire for food remains unchanged. "Now that I see the pleasure of eating as the real obsessive idea," she writes in her diary, "it has pounced on me like a wild beast. I am defenselessly at its mercy. It pursues me constantly and is driving me to despair. . . ."

Her analyst's Freudian interpretations don't seem to help. "The anal-erotic connection is purely theoretical," she writes. "It is completely incomprehensible. I don't understand myself at all."

A consultation is requested with one of the most eminent psychiatrists in Europe, Emil Kraepelin. After examining Ellen, he diagnoses melancholia—what we would now call "major depression." From the vantage point of the 1980s, it seems almost certain that Kraepelin was right; Ellen was experiencing one of the commonest of the bulimia-associated disorders described in Chapter 4. In fact, it would seem that the diagnosis of melancholia should have been clear even at the time: Not only did Ellen display many symptoms of depressive illness, but her family tree was riddled with cases of depressive illness and even manic-depressive illness. Her brother had been hospitalized for depression and suicidal feelings, two of her uncles had shot themselves during periods of "melancholy," an aunt had fallen ill on her wedding day, and a great-grandparent had been diagnosed as manic depressive. On the strength of heredity alone, melancholia would seem a strong probability.

But Ellen's analyst does not accept Dr. Kraepelin's diagnosis, and the analysis goes on—but not for long. Ellen deteriorates so much that her medical doctor orders the analysis terminated and his patient sent to a sanatorium. He notes in his final medical exam that her salivary glands are grossly enlarged—perhaps from self-induced vomiting (discussed in Chapter 2).

In the sanatorium, Ellen's symptoms continue. She is described as suffering greatly "from obsessional impulses to throw herself upon food and gulp it down like an animal (confirmed by observation)." Another internationally recognized psychiatrist, Dr. Eugen Bleuler, the man who introduced the term *schizophrenia*, is called in to consult. Somewhat predictably, Dr. Bleuler concludes that the patient is schizophrenic, in spite of the fact that she has never shown any clear psychotic symptoms and in spite of the fact that she has a positive family history of major affective disorder, and none for schizophrenia. Yet another consultant, who sees the patient along with Dr. Bleuler, decides that Ellen has a "psychopathic constitution progressively unfolding."

But even though they disagree on the diagnosis, everyone agrees that the case is hopeless. Since there is no therapy likely to benefit the patient, she is sent home with her husband.

At first, her symptoms are even worse, but on the third day home she seems transformed: "At breakfast she eats butter and sugar, at noon she eats so much that—for the first time in thirteen years!—she is satisfied by her food and gets really full. At afternoon coffee she eats chocolate creams and Easter eggs. She takes a walk with her husband, . . . is in a positively festive mood, and all heaviness seems to have fallen away from her."

That evening, she takes a fatal dose of poison. She is dead by dawn.

What caused Ellen's bulimia, her depression, and her suicide? The greatest psychiatric minds of Europe had consulted on her, with no consensus. She had undergone two analyses, not to mention treatment by the eminent Dr. Binswanger during her final hospitalization, all without effect. Indeed, the psychiatrists had openly confessed their inability to treat her; she was discharged from the hospital with the full knowledge that suicide was almost inevitable. Nevertheless, despite the failure of all treatment, Dr. Binswanger offers an "existential analysis" of the case, which runs to more than 100 pages of ponderous German prose and concludes with the theory that Ellen was indeed psychotic.

What is disturbing about the theory is that Ellen West—like most people with bulimia—had displayed no evidence of psychotic symptoms, such as delusions, hallucinations, catatonic symptoms, or verbal incoherence. One is left with the uncomfortable feeling that Binswanger deliberately postulates that she was psychotic in order to make her case compatible with his theory.

Another explanation of Ellen's symptoms also strains credibility: Ellen's second psychoanalyst, an orthodox Freudian, had concluded that Ellen's craving to eat chocolate was actually a craving to eat feces, due to her suppressed anal-erotic urges. He carefully explained this to Ellen, as a matter of fact. But, as quoted above, Ellen found this "completely incomprehensible." Indeed, it was at about this time that she made two suicide attempts in rapid succession.

A third theory offered to explain Ellen's symptoms was that she unconsciously feared that by eating she would be fertilized and become pregnant. This theory has often been applied to patients with anorexia nervosa, although it requires a bit of stretching to explain how it would apply to bulimia. We will return to it later.

Finally, there is another fact that would seem inconsistent with any of the above theories: Ellen was normal up to the age of twenty, and even at intervals beyond that time. She had normal weight, normal eating habits, and, we might add, an apparently normal sex life. If she was suffering from major deficits in her functioning, stemming from oral or anal-erotic conflicts in childhood, why did she continue through puberty and her teens virtually asymptomatic? The theories do not explain.

In short, we cannot help but be skeptical of the rather complex theory presented by Dr. Binswanger to explain the case; instead, we would side with the first consultant, Professor Kraepelin. Ellen was very likely suffering from recurrent episodes of major depression. Major depression—Kraepelin's "melancholia"—is a hereditary disorder that had run down Ellen's family tree; it frequently strikes individuals who have previously been completely asymptomatic, as in Ellen's case; it typically runs a relapsing and remitting course, as it did in Ellen; and, as we have seen earlier, it is closely linked to bulimia.

Parenthetically, let us cite another authority who might side with us: Sigmund Freud. In a letter to Wilhelm Fliess, in 1895, Freud had conjectured that anorexia nervosa appeared to be a form of melancholia.[6] Thus, had Freud seen Ellen West, he might well have diagnosed melancholia, even though Binswanger, whose theory was derived from Freud's, did not.

If we, Kraepelin, and Freud are right, modern pharmacological treatments, had they been available at the time, would have had at least a 70%–80% probability of relieving Ellen's depressive symptoms—and probably her bulimia—within a few weeks.

But it is a bit unfair to look back on historical cases with the benefit of modern knowledge. What are today's theories on the cause of bulimia? These divide into four major schools of thought: psychodynamic and family theories, behavioral theories, sociocultural theories, and biological theories. Unfortunately, since bulimia has only recently been recognized as a separate diagnostic entity, much of the scientific literature concerns patients who have anorexia nervosa. But since 50% of patients with anorexia nervosa also display bulimia at some point, we will cover the anorexia nervosa literature as well in the following review.

Psychodynamic and Family Theories

Psychodynamic is approximately synonymous with what most people mean by *Freudian:* Psychodynamic explanations for human behavior are founded on the belief that critical conflicts in one's early life, when unresolved, lead to difficulties in psychological functioning later on. This school of thought stems from the work of Sigmund Freud and his colleagues, who developed the technique of psychoanalysis, in which the patient lies on a couch in the analyst's office four or five hours per week and "free-associates" from one thought to another. Although the classical, "orthodox" psychoanalytic theories—which focused almost exclusively on early childhood conflicts—have now begun to fade somewhat, newer psychodynamic theories have expanded to embrace conflicts at any stage of life, and have increasingly implicated "family systems"—the interactions between the patient and his or her family—in the etiology of psychiatric problems.

In the case of Ellen West, we have already seen one psychodynamic theory of anorexia nervosa—namely, that the disorder represents a fear of oral impregnation. This theory was expounded in great detail in 1940 by Dr. John Waller and his colleagues at the Beth Israel Hospital in Boston.[7] They argued: "The role of the fantasy of oral impregnation in our patients is quite clear, with the mouth as the receptive organ of food symbolizing conception, the gastrointestinal tract symbolizing the womb and the cessation of menstruation being associated with pregnancy."

Waller and his associates claim that in childhood a girl acquires the fantasy that one has babies by eating. The fantasy is normally suppressed and does not cause any problems, but under certain conditions it can resurface at the stressful time of puberty.

However, as in many psychoanalytic theories, there are some facts that do not fit easily into place. If the cessation of menstruation in anorexia nervosa symbolizes pregnancy, then wouldn't the patient, since she is unconsciously afraid of pregnancy, want to eat in order to retain her periods? And if fear of pregnancy causes anorexia nervosa, why does the disorder also occur in men? And why would anorexic patients develop bulimia?

Psychoanalytic theories are very flexible in their ability to handle such apparent contradictions. Bulimia, for example, is explained as "the obverse of this rejection of food . . . a sort of compulsive ritualistic gluttony. With the shifting in the dynamics of the neurotic conflict, the gratification of these fantasies takes place at an unconscious level and the patient periodically indulges in an orgy of compulsive eating. Thus gratification of the fantasy of becoming pregnant may be expressed by overeating or gorging."

In other words, the patient is unconsciously terrified of becoming pregnant, but periodically becomes unconsciously possessed with the desire to become pregnant.

Again, this may sound like a farfetched theory, particularly when it tries to explain simultaneously both anorexia nervosa and bulimia. Therefore, you may be surprised to learn that this is the *only* psychodynamic explanation proposed in the last fifty years that relates bulimia or anorexia nervosa to any *specific* series of events in early childhood; no other classical psychoanalytic theory has yet been offered to take its place.

More recently, in 1970, a breath of fresh air was offered by Dr. Hilde Bruch, one of America's leading researchers in the field of eating disorders.[8] She pointed out that fear of oral impregnation was rarely a feature in her patients or in patients treated by her colleagues. Instead, she most often found that her patients were rather asexual—they exhibited decreased sex drive and little in the way of sexual fantasies. Furthermore, she added that anorexia nervosa patients, "in my experience, are singularly unresponsive to the traditional psychoanalytic approach." Reviewing the literature on the value of psychotherapeutic intervention in anorexia nervosa, she found it "hopelessly inconclusive." She did not specifically extend her statements to bulimia, but it would seem likely that her conclusions might be similar.

Having thus questioned the appropriateness of orthodox psychoanalytic theory, she focuses her attention on interaction patterns within the patient's family:

Detailed analysis reveals that the disturbing experiences are not related to one or another incident, but to an all-pervading attitude of doing for the child and superimposing the parents' concepts of his needs, with disregard of child-initiated signals. This deprives the child of a necessary learning experience, namely, the regular sequence of events, that of felt discomfort, signal, appropriate response, and felt satisfaction. Without such reciprocal and confirming responses to child-initiated clues, he will fail to develop a discriminate awareness of his needs, and a sense of control over his impulses. He may even be lacking in the sense of ownership of his body. He will experience instead that he is not in control of his functions, with an overall lack of awareness of living his own life, and a conviction of the ineffectiveness of all of his efforts and strivings.

This theory sounds more plausible: An overcontrolling family prevents the child from becoming attuned to the rhythm of his or her own bodily needs. Having failed to learn this, he or she is susceptible to a sort of "nutritional disorganization" that can cause both anorexia nervosa and bulimia.[9]

The nutritional disorganization has two phases, absence or denial of desire for food and uncontrollable impulses to gorge oneself, usually without awareness of hunger, and often followed by self-induced vomiting. Patients identify with the noneating phase, defending it as a realistic expression of physiological need. In contrast, they experience overeating as a submission to some compulsion to do something they do not want to do and they are terrified by the loss of control during such eating binges. Patients express this as "I do not dare to eat. If I take just one bite I am afraid that I will not be able to stop."

Bruch suggests that both anorexia nervosa and bulimia arise as part of the struggle to gain control over one's functions during adolescence. In the child who has come from an overcontrolling family, this battle for self-control, for a distinct identity, may fail, possibly leading to the development of an eating disorder.

The beauty of Dr. Bruch's theory, unlike many psychodynamic theories, is that it is *testable*: One can systematically study the parents of a sample of patients with bulimia or anorexia nervosa, and assess whether they are demonstrably more controlling than the parents of normals. Do the parents of patients with eating disorders really sow the seeds for these problems in their children?

In response to this question, dozens of studies, resulting in more than fifty scientific papers on the families of anorexic and bulimic patients, are now available. The great majority of the studies examined anorexia nervosa with or without bulimia, so that again they give us only an approximation of what might be found in the parents of purely bulimic patients. Recently, these studies were thoroughly reviewed in an article by Dr. Joel Yager.[10] Among other findings, he noted that one study found fussy, nervous mothers and alternatively quick-tempered and easygoing fathers. Another found robust, nagging mothers and passive fathers. Yet another found obsessionality in 29% of fathers and 14% of mothers. Still another found that 21% of families showed forceful and robust mothers with weak and remote fathers; 17% displayed tense, neurotic mothers and passive fathers; 5% had domineering, aggressive fathers; 8% had domineering but nonaggressive fathers; and 4% had "psychopathic" fathers who were inconsistently domineering. On the basis of this review, Dr. Yager concludes: "One begins to suspect that if common personality patterns are to be found in these families, they will have to be at more subtle levels."

Studies of parent-child interactions seem similarly contradictory: Some mothers are found to be very attached to their daughters; others are ambivalent toward their daughters; still others are strict disciplinarians; and some are overtly rejecting. Fathers range from lenient, kind, and affectionate to cool, antagonistic, and overtly hostile. Again, it appears that if there are any specific abnormalities in the families of anorexic or bulimic patients, they are not easy to demonstrate.

In an attempt to examine more subtle issues in the family, some studies have suggested that families of anorexic or bulimic children are "enmeshed"—overinvolved with one another. Overprotectiveness and rigidity have also been described in association with "enmeshment." Other researchers have described families with "neurotic constellations" that prohibit adolescent maturation; they argue that the child's symptoms can be seen as "protecting" the father or the mother in some way. Marital disharmony and sexual dissatisfaction are reported in some parents. In another study, comparing families of bulimic anorexic patients against families of "restricter" anorexic patients, the families of bulimic patients exhibited more conflict and expressions of negativity among members; families of restricters were more cohesive and organized.

Again, these studies were of families of anorexic patients with or without bulimia, rather than families of purely bulimic patients. But it seems likely that as studies of bulimic families emerge, the findings will continue to be equally confusing, with no clear agreement among different researchers. However, even allowing that several family studies emerged with similar results, identifying specific parental traits or a particular family pattern in the families of bulimic patients, these studies would still be open to a number of serious methodological questions in the eyes of a scientifically trained reader.

First, most family studies do not use control groups—comparison groups of families of normal children. For example, one study found "sexual dissatisfaction" in 41% of the parents of anorexic children. But what is the level of sexual dissatisfaction among the parents of normal children? Might it not also be in the range of 41%? Without such control figures for comparison, many findings in the families of patients with eating disorders become uninterpretable.

Second, in virtually all studies, the observers who interviewed the family members were nonblind—that is, they were perfectly aware that they were interviewing the relatives of a patient with an eating disorder. Knowing this, it would be all too easy to see pathology in the mother or father because one is expecting to find it. From a scientific standpoint, that degree of bias is very likely to skew the findings.

Third, practically none of the studies attempt to separate what is a cause and what is an effect of the eating disorder in the child. Faced with a bulimic or an anorexic son or daughter, parents may argue as to what should be done, blame each other for causing the problem, attempt to be more protective of the child, or deliberately withdraw somewhat from the child—all of which may be entirely normal responses of parents whose child displays any intractable illness. As Hilde Bruch comments: "There are few conditions that provoke so much concern, but also frustration, rage, and anger, as the spectacle of a starving child refusing food." It would be hazardous, therefore, to assume that the parents' arguments, or their protectiveness, or their withdrawal, is necessarily *causing* the eating disorder; it may instead be a reaction to it.

Fourth, given the evidence that bulimia and its associated disorders have a marked hereditary component (as discussed in detail in the next chapter), it is possible that much of the pathology observed in the parents is a genetic phenomenon, only incidentally related to the environment. For example, take the observation, quoted above, that obsessionality was observed in 29% of fathers and 14% of mothers of anorexic individuals. This parental obsessive-compulsive disorder may have nothing to do with causing the eating disorder in the child, but may simply indicate that the father or mother shares with the child a given hereditary tendency—as was the case with Nadia and her mother, or with Ellen West and her brother, uncles, and aunt.

In summary, we find little agreement among the available studies of family dynamics in anorexia nervosa or bulimia. Furthermore, these studies lack control groups, were performed nonblind, and generally fail to compensate for genetic factors and influences caused by the presence of the illness in the child. At this time, therefore, we cannot find reliable scientific evidence of any specific abnormality in the behavior of families of anorexic or bulimic patients.

Behavioral Theories

Behavioral psychology provides a perspective very different from that of psychodynamic theory, in that it spends little time attempting to discover the cause of a given psychiatric disorder.[11] Instead, it asserts that behaviors arise for unknown reasons in an organism that is effectively a "black box"; one examines only external behaviors and does not attempt to infer what murky processes go on inside. The behaviors may be rewarded (positively reinforced) or punished (negatively reinforced) by the environment. Psychiatric disorders such as bulimia fit particularly well into behavior theory: Like phobias, or obsessive rituals, eating binges are relatively discrete, measurable items of behavior that would seem to be positively or negatively reinforced by identifiable stimuli.

In contrast to psychodynamic theorists, behavior theorists would caution us to limit our speculations as to what causes the binges. Possibly binges occur, and are perpetuated, because some biological stimulus reinforces them—for example, a severe craving for carbohydrates. Or some psychological reinforcement may perpetuate them; the binge may temporarily allay some nagging feeling of emptiness or loneliness, and thus be positively reinforced. But the details of this are of little consequence; the goal of behavior therapy is to treat the symptoms themselves, say by instituting a program that rewards normal eating patterns and punishes binges.

This very pragmatic theory would seem to offer a method of obtaining quicker results with bulimic symptoms than might be expected in a long course of psychotherapy. But behavior theory seems less well suited to explain or treat some of the other aspects of the disorder, such as the episodic major depression so frequently described by bulimic patients. Reward and punishment would also seem less likely to ameliorate such syndromes as manic-depressive illness or panic disorder, which are also common bulimia-associated disorders.

Thus, although we should consider behavior therapy a possible treatment for the binges themselves, we are unlikely to find in behaviorism an explanation of the cause of bulimia and its cluster of associated disorders.

Sociocultural Theories

If you have read any of the numerous articles in the popular press, or watched recent television documentaries on bulimia, it is the sociocultural theories that you probably have heard most often. Typically, they run as follows: Bulimia and anorexia nervosa are becoming increasingly common in our culture, due to the increasing pressure to be thin in a more and more weight-conscious society. Women, so the theory runs, are far more susceptible than men to eating disorders, because they are the principal victims of this cultural pressure.

Among the leading exponents of these views are Drs. Marlene Boskind-White and William White in New York. From their work with eighty women with bulimic and anorexic symptoms (which they have termed "bulimarexia"), they proposed a sociocultural theory of bulimia from a feminist perspective:

These women [with bulimarexia] seem to be trying desperately to fit themselves into a stereotyped feminine role, both in the relentless pursuit of thinness and in their passive, accommodating, and help-less approach to life. . . . Women in our culture are socialized to be passive, dependent, and accommodating, and to value their bodies principally for physical attractiveness. The common fantasy of this group [of women with bulimarexia] was that their lives would be successful if only they were thin and pretty, other personal qualities being relatively unimportant.[12]

Are these theories scientifically verifiable? It is difficult to test them systematically, but the evidence suggests that they probably have at least some basis in fact. For example, a group of researchers in Toronto and Chicago reviewed all *Playboy* centerfold women from 1959 to 1978 and found that their average weight, relative to height, declined by about 8% over the twenty years.[13] Miss America Pageant contestants also grew thinner over the same twenty years; and the winners were thinner still. By contrast, the average American woman under thirty has been growing fatter over the same period, leading to an ever greater discrepancy between her own weight and that which society perceives as beautiful. It should come as no surprise, then, that when these authors counted the number of diet articles in six popular women's magazines, the number had doubled between 1959 and 1978.

Against the sociocultural backdrop, we have certain hard medical facts: All animals, including man, automatically regulate their weight in a narrow range around a "setpoint," much as a thermostat maintains a constant room temperature.[14] If one's weight drops even 5% or 10% below the setpoint, hunger increases and the body burns fewer calories. Any dieter can confirm this: After quickly losing the first few pounds, it becomes much harder to lose further weight. Similarly, if one gains even a modest amount of weight, appetite drops and caloric expenditure rises in order to defend the setpoint; further weight gain is difficult.

What sets the setpoint? Why do some people remain fat and others thin? The process appears largely genetic; you are more likely to be fat if your relatives are. Certain drugs, such as nicotine and diet pills, temporarily lower the setpoint somewhat, but it will promptly increase again if these drugs are withdrawn. Regular exercise lowers the setpoint; inactivity will raise it. In fact, the increasing obesity of modern Americans, just discussed, is probably due to our increasingly sedentary lifestyle.

Dieting has no effect on the setpoint. In fact, the common low-carbohydrate diet—with reduced carbohydrate in proportion to protein and fat—may actually compound the problem: Drs. Richard and Judith Wurtman have shown, in an elegant series of experiments, that low-carbohydrate diets selectively increase the craving for carbohydrate-rich foods.[15]

What happens when one tries to fight one's own biology and aims for a weight far below nature's setpoint? One feels guilty and depressed if one fails to achieve the desirable weight, but chronically hungry if one succeeds. This conflict, it might be argued, could trigger anorexia nervosa and bulimia. Anorexia nervosa represents the ultimate "starvation diet"—an aberration developing in some individuals who overidentify with the societal cult of thinness. Binging, on the other hand, is simply nature fighting back; hunger overrides the rigorous attempts at dieting and the individual finally loses control. The binge is perpetuated because the body does not signal satisfaction when the stomach is full; it demands to return to its setpoint before turning off hunger. Purging is a way to maintain or even lose weight despite binging—a way of having your cake and losing it too. And the depression following binges is explainable as guilt about having failed to conform to societal (or male) expectations.

This theory would seem to fit many of the facts: It explains why anorexia nervosa and bulimia are so much more common in women; it is supported by some interesting data, such as the *Playboy* and Miss America statistics; and in its explanation of bulimia, it neatly combines a well-established body of biological data—the setpoint theory—with sociocultural factors.

We suspect that at least some of the steps in this theory are correct, particularly given that weight loss seems to exacerbate bulimia. But there are several observations that do not fit the theory—particularly the fact that patients with eating disorders seem to lack completely normal control. Anorexic patients, for example, do not merely diet until they achieve *Playboy* dimensions; they continue uncontrollably far beyond that, far below their setpoints, even to the point of death. And bulimic patients do not merely binge until they are full; they go beyond all the limits of any ordinary hunger. In fact, most of our bulimic patients state that they do not even feel true hunger at the time of a binge; it is a different species of sensation. Furthermore, if the setpoint theory is true, why do many bulimic patients continue to binge even after they have gained a good deal of weight? In short, it is hard to believe that dieting to the point of death or binging repeatedly on 10,000 or 15,000 calories could be explained purely by cultural pressures or the setpoint theory.

Finally, these theories do not account for the presence of the bulimia-associated disorders. It seems unlikely that society and setpoint alone could cause manic-depressive illness, panic disorder, agoraphobia, obsessive-compulsive disorder, and so forth. In short, although the society-setpoint theory may help to explain some steps in the evolution of bulimia, it seems unable to explain the underlying *cause* of the eating disorders.

Nutritional Theories

Although we have not seen nutritional theories of bulimia in the scientific literature, we have periodically heard them from our patients, or from their parents. Some have decided, for example, that the abundance of refined sugar in our society is the root evil that has fueled the spread of bulimia. Occasionally, others have claimed that a particular diet, or vitamins, helped with their symptoms. In response to this, all we can say is that there are simply no data available to support such beliefs, nor have we ever seen or heard of a bulimic patient whose binges ceased clearly as a result of dietary manipulation. Until more specific evidence surfaces, we can give little credence to nutritional theories.

Biological Theories

Until recently, most biological theories focused entirely on anorexia nervosa rather than bulimia. For example, in the early twentieth century, physicians noted that patients who had sustained damage to the pituitary gland (the "master gland" in the brain, which secretes a range of hormones) often displayed severe weight loss as a result. For a time, therefore, it was thought that pituitary insufficiency might account for anorexia nervosa.[16] But when the technology became available to measure pituitary hormones in the bloodstream, it turned out that pituitary insufficiency was not the explanation.

In the 1970s, endocrine theories of anorexia nervosa were revived, but this time the malfunctioning gland was theorized to be the hypothalamus, a "higher order" gland in the brain controlling not only the pituitary but a number of the body's other mechanisms. Many of the hypothalamic hormones and other hypothalamic functions have now been measured in anorexic patients, but it is difficult to interpret these findings since weight loss alone can produce hypothalamic abnormalities. Thus, if a given finding is abnormal, one must demonstrate that it is specific to anorexia nervosa and not due merely to weight loss in general.

In response to this, some recent studies have shown that abnormalities in several hypothalamic hormone systems, including those that regulate sex-hormone production, cortisol, and thyroid hormone, cannot be explained by weight loss alone.[17] Furthermore, the endocrine systems controlling cortisol and thyroid hormone have now also been shown to be abnormal in normal-weight patients with bulimia. In fact, we published the first such study of bulimia in 1982;[18] investigators in other laboratories have now replicated and expanded upon our results.[19]

In summary, we are beginning to discover tantalizing evidence of possible biological abnormalities, both in anorexia nervosa and bulimia, in the form of hypothalamic dysfunction. These abnormalities do not by themselves explain the entire symptom picture of anorexia nervosa or bulimia, but any convincing explanation of the cause of the eating disorders must account for them.

The 1970s also saw a biological theory that attempted to specifically explain the cause of bulimia: Drs. Richard Green and John Rau proposed that bulimia might be a form of seizure disorder, or epilepsy.[20] They based their theory on three major pieces of evidence.

First, they noted that in bulimic patients the urge to binge comes on suddenly, appears to be beyond voluntary control, and directs behavior in a specific, patterned way. This is much like the repetitious, "automatic" behavior seen in a certain form of epilepsy, called psychomotor epilepsy, which is caused by abnormal electrical discharges on the surface of the brain, particularly in the region of the temporal lobes.

Second, Green and Rau found that patients with bulimia commonly displayed a specific abnormality on their EEG (electroencephalogram, or brain-wave tracing) called a ctenoid. This is a pattern of six- and fourteen-per-second slow waves, thought to be present in several disorders in which there is a loss of impulse control.

Third, when they gave bulimic patients phenytoin (Dilantin), commonly used in the treatment of seizure disorders, the initial results were astonishing: Nine out of ten patients appeared markedly better.

But the seizure-disorder theory has not held up well over time. First, further studies with phenytoin by Green and Rau did not yield such promising results—less than 50% of subsequent patients improved. A later study of phenytoin, which was placebo controlled (some subjects received active medication and others an inert placebo), found only a 40% response rate.[21] And of the four patients who improved markedly in this study, two relapsed during the follow-up period after completion of the study, despite the fact that they were still taking phenytoin. It was also recognized by this time that the ctenoids, which were supposedly specific for bulimia and other impulse disorders, were often seen in normal adolescents and young adults and thus are what is called "normal variants."

Since 1977, there have been no major studies showing phenytoin to be effective. We ourselves have tried it in about ten bulimic patients, but only one of them described any perceptible improvement—she felt a modest reduction in her urge to binge three weeks after starting phenytoin. However, when we stopped the phenytoin a month later, she did not relapse, but continued to improve. This suggests that probably she was experiencing a gradual spontaneous remission of her disorder, which by chance coincided with her starting on phenytoin—a fine example of how one must allow for the possibility of spontaneous remission before pronouncing a therapy effective! In short, our experience seems to coincide with that of other researchers; there remains little hard evidence that bulimia is a form of seizure disorder.

Some of the theories reviewed in this chapter are attractive in their apparent ability to explain one or another aspect of bulimia or the related disorder, anorexia nervosa. But when subjected to scientific scrutiny, most of the theories begin to break down rapidly. The evidence supporting them proves weak or contradictory, or they prove incapable of explaining plausibly why certain features of bulimia or anorexia nervosa should occur. Although the sociocultural and setpoint theories seem the most attractive, they remain weak in their ability to explain why the many bulimia-associated disorders are present in such a large percentage of bulimic patients.

Of course, we can finesse the whole question of cause by arguing that bulimia is a heterogeneous, multifaceted syndrome, which is multidetermined on multiaxial etiologies. Psychiatric theory is filled with mumbo-jumbo like this. But we doubt that the intelligent reader would be satisfied with a psychodynamo-familio-behavioro-socio-nutritiono-biologico-cultural theory. There has to be a better answer.

There is. In the next chapter, we propose a theory that is based on four independent lines of quantitative scientific evidence, that readily explains the presence of the bulimia-associated disorders, and that has produced an effective new treatment.

1985 Update: Earlier in this chapter (page 80), we expressed our distrust of studies finding abnormalities in the attitudes of families of anorexic or bulimic patients, since these studies have not used control groups. However, since our book first went to press, an excellent controlled study has at last appeared. Dr. Paul Garfinkel and his associates compared the mothers and fathers of forty-two anorexic women (twenty-three of whom were also bulimic) with the mothers and fathers of a matched group of twenty-four normal women. Contrary to their expectations, the authors found no differences between families of anorexics and families of normals on most measures, including family attitudes toward weight and dieting, parental psychopathology, or parents' body-size estimates or body dissatisfaction. Only on certain subscales of one instrument—called the Family Assessment Measure—were significant differences found, and then only for the mothers; fathers of anorexics and fathers of controls remained indistinguishable.

These essentially negative results further challenge the popular theory that anorexia nervosa or bulimia are attributable to abnormalities in the structure or attitudes of the family. Such findings underscore the need for skepticism, and for insistence on properly controlled studies, before we accept any theory of the cause of bulimia.

6

BULIMIA AND MAJOR AFFECTIVE DISORDER

What Is Major Affective Disorder?

Major affective disorder is the name given to a family of psychiatric disorders of which the two principal members are manic-depressive illness (bipolar disorder) and major depression. At present, we know a good deal about major affective disorder, probably more than about any other common illness in psychiatry. Extensive evidence now suggests that it has a biological basis—i.e., that it is caused by some type of chemical imbalance in the brain; in fact, several laboratory tests have now been tentatively proposed to help diagnose it. Major affective disorder is well established to be hereditary, and we now possess a wide range of effective medications to treat it, to the point where a majority of patients with both manic-depressive illness and major depression can get markedly better in a matter of weeks and return to their normal lives.

Why are we so sure that these illnesses are biological? To begin with, look back at the quiz in Chapter 4 and the accompanying descriptions of major depression and manic-depressive illness. Major depression, for example, is completely different from the ordinary depression we experience when something sad happens in our lives; it causes severe disruption of many of the biological functions of the body: sleep disorder, weight loss, impaired concentration, and the peculiar phenomenon of diurnal variation—the daily cycle of mood—that we discussed earlier.

People who have experienced an episode of major depression report that it feels very different from any ordinary depressive period. It often seems to come on at random, when there is no particular external stress. And once the depression sets in, it often has a strikingly autonomous quality: The symptoms remain the same, day after day, unaffected by outside events, good or bad. After some time, major depression will usually spontaneously remit, also for no apparent reason: The symptoms will begin to clear, and in most cases the individual feels completely back to normal again.

In many people, major depression is an episodic illness, with a period of depression lasting six months, a year, or even two years, followed by a remission that may run for many years before another episode occurs. Some individuals experience only a single episode in a lifetime; others may have multiple episodes. Some particularly unfortunate patients may develop chronic symptoms of major depression that go on for years. Finally, a small fraction develop manic-depressive illness, characterized by "highs" as well as "lows"—periods of euphoria, irritability, hyperactivity, and racing thoughts, which alternate with the depressed periods. This is now called "bipolar disorder" because there is a "high" pole as well as a "low" pole in the course of the illness. Figure 1 illustrates these several possible progressions of major affective disorder.

It is the autonomy of the symptoms and the on-and-off course, often apparently independent of psychological factors, which first suggest that major affective disorder is controlled by some biological abnormality rather than by external events. But do we have actual proof of a chemical imbalance that causes the illness? As of 1983 we do not have a final answer. Various theories have been suggested and tested,[1] but it may be another ten or twenty years before major affective disorder is "cracked." We are still in the testing stages.

Among the most intriguing findings recently proposed are certain laboratory tests which are positive in a large number of individuals with major depression, but negative in normal individuals. These include the dexamethasone suppression test, the thyrotropin releasing hormone stimulation test, measures of urinary tyramine excretion, and measures of REM latency (the interval between when one falls asleep and when one begins to dream).[2] Although these findings may eventually provide fur-

FIGURE 1:

Several Possible Progressions of Major Affective Disorder

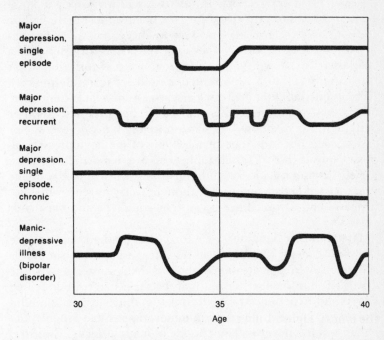

ther support for a biological basis for major affective disorder, they remain too preliminary and too controversial at this point to be interpreted with confidence. Within the next few years, however, more definite answers may emerge.

Heredity in Major Affective Disorders

If the above evidence still seems inadequate to justify the assertion that major affective disorder has a biological basis, one need only turn to the genetic data. There are now scores of studies in the scientific literature strongly demonstrating that major affective disorder has a major hereditary component.[3] In fact, if a patient has the bipolar form of major affective disorder, the chances may be as high as 30% or 40% that a first-degree relative of that patient (parent, sibling, or child) will develop major affective disorder as well.

Upon investigating a family tree carefully, obtaining all possible background information on the relatives and personally interviewing as many as possible, one frequently discovers a dense cluster of cases of affective disorder, as shown in Figure 2. The patient depicted, Mrs. R., now seventy-three, had a postpartum depression after the birth of her son (who is now forty-six), and a "nervous breakdown" when she was in her mid-forties. Both of these almost certainly represented episodes of major depression. Her oldest daughter had a clear-cut case of manic-depressive illness, first manifested when she was in her twenties. Another daughter was diagnosed as schizophrenic, but on review, her case turned out to be one of the many of manic-depressive illnesses misdiagnosed as schizophrenia. She is now almost completely asymptomatic on lithium—but unfortunately, many years passed before any doctor thought to try it. Meanwhile her husband had divorced her because he couldn't stand her manic episodes.

The youngest daughter, now forty-two, has had only a single episode of major depression in her life, so mild that she never even consulted a professional about it. When interviewed, she disclosed that for nearly eight months she'd had trouble falling asleep and experienced loss of appetite, diurnal variation, and inability to concentrate on even minor tasks.

The son has never had an episode of major affective disorder, but he appears to be a "carrier" of the illness; his twenty-six-year-old daughter was recently hospitalized with a severe case of major depression, after she tried to commit suicide with an overdose of barbiturates. She is one of no less than six individuals in the third generation with one or more major depressive episodes.

In the fourth generation, there are seven children ranging in age from one to twelve. None of them is old enough to have had much risk of developing major affective disorder yet, but the chances are that one or more of them will develop symptoms as they grow older.

The thirty-four-year-old woman on the far right, in addition to major depression, had bulimia. We will return to this point—the genetic relationship of bulimia to major affective disorder—later in this chapter.

The reader might argue that such pedigrees still do not prove

FIGURE 2:

A Pedigree for Major Affective Disorder

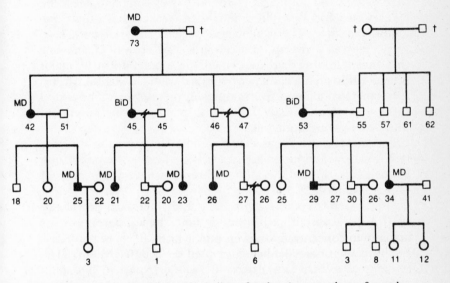

Squares indicate males, circles indicate females. Ages are shown for each individual. A solid square or circle denotes an individual who has developed major affective disorder. "MD" indicates major depression; "BiD," bipolar disorder.

A joined square and circle (□—○) designate a married couple; a double line through a "marriage" (□—//—○) indicates a separation or divorce. A cross beside a square or circle shows that the individual has died.

For simplicity, we have omitted the second wives and children of two individuals who are remarried (the 46- and 27-year-old men). We have also not indicated other psychiatric disorders (specifically alcoholism and panic disorder) that affected some individuals in the same family tree.

that major affective disorder is hereditary or biological; after all, there might be some psychological influences operating in this family that would cause its members to be much more susceptible to affective disorder than ordinary people. This is a legitimate objection, but genetic researchers have devised special research strategies to deal with it.

One of these is to study adoptees. For example, Drs. Julian Mendlewicz and John Rainer found twenty-nine adoptees who had manic-depressive illness and then tracked down their biological parents.[4] These biological parents had not even seen their children grow up, and certainly had no way of knowing that their children had developed the bipolar form of major affective disorder. Yet almost one-third of the biological parents suffered from major affective disorder themselves, a rate almost three times higher than that found in the *adopting* parents of these twenty-nine individuals.

For comparison, Mendlewicz and Rainer also looked at the biological and adopting parents of a comparison group of *normal* adoptees. Both of these sets of parents had very low rates of affective disorder.

Only heredity could explain the greatly increased prevalence of affective disorder exclusively in the biological parents of the manic-depressive adoptees. If psychological factors were operating, or if the process of being adopted contributed to the development of affective disorder, one would expect to find high rates of affective disorder in some of the other three parent groups as well, but this was not the case.

This type of finding virtually establishes the case for a hereditary component in major affective disorder. It seems safe to say that virtually no responsible psychiatric researcher today would question the existence of a significant genetic role in major depression and bipolar disorder.

Of course, these findings do not prove that major affective disorder is entirely hereditary or entirely due to biological factors. Many biological diseases—such as atherosclerotic heart disease, various forms of cancer, and high blood pressure—are strongly affected by environmental influences, and major affective disorder is no exception. But whatever the degree of environmental influence in major depression or bipolar disorder, we would be neglecting the evidence if we did not concede that there exists a major underlying biologic abnormality in these illnesses.

Treatment of Major Affective Disorder

All this would be academic if there were not some type of biologic treatment that actually worked for patients with bipolar disorder or major depression. Fortunately, in the last thirty years or so, researchers have discovered dozens of medications that are effective in the treatment of major affective disorder. These include lithium carbonate; various antidepressant drugs, such as tricyclic antidepressants, monoamine oxidase inhibitors, trazodone, sympathomimetic agents, and others not yet commercially available in the U.S.; various antipsychotic drugs, such as phenothiazines and butyrophenones; certain anticonvulsants, such as carbamazepine; and many other medications that are still in the experimental stages.[5] Then there is electroconvulsive therapy ("shock therapy"), highly effective in both mania and depression and a surprisingly safe treatment, but infrequently used these days because most people get better with medications alone.[6] Finally, there is some research suggesting that certain food substances—a fat called lecithin and an amino acid called L-tryptophan—may be effective in certain cases of bipolar disorder or major depression.[7]

To review all these treatments would require an entire book; information directly relevant to the treatment of bulimia we have placed in Chapter 8. For now, suffice it to say that with this wide range of medical treatments, a large percentage of patients with major affective disorder now can get much better in a matter of weeks, to the point where their sleep, appetite, mood, and energy level return to normal and they are functioning as well as they did before their symptoms began.

We have deliberately avoided going into detail about treatment at this point, because the purpose of this chapter is to present the evidence that bulimia is related to major affective disorder. But in passing, we must note one point: Many people have the misconception that psychiatric drugs merely "cover up" symptoms—that an antidepressant drug "energizes you," or lithium "calms you down" or "stabilizes your mood." This might be correct in the case of a simple sedative, or "tranquilizer," such as diazepam (Valium), but it is completely erroneous in the case of most of the drugs used to treat major affective disorder.

Let us take, for example, an antidepressant such as imipramine. If a normal person takes imipramine, even for a long time, virtually nothing happens. He or she may feel sleepy or light-headed, notice some dry mouth or blurred vision, but there is no effect on mood, even after weeks of taking the drug. However, if a depressed patient takes imipramine, he or she may notice a dramatic improvement in mood, energy, and enthusiasm starting around the third week of being on the medication. In other words, one has to have the illness to notice any effect. Imipramine is not just a "feel-good" drug—it does not produce an artificial stimulant effect. Rather, it actually seems to correct the underlying chemical imbalance that is causing the depressive illness; as the imbalance is corrected, the patient begins to feel normal again. It's analogous to penicillin: If someone who is not sick takes penicillin, nothing happens. But if someone who has pneumonia takes it, the effect is often dramatic. The fact that imipramine does nothing in ordinary people, but displays a clear effect in major depression, is yet another piece of evidence suggesting that major depression is caused by some underlying biological disorder.

The same applies to lithium, most other antidepressant drugs, antipsychotic drugs, and carbamazepine: If a normal person takes them, nothing happens, except for side effects. But in a person with major depression or bipolar disorder, striking improvement may occur: A woman too depressed even to leave her hospital room returns home and throws a cocktail party for twenty-five; a man who was picked up by the police while chasing "Martians" with a hunting knife returns to his family and his job as an insurance salesman, completely back to his senses again. And if you met either of these two people (they are real cases of ours, by the way), you would never be able to tell that the woman is taking tranylcypromine (an antidepressant) or that the man is taking lithium, nor would you be able to guess the ordeals they had been through. In fact, the woman whose cocktail party you just attended or the man from whom you just bought insurance may well be such a person—an individual who suffered from a severe episode of depression or manic-depressive illness and is now well protected with modern psychiatric medications.

We belabor this point because so many people seem to believe that medications simply cause a person to be "drugged," or "tranquilized" to the point where the symptoms are no longer bothersome. Except for a few unusual cases, that idea has been obsolete for at least twenty-five years. Modern drug treatments for affective disorder are quite *specific:* Although we do not know the exact mechanism by which they work, we know that they appear to correct the underlying cause of the symptoms, rather than merely to blanket the symptoms.

In summary, therefore, major affective disorder is a biologically based illness (or group of related illnesses) with a strong hereditary component and for which specific, effective treatments are now available. We propose that bulimia is closely related to major affective disorder, and that by recognizing this relationship, we can greatly improve our understanding, and treatment, of the syndrome.

How does one test the hypothesis that one illness is related to another? There are four methods—so-called validating indices:[8] (1) Phenomenology: Do bulimic patients display the same symptoms as patients with major affective disorder? ("Phenomenology" means the description of presenting symptoms.) (2) Genetics: Is the incidence of familial psychiatric disorders among bulimic patients comparable to that found in patients with major affective disorder? (3) Laboratory tests: Do bulimic patients and patients with major affective disorder display the same biological abnormalities on laboratory tests? (4) Treatment response: Are medications that are effective for patients with major affective disorder also effective for patients with bulimia?

Let us go through each of these in detail.

Phenomenology

We have already discussed phenomenology in detail in Chapter 4. To recapitulate: About 80% of the bulimic patients we have studied have had major affective disorder (bipolar disorder or major depression) at some point during their lifetime.[9]

Furthermore, we have quoted five other studies—from Massachusetts,[10] New York,[11] Minnesota,[12] England,[13] and Japan[14]—

that also noted a very high incidence of depressive symptoms in their samples of bulimic patients.

Does this necessarily prove that bulimia is related to major affective disorder? Perhaps the high incidence of major affective disorder in our study of seventy-four bulimic patients was simply due to chance; after all, it is perfectly possible for someone to have two unrelated disorders, such as pneumonia and a broken arm.

This argument does not hold up: The 80% incidence of major affective disorder in our bulimic patients is so much higher than that found in a random sample of people (a maximum of 26%, on the basis of the two studies of normal populations cited in Chapter 4) that the 80% figure could not be due to chance alone. Specifically, if we assume a population prevalence of 26%, the probability of finding major affective disorder in 80% or more of seventy-three people chosen at random would be less than 1 in 500,000,000,000,000,000,000. Therefore, it would be very hard to claim that our study results (not to mention the results of all the other researchers) were due merely to chance.

Is it possible, then, that we happened to interview an unusual sample of bulimic patients, which was biased in some way to include a grossly disproportionate number of patients who also happened to have major affective disorder?

Certainly there may be some bias. Individuals with mild or transient cases of bulimia—such as students temporarily experimenting with bulimia in a college dormitory—and some other groups, such as individuals with bulimia and obesity, might be less likely to appear at our offices. But if we consider the group of patients who specifically *seek treatment* for bulimia, then our sample appears representative, since it included consecutively interviewed patients from four different sources: hospitalized patients, outpatients referred to us, and two sets of research subjects obtained through two different advertisements in newspapers. All four groups showed roughly the same 80% lifetime prevalence of major affective disorder. Considering that our patients came from so many different sources, it is hard to argue that *all* the groups could be equally biased. And even if one claims that there was such a bias in all our samples, one is still left with the problem of explaining why depressive symptoms were so commonly reported in the other bulimia studies we have reviewed. In short, it is very difficult to dismiss the results as due to a problem in sample selection.

Granting, then, that the high incidence of major affective disorder in bulimia is real, and not due to chance or sampling bias, does this necessarily prove that bulimia is closely related to major affective disorder? Perhaps the depression is merely a consequence of having bulimia.

We have already considered this objection in Chapter 4. To repeat the argument briefly: Nearly half of our bulimic patients experienced the onset of their depressive symptoms more than a year before the bulimia started, and an additional number experienced depressive episodes at later times when they were not bulimic. There is no way to explain these cases if one claims that the bulimia was the cause of the depression. Furthermore, even if one did argue that bulimia causes depression and other symptoms of major affective disorder, we would still be left with the problem of explaining what causes all the other bulimia-associated disorders. It would be difficult to argue that bulimia also causes anorexia nervosa, manic-depressive illness, panic disorder, agoraphobia, obsessive-compulsive disorder, and kleptomania! Surely the simplest, most straightforward explanation—what many scientists would call the "most parsimonious hypothesis"—is that major affective disorder, bulimia, and perhaps many of the bulimia-associated disorders are closely related illnesses—perhaps sharing some specific underlying biological abnormalities.

But there are still some remaining objections to our argument, and to be thorough, we must consider them. First, what about the 20% of our bulimic patients who had *not* displayed bipolar disorder or major depression: Are their conditions related to major affective disorder as well?

In many of these 20%, the relationship may still hold. Since they were quite young, with a mean age of about twenty-six, it is entirely possible that some of them had not yet developed an episode of major affective disorder. In a certain number of people, the first episode of major depression does not strike until the forties, or even until old age. After correcting for this fact, we would project that only a very small percentage of bulimic individuals go through an entire lifetime without at least some manifestation of major affective disorder. Thus, although there may be *some* cases where bulimia is not related to major affective disorder, it seems likely that they represent only a minority.

We must also consider the converse argument: Not only do some bulimic patients lack a history of major affective disorder, but certainly many people with major affective disorder have never displayed bulimia. If bulimia is closely related to major affective disorder, why don't all patients with major affective disorder develop eating binges?

This is fairly obvious: Nobody develops every possible symptom of a given disease. Some people with common colds have runny noses but no sore throat; others have sore throats but no cough. The family of illnesses related to major affective disorder probably creates such a vast range of symptoms that no one could be expected to develop them all. One patient may develop depressive episodes, bulimia, and obsessive-compulsive disorder; another may develop manic-depressive illness and alcoholism. At this stage of knowledge, it is very hard to guess why some people with major affective disorder develop bulimia while others do not. And to some extent the question is academic: If treatments that are successful in affective disorder also prove to work for bulimia, it becomes less important to ask why a given person with affective disorder has developed bulimia as an associated syndrome.

In summary, then, the phenomenological evidence stands up to criticism; it strongly suggests that bulimia is closely related to major affective disorder. But this is only the first of four bodies of evidence, all pointing in the same direction. The next is genetics.

Genetics

Given the extensive evidence, mentioned earlier, that major affective disorder displays a strong hereditary component, and given our hypothesis that bulimia is closely related to major affective disorder, we would predict that bulimic patients would have a high prevalence of major depression and manic-depressive illness in their family trees. In fact, to really establish our case, we would have to show that the prevalence of major affective disorder in the family trees of bulimic patients is comparable to that in the family trees of, say, manic-depressive patients, but much higher than that found in the family trees of control patients who have other types of psychiatric disorders.

In a small study of ten bulimic patients and their families,[15] followed by a larger study of seventy-five patients and their families, this is exactly what we found.[16] In fact, among the seventy-five individuals with bulimia, 53% had a father, mother, or sibling with a history of bipolar disorder or major depression. Had we looked farther out in the family tree—to grandparents, aunts, and uncles—the figure would have been even higher. For comparison, we looked at several other samples of patients, who had been studied previously at our research center. Among forty manic-depressive patients, 43% were found to have a parent or sibling with major affective disorder, a figure actually lower than that found for the bulimic patients. Nevertheless, the 43% and 53% figures do not represent what is called a "statistically significant" difference; the difference is probably due to chance alone.

By comparison, only 9% of forty-six schizophrenic patients, and only 7% of fifteen patients with so-called borderline personality disorder (the latter group screened to exclude any patients with concomitant major affective disorder), were found to have a parent or sibling with major affective disorder. The difference between the families of the bulimic patients and the families of the schizophrenic and borderline patients was highly significant in statistical terms: In both cases the odds are less than 1 in 1,000 that the differences could have occurred by accident.

Putting all this in simpler terms, there again seems to be only one parsimonious explanation that fits the data: Bulimia must be closely related to major affective disorder.

Once more, to be thorough, we must consider possible flaws in the study. First, we interviewed personally only forty-two of the relatives; for the others we had to rely on information from the patient. In most cases, it was fairly easy to identify cases of major depression and other psychiatric disorders in relatives, but in some cases we may have been wrong. Studies have shown, however, that when one uses the family-history method, as we did, rather than personally interviewing all of the relatives (the family-interview method), one tends to *underestimate* the prevalence of psychiatric disorders in a family tree. In other words, if we had been able to personally interview every first-degree relative of every patient, we might have found an even *higher* prevalence of affective disorder in the families of bulimic patients than that which we reported in the study.

Second, what about the possibility that we could have been biased in diagnosing family members? Is it possible that we tended to diagnose virtually all psychiatrically ill relatives as having major affective disorder—as opposed to, say, schizophrenia or personality disorder—just to make our results come out right?

There is no way to prove definitely that such bias did not occur. We are currently conducting a blind study (in which the relatives are diagnosed by a separate researcher who has no knowledge of the diagnosis of the patient) in order to deal with this objection. For the present study, however, suffice it to say that even if one makes the extreme assumption that we were overdiagnosing major affective disorder by a factor of two, the results are still statistically significant in favor of the hypothesis that bulimia is closely related to major affective disorder.

Another objection: Is it possible that some of our bulimic patients induced major depression in their relatives because the relatives were so distressed at having to live with a bulimic family member? This is a silly objection, but we have nevertheless heard it on a couple of occasions. In reply, we simply point out that in the great majority of cases the onset of the affective disorder in the relatives long preceded the onset of the eating disorder in the patient. Once again, therefore, the explanation that best fits the data is that bulimia is related to major affective disorder.

So far, only one other large family study of bulimia has been published. In this study, from the group in Minnesota already cited,[12] 48% of thirty-three bulimic patients were reported to have a positive family history of depression. This compares closely to the 53% figure obtained in our study.

In the scientific literature, there are also four studies (one of which is our own) that looked at the family trees of patients with anorexia nervosa, many of whom probably had displayed bulimic symptoms as well.[16–19] All four studies found a significantly increased prevalence of major affective disorder in the family trees of anorexic patients, very similar to that found in the families of bulimic patients.

However, one recent study in California[20] appears to have

found only a modestly increased prevalence of major affective disorder among the relatives of anorexic patients. It is unclear why this one study failed to find the large increase reported in all of the other four studies; as best as we can see, it was methodologically sound.

In summary, the weight of the evidence suggests that patients with anorexia nervosa or bulimia have a markedly increased prevalence of major affective disorder in their families. This suggests that anorexia nervosa, like bulimia, may be closely related to major affective disorder.

Do patients with bulimia have relatives with bulimia?

Yes. Among our seventy-five bulimic subjects, 12% had a first-degree relative with bulimia, and 8% had a first-degree relative with anorexia nervosa. Of course, one might immediately ask whether these were "copycat" cases in which, say, a girl developed bulimia because she started to imitate the bulimic behavior of her sister. Certainly this may occur, but we have found several families in which the two relatives were completely unaware of each other's symptoms. Both had binged in secret, and were astonished to find that another member of the family was doing the same thing. The existence of families with more than one case of eating disorder raises the possibility that there are additional genetic factors which may contribute specifically to bulimia, but the evidence is too slim to permit conclusions on this point.

Admittedly, the prevalence of eating disorders in the family trees of bulimic patients is not as dramatically high as the prevalence of major affective disorder. But this is presumably because the eating disorders are rarer syndromes. Since they appear to represent only one of many syndromes related to major affective disorder, it is not surprising that they should be less frequent than affective disorder itself.

Laboratory Tests

The evidence goes on. You will recall our earlier mention of the various laboratory tests now being evaluated in major affective disorder. Two of these tests—the dexamethasone suppression test and the thyrotropin releasing hormone stimulation test—have been found positive in bulimic patients with the same frequency as in patients with major depression.[15,21,22] However, on both tests, the bulimic patients have shown a higher frequency of positive tests than would be expected in a normal control population. Again, this finding would seem to favor a relationship between bulimia and major depression.

However, there are many caveats associated with these data. For example, is it possible that the stress of frequent binging and vomiting, the metabolic abnormalities produced, or the rapid fluctuations of weight in bulimic patients might cause "false positive" results on these tests? To check this, we examined the correlation between frequency of binging and dexamethasone suppression test results in a sample of forty-seven bulimic patients. There was no correlation; in fact, even those patients who were in the hospital, who were entirely prevented from binging, demonstrated the same prevalence of positive tests as patients who were binging several times a day. Thus, the positive tests in bulimic patients may not be an artifact, and the finding may reflect a genuine relationship between bulimia and major affective disorder.

Nevertheless, we must emphasize that the meaning of both the dexamethasone suppression test and the thyrotropin releasing hormone stimulation test remain in dispute. It is possible that neither of the two tests is a marker for affective disorder at all, and that they are merely nonspecific reactions to stress or other factors. We have therefore accorded them only a minor place in this chapter. However, if the tests do have meaning, then the findings are consistent with the hypothesis that bulimia is related to major affective disorder.

Treatment Response

Finally we come to the most important question of all: Does bulimia respond to the same treatments that have been found effective in major affective disorder? We have already explained that drugs such as lithium or antidepressants have essentially no effect on normal people; however, they are highly effective for people suffering from major affective disorder. Therefore, if bulimia were to respond to these medications, this finding might again suggest a relationship between bulimia and major affective disorder.

We have performed four studies showing that antidepressants are indeed effective in bulimia. These findings are so important that we will devote an entire chapter to describing them in detail. For now, we point out simply that binge eating has markedly decreased or completely vanished in a large percentage of our patients treated with any of several different medications used in the treatment of major affective disorder, including imipramine, desipramine, tranylcypromine, phenelzine, trazodone, lithium carbonate, and carbamazepine. The success of these medications adds to the argument that bulimia is related to major affective disorder.

Once again, we must consider a possible objection: Is it possible that bulimia might *not* be related to affective disorder but nevertheless respond to antidepressant drugs for some reason *other* than their antidepressant properties? In other words, can we establish that the medications' antidepressant effects and antibulimic effects are one and the same?

There are at least three arguments favoring this assumption. First, our bulimic patients have responded not to just one antidepressant medication but to several unrelated drugs. Imipramine, tranylcypromine, and trazodone have little in common in terms of their chemical structures. The principal attribute they share is their ability to relieve the symptoms of major depression. Therefore, if they all work for bulimia, it seems likely that this must be due to their common antidepressant properties, rather than to some novel property they all happen to share.

A second argument is that there is a close correlation between improvement in depressive symptoms and improvement in bulimic symptoms in our patients: Those who get better in one respect also get better in the others; those who fail to feel an improvement in depression are also unlikely to notice any improvement in their bulimia.

The third observation is that the antidepressant effect and antibulimic effect take about the same time to appear—usually three to four weeks. This would again suggest that the two effects are one and the same.

Adding all three of the above observations together, we have a strong argument that antidepressants work in bulimia because of their antidepressant properties, and not because of some novel property that they accidentally have in common. Thus, the effect of antidepressants in bulimia adds yet another piece of evidence to the growing case that bulimia is related to major affective disorder.

Do drugs used for manic-depressive illness, such as lithium and carbamazepine, also work for bulimia? We have had success with both these drugs in isolated cases, but since the majority of bulimic patients get better with ordinary antidepressants, we have had little occasion to use them.

What about antipsychotic drugs, or "major tranquilizers," such as Thorazine (chlorpromazine)? These drugs, first of all, are not "tranquilizers"; they are designed to counteract psychotic symptoms, such as paranoid delusions or auditory hallucinations. Furthermore, unlike antidepressants or lithium, they are effective for psychotic symptoms in a broad range of psychiatric disorders other than major affective disorder, including schizophrenia, organic psychoses, and drug-induced psychoses. Therefore, even if they were effective in bulimia, this would not give us any diagnostic information one way or the other. In any case, they are almost certainly ineffective in the great majority of bulimic patients. Once again, ordinary antidepressants are so frequently effective in bulimia that we have had few occasions to try other medications.

The use of antidepressants in bulimia is new—so new that relatively few studies other than our own have been published. However, physicians in New York, Philadelphia, and California have now also reported successful antidepressant treatment of bulimia. These reports will be described in detail in Chapter 8.

The Evidence of
Four Validating Indices

Our argument that bulimia is closely related to major affective disorder may be growing rather repetitive, as we have presented study after study in the areas of phenomenology, genetics, laboratory tests, and treatment response. Is it really necessary to go through all four of these validating indices in order to make our point?

Although it may seem like scientific overkill, we do feel that it is necessary, because a sound theory should be shown capable of standing up to rigorous examination, using as many different tests as possible. In fact, we feel that there should be even more data: Further blind family-interview studies should be performed in both anorexia nervosa and bulimia; further evaluation of laboratory tests (particularly REM latency and tyramine excretion) is imperative; further phenomenological studies should be conducted with differing populations of bulimic subjects (particularly those with mild bulimia and those with obesity) and additional placebo-controlled double-blind studies of antidepressants, lithium, and carbamazepine in both bulimia and anorexia nervosa are urgently needed.

Nevertheless, we feel that the evidence, even at its present preliminary stage, is enough to make a persuasive argument that many or most cases of bulimia are closely related to major affective disorder. Furthermore, this evidence is already far more extensive than that supporting any other theory of the cause of bulimia. Psychodynamic, family, or sociocultural theories, persuasive and intriguing though they may be, rest on a far more tenuous empirical foundation.

7

THE TREATMENT OF BULIMIA: PREVIOUS APPROACHES

A Treatment Odyssey

In the previous chapter, we mentioned our findings that anti-depressant medications appear highly effective in the treatment of bulimia. But before discussing our own approach, it seems only fair to present a careful review of the other treatments that have been proposed for bulimia, together with an appraisal of the scientific evidence regarding the effectiveness of each.

Many of our bulimic patients—particularly those who have suffered for many years and tried countless courses of therapy— have told us stories that in themselves are virtual reviews of the various treatments of bulimia. A typical example is the treatment odyssey recounted below by a twenty-eight-year-old woman named Helen. She came to our office in response to a newspaper advertisement seeking subjects for one of our studies.

Eight years ago I began to binge eat—March 24, 1974. I know the exact date, but not because anything in particular was going on in my life. Just the opposite. Everything was fine. I had been working for a year and a half in my new job as an assistant editor at a publishing company in New York. Things were not very pressured then, cer-tainly less so than now—and much less so than before I started working, when I was in all sorts of turmoil as to what I would do after college. But in March of 1974, everything was completely fine. If I appear to protest too much, it's because I had no answer then and I have no answer now as to why the binging started. But it's not been for lack of searching.

At first, I was shocked by it. I couldn't believe that every night I would come home and binge. I often got a horrible sense of anxiety and binging would somehow relieve the anxiety, but then I'd feel awful afterward. I knew I needed help. I told my mother I was having a tough time handling the pressure of my job (which wasn't true) and that I wanted to see someone. She told me that, of course, she and dad would pay for treatment and she recommended someone at a psychoanalytic institute who had helped a friend of hers cope with stress.

He was a very sympathetic, middle-aged man. I should start by telling him what the difficulties were, he said. Then together we would follow the patterns that emerged and see the underlying meaning of them. The process would take a long time and I was warned not to expect too much too soon. I might even get worse before I got better. So I began seeing him weekly. Gradually, I got the feeling he was more interested when I talked about my family and my upbringing than when I talked about my binge eating and vomiting. But after six or eight months, it still seemed like we were "setting the stage."

I finally got enough courage to ask him what *he* thought were the goals of the therapy and how long they would take. He asked, "Why do you suppose you are bringing up questions like this now?" Then he told me that in therapy there is usually a time, after six months to a year, when the patient becomes very concerned with how the therapist is reacting, and afraid of a growing attachment to the therapist, and will show this in any number of ways. This included becoming "a little rebellious," often in a childlike way, as if reacting to a parent.

I felt pretty embarrassed because he was right—he did remind me of my father in some ways, and here I was playing the spoiled little girl again. He did say this was a necessary process for the therapy, and that, as a way of "approaching" my question, therapy for my problems could take many years. He would recommend I undergo psychoanalysis, which would mean coming four days a week, lying on the couch, and saying everything that came into my mind. He said he thought that my binging reflected "intense oral needs" that were never satisfied and were a consequence of events very early in my childhood. The reason I had fared so well in the meantime was that I had no real demands placed on me until I began working and had to face the adult world. Because of a serious developmental flaw, however, I was destined to be unable to function as an adult until I had resolved this early conflict. This would probably take many years.

I was so shaken after that session, I could hardly get home. I couldn't stand up at the bus stop, so I took a cab, wailing in the back seat. Once home, I unplugged the phone and cried myself to sleep. I called in sick at work the next day. I didn't know what to do, where to turn. Years? Psychoanalysis? Attachment to him? I was so confused. It was eight months and I had made no progress. How could I work and see him four times a week? My parents couldn't afford it and neither could I. Besides, I was binging and vomiting every night and no one could possibly know what it was like.

That afternoon Martha came over. She was sort of a partial friend of mine—one of those people who was always into everybody's business. I almost didn't let her in, but I needed someone there. So I told her the whole story. She wasn't shocked. In fact, she said that she knew many women who had the problem; there were even a couple in her consciousness-raising group.

For the first time, another human being seemed to know what I was struggling against. She said that the women in her group had also tried traditional psychotherapy with male therapists. "A man just can't understand," she said. "It's a women's issue. Society is run by men who expect women to be thin and pretty, to be available to have sex with when desired, and then to get married and get pregnant. You've violated that expectation, Helen! You are a successful editor in a male-dominated world. Every day you feel the pressure to look nice and be deferential. That kind of stress, turned inward, gives you tremendous conflicts, and that comes out in the form of binge eating. Then you feel guilty because you'll look fat and not meet male expectations, and that leads to purging and depression. I've heard the same story from two of the women in my group. In fact, why don't you come to our Tuesday evening meeting?"

Well, I did go for a while with Martha. All the women were very sympathetic, and it was with their help and support that I was able to disentangle myself from my male therapist and get over my difficult experience in therapy. But the trouble was, I was still binging, and so were the two other women with bulimia in the group, although they seemed to be happier and very committed to the group and its purpose.

I don't know why I stopped going. I guess I wasn't really that close to Martha and I felt under some pressure to demonstrate and sign petitions for causes I basically thought were okay but didn't believe in completely. I did ask one of the women with bulimia if she knew of any place where I could get more information about bulimia.

She referred me to the local chapter of a self-help organization for eating disorders. There, the staff—two women, one of whom had had anorexia nervosa herself and one who had a daughter with bulimia—were very kind to me. They instantly seemed to understand how I felt. They said they did not endorse any particular form of treatment, but that there were a number of approaches which seemed to be helpful. They were quick to point out that many so-called experts in the mental-health field had little knowledge of the eating disorders, and that they would, if I wished, give me the names of some therapists or programs that were particularly experienced in treating bulimia.

It was a wonderful relief to talk to them. From their list, I got the name of a woman therapist, Dr. L., and made an appointment, hoping that my experience would be better this time. I went to see her with the idea that at least I wouldn't waste nine months on something I felt wasn't going anywhere.

Well, I didn't really have to worry. We hit it off right from the beginning. She seemed to respect me as an adult. I didn't feel infantilized as I had with my first therapist. She had seen many women with bulimia, she said. In contrast to focusing exclusively on my early childhood, she was very concerned about what I was doing now with my life, what I wanted in life, how miserable I was with binging. She said that the major issue was one of control; that my lack of control of my eating mirrored the chaos of my internal psychic state; and that by understanding more of what I wanted and working out how to accomplish it, I could also learn to control my binging.

We worked on ways to understand the stresses I was under at work and how to diminish them. We also talked about my family. Much to my surprise, I was able to see that some of my passivity, both at work and in dealing with friends, did seem to stem from the way I had always been toward my parents. I even thought I was beginning to gain some control over my binging, but unfortunately it seemed to plateau. I should say, however, that while I have had my ups and downs in therapy, and there have been times in the last four years when I have considered quitting, all in all it has been a good experience, and I think it's the only thing that's kept me from killing myself. But, as you know, I'm still binging.

There was one time, two years ago, when I really began to get worse. Dr. L. was getting concerned, too. I had become very irritable and depressed. I started to dream about death. I got drunk every weekend at parties. I started to snap at my colleagues at work, and they began to treat me as if I were very touchy. I was getting nowhere in therapy—often I would show up late, or not talk for ten minutes at a time. Dr. L. and I both agreed this could not continue. She knew of an intensive behavior-therapy program at a local hospital. It would require being admitted as an inpatient, but the ward was specifically designed for patients with eating disorders. I looked into it, and felt that it was worth a chance. It was not easy taking two months off from work, but I thought that if I could apply all my energies to this one problem, perhaps I could finally gain control.

I came in with great enthusiasm, bordering on euphoria. My eating was supervised; I was not allowed to choose my menu. I had no opportunity to binge. Initially, a woman staff member was with me in the bathroom to see that I didn't throw up. For four days I had no urge at all to binge. I was very encouraged. During the entire time I was there, I only binged once. When it happened, I told the staff about it, and lost my privileges to leave the hall unescorted for a week. That seemed to do the trick.

Each week I would make a "contract," as they called it, and at the end of the week it would be evaluated. My primary goal was to "normalize eating behavior," and I would make a contract not to vomit, to monitor my mood and to talk to a staff member when I had the urge to binge.

I gradually took more charge of my menu planning, and my meals were not supervised. I also had other goals—for example, to deal more effectively with stress and to resolve certain problems with my family. I learned relaxation techniques and underwent assertiveness training in a group. And then there was also a women's group. I learned behavioral techniques of impulse control—how to delay acting on an impulse, such as the urge to binge eat, by substituting other behaviors in place of it.

Finally, my parents came in to meet with me and the social worker once a week. My whole day was packed with scheduled activities. I was able to stop binging, I was succeeding in my program and got a lot of what they called "positive reinforcement" for this, and although it was a struggle, I seemed to be moving in the right direction for the first time in years.

I particularly remember the family work. At first, my parents and I were not very enthusiastic. But having a family evaluation was a precondition for treatment there, so my mother dragged my father down to meet with the social worker and me. Since I had been alone with my problem for years, it was hard to let my parents in on what I had been going through. My mother felt so guilty, and my father seemed ashamed that a daughter of his had to go to a psychiatric hospital. A couple of times we had our meetings in the hospital cafeteria—so we could look at our interactions at meals. They were a bit heavy-going. I think all of us had indigestion afterward. The social worker made comments about how our abnormal communication, particularly at mealtimes, helped to cause and foster my attitudes toward food and my bulimia. Somehow that all seemed forced. As near as I can recall, meals were pretty ordinary events when I grew up, and not particularly stressful.

I think the family work was most helpful in simply educating my parents about what I was going through. It was least helpful when it made my mother feel that she'd caused my problems. She'd cry, then yell at my father, and he'd be bewildered and tongue-tied. At home he would have told her she was simply taking it too hard and it wasn't her fault, but I think he felt like he couldn't say that in the therapy session. We often all felt so hurt, guilty, and inadequate. Maybe if family therapy had gone on longer, it would have been helpful. I don't know.

I was discharged after eight weeks. They said I should really have stayed four months, but I felt I couldn't take any more time from work—and besides, I had stopped binging. I was still anxious and had trouble sleeping, but I could finally keep my impulses under control.

Then, three weeks after I left, on a Saturday afternoon, I felt it come back again—the urge to binge. It had really never left me entirely, and I guess I just lost control over it again. I spent the next ten hours binging and vomiting, as if in a trance.

Over the next two months, I tried to practice all the techniques I had learned. I was still in a follow-up group, and though I told them I only binged occasionally, it was more like twice a week. After another month, I was back where I started. I asked to be released from my commitment to a year of follow-up, but was encouraged to stick it out, and I did. By the end it got to be torture. I had obviously failed. I should have been able to control it, and I couldn't. I was also angry. I had gone to considerable lengths to be able to take off the time to go into the hospital. I had tried so hard. I thought I was doing so well. But maybe I never was, maybe I was fooling myself. But how could I try harder? If a twenty-four-hour-a-day program didn't work for me, how could anything else help?

But I kept trying. I had to. It's either that or admit that I've got this problem forever, and somehow I just can't do that. So in the last year I tried some treatments that were not on the list of the self-help organization. I went to a special place in California for a ten-day retreat. Meditation, brown rice, harmony with nature. It was a great experience and I felt refreshed. But I still binged. I went to a nutritionist, and she said that it was due to too much carbohydrate and food additives in my diet. That was a horrible experience, let me tell you. A low-carbohydrate diet made my urge to binge worse instead of better. It lasted only five days. Maybe I didn't give it a chance.

I guess you're next in line. I'm not thrilled about taking a pill, but I can't afford not to keep trying, even though each failure is so hard to take.

Helen's story may seem hard to believe, but many of our patients give similar accounts of treatment after treatment, technique after technique, and therapist after therapist over years of time, with the same results: repeated failures; a growing sense of guilt and shame at being unable to overcome their problem; and finally, an entrenched skepticism that any treatment could possibly help. Such stories illustrate how persistent bulimia can sometimes be in the face of standard treatment approaches.

How to Evaluate Treatment Claims

Of course, we have seen patients who described experiences quite opposite to Helen's, who raved about how some particular therapy—even a rather exotic one—relieved their symptoms. Clearly, we cannot draw conclusions from individual anecdotal accounts, in which one person claims that a given therapy succeeded, while another claims that it failed. If a therapy is truly effective, there should be studies in the scientific literature that demonstrate its effectiveness, not just word-of-mouth reports from people who claim to be cured.

How do we evaluate studies in order to judge whether a given treatment is effective or not? Various treatment claims for all kinds of ailments come and go. Long ago it was believed that complete dental extraction would cure rheumatoid arthritis! Lately it has been laetrile for cancer; tomorrow it may be biofeedback for diabetes. What criteria should we use to decide whether a given treatment is truly legitimate or just another form of snake oil?

A good study of any treatment technique should meet at least four criteria: It should be (1) *quantitative,* (2) *prospective,* (3) *controlled,* and (4) *blind.*

A *quantitative study* states, very simply, what percentage of treated patients got better, or by what percentage their symptoms declined. For example, if someone writes that three patients with bulimia were cured by primal-scream therapy, this means nothing. Maybe there were thirty-seven other patients, also treated with primal-scream therapy, who failed to get better, or even got worse! Thus, we can draw no conclusions from individual case reports that fail to provide such quantitative information. Case reports will almost always give us a biased view, since someone with a successful case is likely to write it up, while other people, who were unsuccessful with the same treatment, are not likely to publish their negative results.

By insisting on quantitative studies rather than anecdotal reports, we have already greatly reduced the number of scientific studies that can be considered useful.

A *prospective study* selects a group of patients in advance, applies the treatment, and then reports the results. The opposite is a *retrospective study,* in which someone looks back on a number of patients who have been treated and comments on how many got better. The retrospective study may appear harmless, but it contains hidden flaws.

First, there may be biases in the selection of patients: Perhaps the treatment was not offered to patients who seemed unlikely to benefit from it, or perhaps some patients began the treatment but dropped out at an early stage because they weren't improving.

Second, as mentioned above, the literature will contain a disproportionate number of positive results. If four out of the first five of someone's patients get better, he will probably publish the results. But other therapists, using the same technique, might succeed with only one, or zero, out of five, and will be unlikely to publish. Reading the literature, we will get the impression that the treatment is 80% effective, when in fact it may work for only 15% of patients. The proper way to deal with this problem is to do the experiment prospectively. Select, say, twenty patients at random, without regard to whether their cases seem promising or not. Apply an identical treatment to all twenty patients, keeping track of those who drop out for any reason. At the end of the study, report on all cases, successes and failures alike. Only by this method can one avoid the pitfalls of the retrospective approach.

By insisting on prospective study designs, we have whittled down even further the number of published studies that we can consider acceptable and useful.

A *controlled study* is so named because it controls for the rate of *spontaneous* improvement in the illness. This is terribly important, yet few lay people take it into account when they listen to the results of a study. Suppose twenty people take vitamin X for a common cold, and sixteen of them feel dramatically better in seven days. Does this mean that vitamin X works? No. Sixteen out of twenty people with a common cold feel dramatically better in seven days anyhow. Going back a century or two, suppose twelve young women with recent-onset cases of rheumatoid arthritis undergo the painful treatment of complete dental extraction. Within a year, several of them are almost completely free of joint pains. Would you have all your teeth removed on the strength of this study? We hope not. Up to 20% of all recent-onset cases of rheumatoid arthritis go into remission within one year, even with no treatment. If more than 50% of patients with anorexia nervosa are completely better after five years of nude encounter groups in a hot tub, should all therapists install hot tubs? Forget it! More than 50% of people with anorexia nervosa get better within five years all by themselves, without any treatment.

It is amazing how few scientific studies bother to control for the fact that in most illnesses a certain percentage of people get better spontaneously. To do a proper controlled study, one must take two matched groups of patients—a *treatment* group that receives the proposed treatment and a *control* group that receives no treatment but is followed in parallel with the treatment group. If, say, 40% of the people in the treatment group get better after a year, but 41% of the people in the control group are also better, it would be hard to argue that the treatment is effective. If, however, only 10% of control patients get better, but 87% of treated patients get better, then we probably have a meaningful finding.

That sounds easy, does it not? Then you may be surprised to learn that, as of the end of 1982, only one study of any treatment for bulimia, published anywhere in the world, had ever used a control group simultaneously with a treatment group. Clearly, the requirement for a control group drastically reduces the number of studies whose results we can trust.

A *blind study* is one in which neither the patients nor the therapists know who is receiving the real treatment and who is in the control group. For example, in a "placebo-controlled double-blind study" of a new medication, half the patients receive the real medication, while the other half receive a placebo, a "sugar pill" that looks identical to the real thing but has no effect at all. Only when the study is over does the patient find out whether he or she was receiving the active medication or the fake.

Such blindness is easy to maintain when studying drugs; it is harder to maintain when studying other therapies—but not impossible. For example, suppose we wish to study the effect on bulimia of a particular form of impulse-control training. We might choose two matched groups of subjects—prospectively, of course—and put one group into ordinary psychotherapy and another into psychotherapy *plus* impulse-control training. That way, the patients in the control group—with psychotherapy alone—would be blind to the fact that they were not receiving the test treatment, the impulse-control training. Of course, the therapists treating the patients would not be blind; they would know perfectly well which patients were receiving the test treatment. But we could get around this too. At the end of the study, the patients' improvement could be rated by an independent researcher who was kept blind as to which treatment each patient had received.

Why such elaborate methods to maintain blindness? It is to correct for the power of suggestion, or, as researchers call it, the "placebo effect." Human nature being what it is, any researcher testing a new treatment is going to be anxious for it to work, and anybody who volunteers to try the new treatment is also going to want it to succeed. Under such conditions, the power of suggestion can be incredible. In many medical conditions, 20% or 30% of patients given inert placebos will promptly feel better, and swear that it's due to the pills. An entirely ineffective treatment may thus appear to be quite helpful for many patients, simply because they (and those treating them) expect it to work and want it to work. It becomes obvious that blindness is very important in any study in order to be sure that improvement is genuinely due to the treatment, and not to suggestion alone.

What about studies of psychotherapy? As we have pointed out, it is hard to do such studies blind; obviously, the patients are going to know whether they are receiving psychotherapy or not. But we can still ensure partial blindness, as mentioned above, by having the patients' progress rated by an independent researcher, or some other individual who deliberately does not ask the patient whether he or she has been receiving psychotherapy.

The importance of such blindness is abundantly illustrated in the scientific literature. One famous example is the Cambridge-Sommerville Youth Study.[1] This study took a group of youngsters who seemed destined to become juvenile delinquents, and put half of them in intensive therapy with Freudian and Rogerian psychotherapists, while essentially leaving the other half on the streets. So far, so good: This is quantitative, prospective, and controlled. At the end of two to eight years of therapy, the therapists rated about two-thirds of their boys as having "substantially benefited" from therapy, and about half of these were rated as showing "outstanding" benefit. A majority of the boys—62%—also rated themselves as improved; they felt that the therapy "kept them out of trouble." This sounds very promising, doesn't it? Psychotherapy helped to reduce delinquency. Wrong! When we look at a couple of "blind" measurements, which were independent of the therapists' and patients' bias, we see quite a different picture. Over the period of the study, the boys in the therapy group actually chalked up *more* court appearances than the boys left on the street. The treated boys were charged with a total of 264 offenses, while the control boys had only 218. This illustrates the pitfalls of taking nonblind ratings at face value.

Control and blindness are so important that they deserve one more example. A recent psychotherapy study[2] used a particularly ingenious design. It took a group of "neurotic" college students who wanted therapy and divided them into three groups. One group was left untreated (put on a waiting list); a second was treated in twice-a-week psychotherapy by highly experienced, senior psychotherapists; and the third, interestingly enough, was sent off to see college faculty members—English teachers, math teachers, and the like, who had no formal training in psychotherapy—for friendly talks on the same twice-a-week basis. Here we have a study that is not only quantitative and prospective but is in a sense doubly controlled: It has not only the usual control group but also a second control group receiving "pseudotherapy" from teachers. There is even a sort of blindness here, in the sense that the study tries to measure the "placebo effect" of merely seeing a caring person, as opposed to a trained therapist, on a regular basis.

At the end of three to four months, improvement was measured by blind raters. The students in the psychotherapy group had improved much more than those in the untreated control group. The students who saw the math teachers and the English teachers *also* improved more than those in the control group. And there was no significant difference between those who saw the senior therapists and those who saw the teachers.

Of course, we can make all kinds of speculations on the basis of such results, but our point is simply this: We must be very cautious and very skeptical in interpreting the results of any study that is not quantitative, prospective, controlled, or blind.

With these caveats, then, let us look critically and systematically at published studies of the treatment of bulimia. Again, because anorexia nervosa has been more extensively studied than bulimia, and because nearly half of anorexic patients display bulimia at some point, we shall borrow from the literature on anorexia nervosa as well.

Psychodynamic and Family Therapies

As mentioned in Chapter 5, there are many different psychodynamic and family theories that might be used to explain bulimia. All share the belief that life events, particularly in early childhood or in certain family interactions, cause the symptoms of the eating disorder to appear. In therapy, therefore, the patient tries to gain insight into what conflicts may have caused the symptoms; once these conflicts are understood and discussed, they can eventually be resolved, and the eating disorder will hopefully disappear. It is usually expected that such therapy will work over a matter of years.

For both anorexia nervosa and bulimia, there are various reports of individual patients who have done well with classical long-term psychoanalytic psychotherapy.[3] On the other hand, there are a number of experts, including Dr. Hilde Bruch[4] at Baylor University and Drs. Nancy Rollins and Amelia Blackwell[5] at Children's Hospital in Boston, who recommend other forms of psychodynamic therapy for eating disorders, and argue that classical psychoanalytic therapy may be ineffective in anorexia nervosa. In 1965, a well-known researcher, Dr. Shervert Frazier,[6] wrote: "The usual psychoanalytic technique is not appropriate for these persons. Providing insight for these patients through motivational interpretations is not only useless but reinforces the basic defect—the inability to know what they themselves feel."

Setting aside these contrasting impressions, what are the results of actual studies of psychodynamic therapy in the eating disorders? You may be surprised to hear the answer: There are no such studies. There are reports describing the results of overall treatment programs for anorexia nervosa.[7] And there are anecdotal descriptions of one or a few cases. But we have been unable to find any major study of any specific type of individual psychodynamic treatment for anorexia nervosa or bulimia that meets even one of our four criteria for a reasonable scientific study. Of course, we cannot conclude from this that psychodynamic therapy is ineffective. It may be highly effective for some patients. But, to date, no one has tried to demonstrate this in a proper scientific study.

What about the effectiveness of family therapy? Here, in addition to the usual anecdotal reports pro and con, we fortunately do have one study to review. Since the early 1970s, Dr. Salvador Minuchin and his colleagues in Philadelphia have been evaluating the effectiveness of family therapy in anorexia nervosa.[8] In a recent report, they summarize the first fifty-three cases treated. All were adolescents who had had anorexia nervosa for a relatively brief period, usually six months or less. Treatment lasted an average of six months, and the patients were followed up after three months to four years; only 25% of cases had been followed more than two years. The results seem impressive: 86% of patients returned to normal eating patterns and normal weight; 88% were judged to have achieved a satisfactory family, school, or social adjustment.

How do these results stand up to scientific scrutiny? Clearly, the study is quantitative, and although it began as a retrospective study, it has more recently evaluated patients prospectively. Apparently, the follow-up information was not obtained by personal interviews, so some serious psychopathology might have been missed. But this is only a minor problem with the study.

It is on the issues of control and blindness that the reader is forced to become increasingly skeptical. There was no control group—a serious problem, because the study examined only young patients who had been ill for a short time. In an illness that tends to remit spontaneously, such remissions are likely to occur early in the course of illness rather than later. For example, someone who has had rheumatoid arthritis for only three months is much more likely to have a spontaneous remission in the near future than someone who has been ill continuously for the last ten years. This may help to explain our findings on anorexia nervosa among students, mentioned in Chapter 3: Of nineteen young women who reported anorexia nervosa at some time in their lives, only one reported anorexia currently. The other eighteen—95% of the group—had got better, even though the great majority of them reported that they had never sought psychiatric help. These observations suggest that we might expect a majority of young, briefly ill anorexic patients to get better of their own accord. Without a control group, therefore, can we be certain that family therapy is better than what might be caused by chance alone?

Two additional findings should make us even more wary. First, two of the three dropouts from treatment and five of the seven patients with unsuccessful or partially successful outcome had been ill more than a year. Second, most of the reported improvement occurred within the first two to eight weeks of treatment, and the entire treatment usually lasted only about six months. This contradicts psychodynamic theory, which would lead us to expect little improvement at first and the bulk of the improvement much later on, as insight is gained and conflicts resolved.

The picture grows even murkier when it is revealed that half the patients were treated with hospitalization and behavior therapy. As we shall see, hospitalization by itself, with or without behavior therapy, has excellent short-term results in many large studies—usually in about two to eight weeks, as a matter of fact. Therefore, how much of the patients' improvement was due to family therapy itself, and how much might be explained by these other factors?

Clearly, to properly evaluate the findings of the study, it would be very desirable to have a matched control group. But this is not all: The study was also nonblind. All the investigators had a personal stake in proving that family therapy works. And it was the investigators themselves who rated the degree of clinical improvement in their patients—just like the therapists in the ill-fated Cambridge-Sommerville Youth Study. Of course, body weight on follow-up was a more objective measurement, but that had usually been corrected within the first two to eight weeks.

We have discussed this study at some length, not because it is a bad study—in fact, it is a very important study, and is methodologically better than many we shall subsequently discuss—but because it illustrates the critical need for control groups and blind outcome ratings. If, in the future, researchers undertake other psychodynamic or family studies of the treatment of bulimia, it is important that they take these details into account.

In summary, therefore, there is as yet no fully satisfactory scientific evidence that psychodynamic or family therapy is effective in anorexia nervosa or bulimia. We must reiterate that this does not prove that such therapy is ineffective. It might be effective, but to date no one has demonstrated this clearly.

1985 Update: Since our book first went to press, the first *controlled* study of psychotherapy in anorexia nervosa has appeared. Dr. Arthur Crisp and his associates compared patients treated with brief psychotherapy to patients who did not receive such treatment. Although the psychotherapy patients improved more than control patients on some measures, the control patients were actually slightly more successful at gaining weight, both short-term and on follow-up, than the patients receiving psychotherapy! Given the mixed results of this study, the effectiveness of psychotherapy in eating disorders continues to remain open to question.

Behavior Therapies

Most behavioral programs take place in a hospital setting. In anorexic patients, they work by using such rewards as increased freedom, visiting privileges, and physical activities to reward weight gain, and by using such things as room restriction, prohibition of visits and exercising, and even tube feeding to "punish" weight loss.[9] Behavioral programs have now also been developed specifically for bulimia. These generally include rewards for not bingeing or vomiting, and for maintaining a normal weight; and punishments for bingeing, vomiting, or deviating from the normal weight range. However, there are fewer reports describing behavior therapy for bulimia than for anorexia nervosa.

What is the evidence for the efficacy of behavior therapy? Many studies of anorexic patients report dramatic short-term success, with an average weight gain of twelve pounds in the first month of treatment. But although these studies are generally quantitative, most are retrospective, uncontrolled, and nonblind, and hence not very meaningful from a scientific standpoint. We have been able to find only three studies of anorexia nervosa that have a control group—one in French and two in English. One of these looked not only at weight gain in the hospital but also at how the patients performed on other measures of outcome long after hospitalization.

In the first study, a group of researchers in Lausanne, Switzerland, compared eight anorexic patients treated with standard hospital treatment to nine others treated subsequently with behavior therapy.[10] Although initial weight gain was faster in the behavior-therapy group, there was no difference between the two groups in total weight gain at the end of treatment. Furthermore, the study was retrospective, did not measure any aspect of outcome other than weight gain, was nonblind, and did not use a simultaneous control group; instead, the control group of eight cases represented patients who had been treated several years earlier at the same hospital.

A much more rigorous study was performed by Dr. Elke Eckert and a number of other sophisticated American researchers at three separate institutions: the University of Minnesota Hospitals, the University of Iowa Hospital, and the Illinois State Psychiatric Institute.[11] They assigned eighty-six patients randomly to either inpatient hospital treatment with behavior therapy or to the same treatment without behavior therapy. After thirty-five days, both groups had gained weight, but there was no "statistically significant" difference between them—that is, the difference in weight gain between the two groups was likely due to chance alone.

This is an excellent example of why it is so important to have a matched control group. Looking at the behavior-therapy group alone, we might think that their substantial weight gain represented a beneficial effect of behavior therapy. Only when we look at the control group do we discover that they, too, gained weight, and that behavior therapy did not offer any additional benefit.

Two other studies have looked at the long-term outcome of behavior therapy for anorexic patients. In an uncontrolled study, Dr. Michael Pertschuk reviewed twenty-nine cases of anorexia nervosa treated with behavior therapy at the Hospital of the University of Pennsylvania.[12] In the short term, behavior therapy looked good: Twenty-five of the twenty-nine patients gained weight while in the hospital—an average of over eleven pounds. But on long-term follow-up (an average of twenty months after hospital discharge), Pertschuk found that the patients who had initially done well with behavior therapy were no better off than those who had initially done badly.

For example, all four patients who had failed to gain weight in the hospital turned out to have gained a good deal of weight on follow-up. The other findings were even more striking. Twelve of the twenty-nine patients had had to be rehospitalized at least once—six for relapses of anorexia nervosa, and six for suicide attempts or depression. Although most patients were of normal weight at follow-up, almost all were still plagued with psychiatric problems—twelve had developed bulimia and/or purging and only two "could be said to be completely recovered in the sense of maintaining near normal weight, functioning well, and eating normally." Thus, the study suggests that the short-term benefits of behavior therapy, when examined over the long term, seem to evaporate.

The other long-term follow-up study, which included a control group, found a similar result.[13] Dr. Paul Garfinkel and his colleagues in Toronto compared seventeen anorexic patients who had received behavior therapy in the hospital with twenty-five others who had received only standard hospital treatment. At the time of follow-up, an average of thirty-two months after hospital discharge, using a number of measures of function, the two groups were indistinguishable.

In summary, then, the only prospective, controlled study of behavior therapy in anorexia nervosa found it no more effective than ordinary hospital treatment. And even if there are beneficial effects, both of the two long-term follow-up studies suggest that, with the passage of time, these effects vanish.

By extrapolation from the anorexia nervosa studies, we might expect an equally lackluster track record for behavior therapy in bulimia. Interestingly, however, the only quantitative study of behavior therapy in bulimia produced impressive results.[14] Dr. Christopher Fairburn, now at Oxford University in England, treated eleven bulimic women with standard behavior-therapy techniques, plus a special modification of behavior therapy called "cognitive therapy."[15] Unfortunately, in his brief report, Fairburn is not specific about how cognitive therapy was used with his patients. Apparently, they set a weekly goal with the therapist, and progress toward this goal was assessed at the next meeting. In addition, "cognitive change methods are used, with the patient being trained to challenge and replace maladaptive thoughts."

Fairburn states that nine of the eleven women stopped binging after three to twelve months of this treatment. And, unlike the anorexia studies, his study suggests that these results held up on follow-up after a further four to twelve months. Of the nine cases followed up, the reduction in binge eating had been maintained in all cases in which treatment had been successful.

This appears promising, but although the study is quantitative, it is not clear whether it was prospective, and it certainly was not controlled, nor blind. We need only recall the phenytoin (Dilantin) story, discussed in Chapter 5 and again later in this chapter, in which nine out of ten patients appeared much improved in the first uncontrolled treatment study. Like Dr. Fairburn's report, this first phenytoin report was also retrospective, uncontrolled, and nonblind. And as further studies of phenytoin appeared, the initially spectacular results gradually fizzled.

Thus, before we jump to conclusions, it is important that Dr. Fairburn's promising technique be studied prospectively, with a matched control group, and with outcome rated by an investigator blind to the treatment received. Possibly such a study is in progress; we eagerly await the results.

There is another problem. Even allowing that behavior therapy, in contrast to its record in anorexia nervosa, does prove effective in bulimia, can it help with the severe depression, manic-depressive illness, panic disorder, agoraphobia, and other symptoms experienced by so many bulimic patients? Remember Pertschuk's follow-up study of anorexia, in which virtually all patients regained normal weight, but remained profoundly ill in other respects. By analogy, if we merely reduce the binging through positive and negative reinforcement, are we really curing the whole patient?[16]

In syndromes such as isolated phobias—a fear of snakes, for example—behavior therapy often seems wonderfully effective, because the typical patient has no major psychopathology except for the phobia. But in the bulimic patient, who often suffers from one or even several of the many bulimia-associated disorders described in Chapter 4, it is hard to believe that merely eliminating the binges will end the patient's problems. In any event, this question must be addressed by any study suggesting that behavior therapy is effective in bulimia.

Tallying up the available data, then, the weight of the evidence indicates that behavior therapy is ineffective for anorexia nervosa, especially over the long term. And although we have a single report of promising results in nine women with bulimia, it remains to be seen whether this result will stand the test of a more rigorous study. If it does, the question remains as to whether behavioral therapy would be of value for the many other psychiatric problems suffered by bulimic patients.

Other Forms of Psychotherapy

Psychodynamic and behavior therapies are not the only treatments on the market; at last count, there were at least 250 "therapies" available in the United States, ranging from gestalt therapy to pet therapy to primal scream. Practitioners of each of these techniques might well claim that they could achieve great success in bulimia. And, we must admit, we have seen many bulimic patients who claimed to have derived great benefit from all manner of different therapies, ranging from the standard to the bizarre.

But needless to say, until we are presented with published scientific evidence for a given approach, we have to remain skeptical. After all, for centuries people believed that leeches and emetics were useful for serious medical conditions. Reputable physicians even argued that it was criminal to *deny* leeches to a seriously ill individual. Unfortunately, no one was able to come up with a quantitative, prospective, controlled, blind study to prove that leeches were effective, and so you probably won't be offered any when you next visit your local doctor. The moral is: Don't be convinced about any treatment technique until methodologically sound studies are published to substantiate it.

Among the alternative psychotherapies for bulimia, we find that only two have produced a published study of any type. First, two psychologists, Drs. Marlene Boskind-White and William White, applied an "experiential-behavioral" approach in group therapy of bulimics. They have published two reports. In the first, twelve women college students with bulimia were treated by a woman therapist (Dr. Boskind-White?) in eleven weekly two-hour sessions, with a six-hour "marathon session" midway through the treatment.[17] The behavioral component of the treatment consisted of weekly contracts, assertiveness training, sensory-awareness exercises, and personal daily journals to record feelings and events before binges. The experiential component is best described by the authors themselves:

During the course of treatment, the first issues discussed were personal isolation and shame regarding their behavior. Great relief was expressed at finding others engaged in the same compulsions. Hostility toward parents and their struggle for independence was then encountered. Along with parental issues, problems with men, including fear, hate, and excessive demands and expectations of either real or fantasized boyfriends were examined. In each of these areas connections were made between feelings and eating. Once progress was begun via catharsis, insight, and assertiveness training designed to modify interactions with men and parents, sex became a major focus. The issue of one's sexuality developed concurrently with feelings of trust, friendship, and "sisterhood" that occurred in each group. As the women moved out of their convoluted worlds of self, they shared their sexual hopes, fears, and fantasies with the other group members. Thus, an active support system developed outside as well as inside the group.

At the end of the eleven-week treatment, four women reported that they had ceased binging, six reported "less frequent" binging, and two were unchanged.

In the second study, Drs. Boskind-White and White reported a five-day intensive treatment involving five hours of group therapy per day, divided into morning and afternoon sessions.[18] The subjects for this study were fourteen women who had come asking for treatment after seeing an article the Whites had written for a popular magazine. The group therapy employed fewer behavioral and more experiential elements than in the first study. The authors do not provide us with detailed data on how frequently the subjects were binging before and after treatment, but merely state that before treatment "most binged daily, at least twice, and were purging one or more times during an 8-hour interval." There is no mention of how the subjects performed immediately after treatment; but six months later, three women had reportedly ceased to binge, seven had "less frequent" binges, and four were unchanged. Drs. Boskind-White and White explain the failure of the four unchanged women as follows:

> Those who failed to continue taking the risks necessary to attenuate this habitual response pattern possess one major commonality. They were especially eager to create a favorable impression; to be viewed as "good girls," obsessed with what others thought of them. Further-

more, these women may have been less motivated to change because they were stimulated by their vocations and by heterosexual relationships with extremely supportive men who were aware of their problem.

How do these two studies stand up to scientific scrutiny? First, they are only minimally quantitative. We are given only the bare outlines of the subjects' response to treatment. Specific information on pre- and posttreatment frequency of binging is lacking. We are simply told that some subjects stopped binging, some binged less (90% less, 5% less?), and some were unchanged. In the second study, we are not even told what changes had occurred at the end of treatment, but only how well the subjects were doing six months later.

Furthermore, although twenty-six subjects were involved in the two reports, they actually represent only two groups. In one sense, this is like reporting two cases, since in group therapy it is difficult to be certain that what happened with one group will apply to another. A particular group might develop some unique rapport or understanding that would make it unusually effective. The only way to determine the performance of this treatment with groups in general is to study many groups under the same conditions.

Second, are the studies prospective? Yes, in the sense that the same treatment was administered to all subjects within a particular group. But the studies are not truly prospective in that the authors decided, after the fact, to report their experience with these particular groups and not with other groups. Why? Could it have been that these two groups were particularly successful? Since the authors tell us that they have seen over 300 bulimic women, it seems likely that they would have treated many other groups of women in addition to the two that they report. What happened to those other groups?

Third, were the studies controlled? No. We have no comparison groups to ascertain what the spontaneous remission rate would be. In the second study, the authors argue that a control group is unnecessary, since a change observed abruptly after a one-week treatment is unlikely to have been due to the natural course of a subject's illness. This would be a plausible argument but for the fact that the authors do not provide us with immediate posttreatment data on binging, although they do give us scores on two psychological batteries of no proven relevance to bulimia. Instead, they give us only six-month follow-up. After six months, it is very likely that the natural course of bulimia would have had a substantial effect, perhaps even more than that of the original one week of therapy.

But even supposing that such immediate posttreatment information were provided, the study would still be seriously crippled by the lack of a control group. The reason for this is that the authors did not simply go out and administer their treatment to a group of bulimic individuals chosen at random. Instead, their group was highly *selected*—it consisted of women who spontaneously contacted the authors, specifically requesting group therapy, after having read about it in a magazine article. These women must have been highly motivated for change at that particular time, and ripe to try the methods used by the therapists. Given this enthusiasm, they may well have been at a point in their illness where they were starting to get better anyway. Or they may have had any number of other characteristics that would differentiate them from average patients with bulimia. In short, because the groups were in fact preselected, a control group would have been extremely valuable in order to correct for all these possibilities and permit valid conclusions about the treatment's effectiveness.

Finally, was the treatment blind? No. The authors themselves developed the treatments, conducted the treatments, and rated the outcome of the treatments—in the same manner as the therapists in the Cambridge-Sommerville Youth Study.

Thus, on the basis of rigorous scientific standards, we must conclude on four different counts that neither of the two studies by Drs. Boskind-White and White has yet demonstrated their treatment to be effective. Promising as these techniques may appear, they have never undergone anything approaching an adequate scientific test of efficacy.

A more systematic study of a treatment program involving group therapy has just emerged from England.[19] Dr. J. Hubert Lacey described thirty bulimic women treated with a ten-week program of brief individual sessions, group therapy, graduated contracts to modify diet and behavior, and dietary diaries. Half of the women were placed directly into the ten-week program. The other half were first given a "control" period of ten weeks using the dietary diaries, but without therapy, in order to see whether any degree of spontaneous improvement would occur. During the control period, no improvement in the incidence of "dietary abuse" or vomiting was noted. Following the control period, these fifteen patients were entered in the same treatment program as the other group.

In both groups, binging and vomiting declined dramatically. Prior to treatment, the women averaged twenty-three instances of "dietary abuse" and twenty-seven instances of vomiting per week; after treatment both of these figures dropped to an average of just over once per week. Even more importantly, the improvement persisted in most cases for up to two years of follow-up. However, one patient had to be hospitalized for "further treatment."

These results are gratifying, but the author notes certain negative factors. First, although twenty patients displayed no binging or vomiting during the follow-up period, the report states that "most of these patients felt the impulse to binge eat but resisted the compulsion." In other words, although the overt symptoms were absent, some of the underlying syndrome was still alive. It would be of interest to know if the patients still suffered from preoccupations with food and with weight—two features of the bulimia syndrome which we have often found as disabling as the binges themselves. No formal assessment of these problems is given.

However, the author did assess the patients' level of depression—and found that it *rose* with treatment. Although the study does not present this data in detail, an analogue scale for depression shows a rise from a score of about forty, during the first two weeks of treatment, to about sixty during the final weeks, when binge eating had declined. The author describes this phenomenon as "unmasking a now-declared depression," and states that "pronounced tension, anger, and depression . . . follows giving up the symptoms of bulimia nervosa."

In short, the treatment seems to have been a mixed blessing; although objective instances of binging and vomiting almost vanished, the subjective experiences of bulimia apparently did not. And it seems that many patients traded their binges for an increase in depression and other symptoms. Lacey suggests that this is a necessary "unmasking" process, and recommends further psychotherapy to deal with the newly exposed symptoms. Unfortunately, only one of the thirty women chose to enter psychotherapy after the study.

Setting aside the somewhat mixed results, what about the study's methodology? We find it generally very sound, but two issues deserve discussion.

First, the patients were apparently self-selected individuals requesting therapy, much like those in the Whites' group studies, just discussed. As we explained earlier, such patients might be particularly anxious to improve their behavior at the time that they contacted the clinic, and enthusiastic about treatment. Thus, they might be more likely to improve than a random sample of individuals with bulimia.

Dr. Lacey clearly recognized this phenomenon, and, in an attempt to test for such factors, placed half the women into a ten-week waiting period, as described above. The failure of these women to improve during the waiting period, and their subsequent improvement with treatment, is offered as a type of control in the study.

However, it is difficult to argue that the study was completely controlled, and it certainly was not blind. Although they received periodic evaluations, the women in the control group were apparently well aware that they were not receiving the therapy during the waiting period, and had little reason to expect that they would improve. At the end of the ten weeks, once they started the therapy, they presumably expected results. In short, the waiting period does not compensate for the placebo effect.

An ideal method to control for the placebo effect—although difficult in practice—would be to assign half the patients to the treatment program, while assigning the other half to a sham treatment which they fully expected to be effective. For example, in the next chapter we shall see another study, also recently conducted in England, in which twenty-two bulimic patients received placebo pills and no therapy at all—and experienced marked, statistically significant improvement in anxiety, depression, eating attitudes, and on a "bulimia rating scale." In short, the power of suggestion may be strong in bulimia, and one cannot tell to what degree it may have influenced the results of Lacey's study.

Is this just a methodological quibble? After all, the fact remains that most of the patients achieved dramatic reductions of binging and vomiting. In the final analysis, does it really make any difference whether they got better because of the therapy or because of suggestion? We think it does make a difference: One cannot exclude the possibility that the treatment relieved the symptom but not the disease; the impulse to binge remained, and depression worsened.

Nevertheless, Dr. Lacey's technique may hold much promise, and clearly deserves further study. In fact, an American study, using somewhat similar techniques, has already been conducted: At the May 1983 meeting of the American Psychiatric Association, Dr. Craig Johnson presented promising preliminary data from the treatment of two groups of bulimic women.[20] As in the British study, one group was given a waiting period before starting treatment, and did not improve until the actual treatment began. Interestingly, both groups displayed an instant decrease of 50% in their binging behavior on the first day of treatment. Further improvement occurred as the treatment progressed. The sharp initial decrease, Dr. Johnson conjectured, reflected the "hopeful anticipation" of the subjects that the therapy would work—another testimony to the power of suggestion.

Particularly encouraging was the observation that Johnson's patients, unlike Lacey's, apparently experienced a decrease in depression during treatment. Clearly these findings, and others like them, deserve close attention and analysis as they appear in the literature. It is particularly important to ascertain whether group techniques are as successful at reducing the subjective symptoms of bulimia, and the symptoms of depression and other bulimia-associated disorders, as they may be at reducing the actual frequency of the binges themselves.

Biologic Treatments

You have now read about every study, beyond mere anecdotal case reports, that has ever (to our knowledge) been published, through the middle of 1983, on *any* specific psychological, or "talking," therapy of either anorexia nervosa or bulimia. Considering how much we hear about the alleged causes and cures of the eating disorders, both in the scientific world and in the popular press, and the ubiquitous use of talking therapies in actual treatment, it seems surprising that there is not more evidence available.

Can biologic treatments do any better? Starting again with anorexia nervosa, several types of drugs have been studied systematically, including cyproheptadine, Δ^9-tetrahydrocannabinol, antipsychotics, naloxone, antidepressants, and lithium carbonate.

Although there does not seem to be any clear evidence that patients with anorexia nervosa have a reduced appetite, a number of researchers have tried appetite-stimulating drugs in the hope that they might induce anorexic patients to gain weight. Only one of these drugs, an antihistamine called cyproheptadine (Periactin), has actually been studied in detail. There have now been three studies, all quantitative, prospective, controlled, and even blind.

The first, in Peru, found that cyproheptadine worked: Ten anorexics on cyproheptadine gained significantly more weight than ten who received placebos.[21] But two larger subsequent studies in the United States have both failed to replicate this result.[22,23] Thus the bulk of the evidence is against cyproheptadine. And even if cyproheptadine did work for weight per se, would it be of any value for all the other symptoms of anorexia nervosa? It is hard to believe that this putative appetite stimulant would help to reduce the bulimic symptoms experienced by half of anorexic patients! Not surprisingly, cyproheptadine is rarely used at present, although another study of it is in progress in New York and Minnesota, apparently with somewhat more promising results.[24–26]

Another rather exotic recent study, also based on the principle of appetite stimulation, used Δ^9-tetrahydrocannabinol in a placebo-controlled double-blind trial.[27] Tetrahydrocannabinol is the active ingredient of marihuana, which, as any smoker will attest, is well known to cause the "munchies." But tetrahydrocannabinol produced no benefit in the eleven anorexic patients studied. In fact, several patients found the "high" very unpleasant; they became paranoid and felt out of control.

Antipsychotic drugs, such as chlorpromazine (Thorazine), have also been claimed useful for anorexia nervosa.[28] In the only placebo-controlled double-blind study of such a medication—using pimozide, a drug not available in the United States—the authors reported a trend in favor of the drug, but it did not reach statistical significance.[29] Even allowing that antipsychotics are helpful in anorexia, however, they often have very annoying side effects (as described, for example, by Sally in Chapter 1), and they also may produce a syndrome of involuntary movements called tardive dyskinesia, which may sometimes be irreversible even after the drug is stopped. Overall, therefore, antipsychotics appear unpromising as a treatment for anorexia.

Naloxone, a drug used to antagonize the effects of opiates, has also been claimed helpful for anorexic patients in one preliminary study.[30] But this was largely uncontrolled and nonblind; we must await more detailed studies before reaching conclusions. It is of interest that all the patients in the naloxone study were simultaneously treated with antidepressants, though at low doses.

What about antidepressant drugs in anorexia nervosa? If, as we have argued in Chapter 6, anorexia nervosa, like bulimia, is closely related to major affective disorder, antidepressants should perhaps be helpful to anorexic patients. Unfortunately, even though there have been several case reports of anorexia nervosa successfully treated with antidepressants,[31] only two controlled studies have been performed.[24-26, 32] The first, in London,[32] found no improvement in eight anorexic patients treated with the tricyclic antidepressant clomipramine—but used only 50 mg of the drug per day, a dose almost certainly too low to produce an antidepressant effect. The use of such a low dose virtually precludes any conclusions about the effectiveness of clomipramine in anorexia nervosa. The other controlled study,[24-26] in New York and Minnesota, used probably adequate doses of the tricyclic antidepressant amitriptyline, with better results. However, the study is still in progress; until the data are fully analyzed, it would be premature to draw final conclusions. Our own studies of antidepressants in anorexia nervosa also show promise, but our results are still preliminary.[31]

Although it is unclear why antidepressants have not been more systematically studied in anorexia nervosa, we think there are at least two reasons. First, antidepressants were initially employed, as in the clomipramine study, not for their antidepressant effects but in the hope that they would prove to be appetite stimulants. Thus, low doses were used, no true antidepressant effects were observed, and researchers were not encouraged to embark on further studies.

Second, the most commonly used antidepressants—the tricyclic antidepressant drugs—have side effects that can be bothersome in an already weak, emaciated patient with anorexia nervosa. Unfortunately, tricyclics were the only antidepressants used in the studies, and the side effects made it difficult to raise the dose to a level at which it would be truly helpful. Therefore, researchers may again have been discouraged from pursuing further studies with these medications in anorexia nervosa.

Turning to other medications, another drug used in major affective disorder, and one with fewer side effects, is lithium carbonate. Lithium is not exclusively an antidepressant; it is effective for both the manic and the depressed periods in manic-depressive illness. In patients with recurrent attacks of mania or depression, lithium often prevents new attacks.

In 1975, Dr. A. Barcai at the University of Haifa in Israel reported that two anorexic patients treated with lithium carbonate gained twenty and twenty-six pounds respectively within six weeks, and had maintained their weight after one year of follow-up.[33] This encouraging report prompted a team of investigators at the National Institute of Mental Health, led by Dr. Howard Gross, to conduct a prospective, placebo-controlled, double-blind study of the effect of lithium carbonate in anorexia nervosa.[34] The subjects were sixteen anorexic inpatients. Eight were assigned at random to receive lithium, and eight to receive inert placebo capsules. Neither the patients nor those who rated the patients' outcomes knew which of the two treatments they were receiving. In addition to lithium or placebo, each patient also received standard behavior therapy for a total study period of four weeks.

At the end of the first and second weeks of treatment, there were no differences between the two groups in the amount of weight gained. But at three weeks and four weeks, there were significant differences. The group receiving lithium had gained an average of 15.0 pounds, whereas the group receiving placebos had gained an average of only 11.4 pounds. Although the difference appears modest, the probability is less than one in twenty that it was due to chance alone.

This study is methodologically sound. It meets all the criteria that we have discussed for a rigorous study of treatment effectiveness. But even here we must be cautious. The eight lithium patients weighed slightly more, and were eating more, even before they started on lithium. The authors offer statistical arguments that lithium was effective even if we correct for this problem, but it remains an issue.

On the other side of the balance, the study contains two promising features. First, the effect of lithium was observed after three weeks of treatment—just about the same amount of time that lithium often takes to work when treating the manic or depressed phases of major affective disorder. Second, a statistically significant effect was observed with only sixteen patients, a relatively small sample, after only four weeks, which is just two weeks after the drug seemed to start working. Obviously, it would be very interesting to see a study that treated more patients over a longer period of time. Perhaps the modest effect observed in this study would become much more pronounced.

Adding all these observations together, we have an intriguing finding, but one that must be subjected to more detailed study.

Turning from the scientific to the popular literature, we find an interesting testimonial on the effects of lithium: Cherry Boone O'Neill, the daughter of entertainer Pat Boone, describes her experience with lithium in a fascinating personal account of anorexia nervosa and bulimia, entitled *Starving for Attention.*[35] Mrs. O'Neill first developed anorexia nervosa and bulimia at the age of sixteen. She also describes shoplifting, although it is not clear that this was true kleptomania, since she stole only food and laxatives. Finally, she describes being "on an emotional roller coaster, the highs getting higher, the lows increasingly lower. . . ." At the time, apparently, no one had considered the possibility that these might be symptoms of mild manic-depressive illness—one of the bulimia-associated disorders described in Chapter 4.

She describes a partial remission of the symptoms when she was around twenty, then a severe exacerbation of the bulimia a year later. By age twenty-two, she had developed incapacitating symptoms of both anorexia and bulimia and was admitted to the hospital for two weeks. Following this, she began to see a psychiatrist, and soon she developed a psychological theory of the cause of her eating disorder:

Obviously there had been unfulfilled emotional needs in my life. The need for acceptance and approval—the need to be perfect—had been a driving force that ultimately brought me to the brink of death. In my early years I equated my worth as a person with the level of my performance and I felt that the love and approval of other people would be conditional on my perfection. Therefore I expended every effort to be the best I could possibly be in any given area of endeavor, only to repeatedly fall short of my goals and risk losing value in the eyes of others. Trying even harder, only to miss the mark again and again, resulted in compounded guilt and self-hatred.

This is similar to the theories we hear frequently from our own bulimic and anorexic patients. It sounds very reasonable and, as we mentioned in Chapter 2, it gives the patient the satisfaction of having some explanation for what is going on. But Mrs. O'Neill, despite achieving this self-insight in June of 1977, continued the binging, self-induced vomiting, and shoplifting, and even made a suicide gesture, during the following three months.

The real turning point seems to have occurred at the end of September 1977, when her doctor started her on lithium. She writes:

> Could it be true? Could my radically changing moods and behavior actually be the result of something biological? The thought was encouraging! Perhaps my bad judgment, impulsiveness, and depression were partly the result of a physical condition. I was thrilled to think that I may not be such a terrible person after all!
>
> ... People with bipolar manic depressive illness experience extreme highs and lows effecting observable changes in their moods and behavior. It was not an uncommon phenomenon, Dr. Vath had explained, and I was in good company with the likes of Abraham Lincoln and Winston Churchill. . . .

Within three weeks after starting lithium, both she and her husband saw a marked difference in her temperament, and the problems of anorexia, binging, and vomiting declined dramatically. She was able to discontinue the lithium about six months later, and has apparently maintained a fairly good remission ever since.

Of course, this is a personal account, and hardly a formal study. As we have stated earlier, anecdotal accounts should not be considered scientific evidence. But the story is worth mentioning, not just because lithium appeared to help, but because it also suggested to this patient that she might have a biological illness and was not just a "terrible person." Many of our own bulimic patients, when they responded to antidepressants or to lithium, experienced a similar liberation from their accusatory theories about themselves.

*   *   *

Returning to our review of studies of biologic treatments, we have one more set of findings to discuss. This is the story of phenytoin (Dilantin) in bulimia, already mentioned in Chapter 5.[36] It is worth examining the phenytoin results once again, because they illustrate how a group of careful and responsible scientists, starting with what seemed a dramatic finding, gradually subjected their impressions to more extensive and better-controlled studies. And by insisting on rigorous scientific evidence, these researchers eventually proved that phenytoin was not nearly as effective as they themselves had once thought.

In a retrospective, uncontrolled, nonblind study, Drs. Richard Green and John Rau initially reported that nine out of ten bulimic patients responded to phenytoin. However, by 1977 they had treated another twenty-six patients, among whom they found only seven responders. Then, in an excellent placebo-controlled double-blind study stimulated by Green and Rau's findings, the results emerged as even less promising: Only 42% of nineteen patients showed a moderate to marked response to phenytoin, and of the four phenytoin responders followed long-term, two relapsed despite continuing to take the drug. Since this study in 1977, no major studies of phenytoin have appeared. As mentioned earlier, we ourselves have tried phenytoin in about ten bulimic patients over the last six years and have had no success with it.

The phenytoin findings make a fitting conclusion to this chapter, since they emphasize that prospective, controlled, and blind studies are critical in order to judge legitimately the success of any treatment. Had the first report, with its 90% response rate, been accepted at face value as a demonstration that phenytoin worked, it might have led to widespread use of a treatment that actually fails in a majority of cases, and it might have led us to the erroneous theory that most bulimics have a seizure disorder. But the scientific method prevailed, and researchers eventually established that phenytoin was not the cure.

Unfortunately, most of the other treatments described in this chapter, as we have seen, have not received such careful scrutiny. And so we must be careful not to presume that they are effective until more definitive studies come in.

8

ANTIDEPRESSANTS:
AN EFFECTIVE NEW TREATMENT

The Evidence

As we have seen, the scientific evidence behind existing therapies of both anorexia nervosa and bulimia remains scanty. Although some treatments, such as behavior therapy and group therapy, may reduce the number of binges in bulimic patients, it is less clear whether these treatments reduce the distressing subjective symptoms of bulimia or the symptoms of the bulimia-associated disorders. In particular, the largest published study of group therapy reported a marked decrease in binges, but a considerable increase in depression. Clearly, a rapid, dependable, and inexpensive treatment, effective for both bulimia and its associated symptoms—especially depression—would be welcome. Now we may have one: antidepressant medications.

We have already discussed, in Chapters 4 and 6, the large body of evidence suggesting that bulimia is closely related to major affective disorder. This would be of only academic interest, however, if it did not lead us to a new treatment for bulimia—and perhaps for anorexia nervosa as well. In Chapter 6, we mentioned that antidepressant medications, originally developed for treatment of major affective disorder, have now been shown to be remarkably effective in bulimia. What are the facts?

The first report came from Dr. Daniel Moore at Yale.[1] Treating a twenty-year-old college senior who had both anorexia nervosa and bulimia, he first used phenytoin. This failed. Next, he tried the antidepressant imipramine, again without success. However, with a subsequent antidepressant, amitriptyline, marked improvement occurred: During a four-month period on amitriptyline, she had no further binges and only one episode of vomiting per month. Amitriptyline was then stopped; two weeks later,

> she became preoccupied with food, calories, eating, and vomiting, to the exclusion of the other therapeutic issues on which she had worked so well for the past four months. The next week, she called in tears to say that she had been eating and vomiting continually and would like to resume the amitriptyline. The bulimia stopped within two days, and her preoccupation with weight became a background issue once again.

A similar report came from Dr. Charles Rich in Pittsburgh in 1978.[2] He described a twenty-one-year-old woman who experienced a typical progression of symptoms, starting with two episodes of major depression, the second accompanied by bulimic symptoms. However, it was not until the third episode that she was finally treated with medications. The first antidepressant, desipramine (Norpramin), failed. But with the second antidepressant, phenelzine (Nardil), her binging and purging vanished in four weeks. When she stopped the phenelzine, the bulimia reappeared; she resumed taking the phenelzine, and it vanished again.

Although these two reports are admittedly anecdotal observations, they are "controlled" in a sense: The patients acted as their own controls by discontinuing the antidepressants and then resuming them. The response to both antidepressants seems unlikely to have been a chance improvement, since binging promptly reappeared when the drugs were stopped and disappeared again when they were resumed.

During the next four years, only one other case report described antidepressant treatment of bulimia.[3] Finally, in October 1982, we published the first study of a group of bulimic patients treated with antidepressants.[4] The results of this study are shown in Table 3. The study was uncontrolled, but six of the eight patients improved in a matter of a few weeks, despite having binged continuously for as long as four years prior to receiving antidepressants. Such a rapid response in previously chronic patients is quite unlikely to represent merely a chance spontaneous

TABLE 3

Response of Bulimic Patients to Antidepressants

Patient	Age (years) and Sex	DMS-III Diagnoses	Duration of Bulimia	No. of Binges per Week Pretreatment	Drug and Dose per Day (mg)	Serum Level (ng/ml)	Response[a]	Follow-up Interval (months)
1	21, F	Bulimia, cyclothymic disorder	Chronic, 4 years	2	imipramine 200 nortriptyline 100 phenelzine 60	228 127	0	16
2	31, F	Bulimia, borderline personality disorder	Episodic, 2 years	4	amoxapine 300 maprotiline 350	354	0	10
3	33, F	Bulimia, major depression	Chronic, 4 years	14	imipramine 300 lithium carbonate 1200	163 0.6–1.2 meq/l	+ ++	7
4	49, F	Bulimia	Episodic, 4 years	4	imipramine 150 desipramine 250	167	+ +	7
5	29, F	Bulimia, dysthymic disorder	Chronic, 1 year	2	imipramine 175	324	+	6
6	21, F	Bulimia, major depression	Chronic, 1 year	14	imipramine 250	317	++	5
7	19, F	Bulimia, major depression	Chronic, 4 years	7	imipramine 175 desipramine 150	196	+ +	5
8	24, M	Bulimia	Chronic, 6 months	1	imipramine 200	166	++	2

Note: Serum levels reflect sum of parent drug plus active metabolites (i.e., sum of imipramine and desipramine).

[a] Marked response, greater than 90% reduction or complete disappearance of eating binges (++); moderate response, greater than 50% reduction of eating binges (+); equivocal or no response, no definite reduction of eating binges (0).

remission. Also, at the time the study was written, these patients had maintained their good response for two to seven months, which argues that the antidepressants gave lasting protection against the bulimic symptoms, and not simply a transient benefit.

One of the cases was described as follows:

A 21-year-old woman had a 1-year history of increasingly severe episodes of eating binges. Prior to treatment with imipramine, she engaged in two binges a day, during which she would consume 1 gallon of ice cream mixed with one-half gallon of maple syrup, accompanied by candy, doughnuts, and other sweet foods. Episodes terminated with self-induced vomiting. To control her weight, she consumed as many as 20 diuretic pills and 500 ml milk of magnesia per day. She experienced depression, initial and terminal insomnia, and marked suicidal ideation which was particularly severe after binges. Imipramine was started and the dose raised to 150 mg/day. Within 3 weeks, binges had decreased to once every 2 days and suicidal ideation was much reduced. Several weeks later, the serum level of imipramine plus desipramine was 182 ng/ml: imipramine was raised to 200 mg and later to 300 mg/day. During the 3-month period after imipramine was raised to 300 mg/day, binges averaged only once per week. The patient also reported improved mood and a complete disappearance of her suicidal ideation.

Of course, this case does not represent a complete remission: The patient still did binge once a week, although this was a small fraction of her former twice-a-day level. Does this mean that antidepressants are only partially effective?

As if in answer to this, a second study of antidepressant treatment in bulimia appeared in the scientific literature only two months later, in December 1982.[5] This study, from Dr. Timothy Walsh and his colleagues in New York, reported a complete disappearance of binges in four of six patients, and a drastic decrease in the other two patients, when they were treated with a particular type of antidepressant medication called monoamine oxidase inhibitors. The results from the New York study are summarized in Table 4.

Dr. Walsh and colleagues described the impressive response to antidepressant medication in one of their cases, a thirty-seven-year-old nurse who had experienced bulimia for ten years, with episodes of binging and vomiting three to four times per day. Her food bill ran up to $300 a week. She had been treated with

TABLE 4

Response of 6 Women with Bulimia to Monoamine Oxidase Inhibitors (MAOIs)

Patient	Age (years)	Treatment	Duration of Bulimia (years)	Episode Frequency	Eating Attitude Test Score[a]	AFTER MAOI TREATMENT		
						MAOI	Episode Frequency	Eating Attitude Test Score[a]
1	37	Individual psychotherapy, behavior modification	10	3–4/day	49	Phenelzine, 90 mg/day	1/month	31
2	28	Individual psychotherapy	3	3–5/day	69	Phenelzine, 60–90 mg/day[b]	1–2/month	14
3	21	Minimal psychotherapy	4	4/day	35	Phenelzine, 90 mg/day	None	8
4	34	Individual psychotherapy	15	3/day	77	Tranylcypromine, 40 mg/day	None[c]	33
5	25	Group psychotherapy	7	3–4/day	69	Phenelzine, 60 mg/day[b]	None	22
6	24	Individual psychotherapy	7	2/week	63	Phenelzine, 60 mg/day	None	32

From B.T. Walsh, et al., *American Journal of Psychiatry* (December 1982) 139:1630. Reprinted by permission of the American Psychiatric Association.

[a] A self-rating instrument designed to measure symptoms of anorexia nervosa; normal women score between 2 and 38; patients with anorexia nervosa score between 32 and 90.

[b] Treatment begun while patient was in the hospital.

[c] Patient relapsed after 1 month.

psychotherapy for six years, behavior therapy for eight months, and small doses of tranquilizers and tricyclic antidepressants—all without any significant effect. The authors continue:

> Ms. A was treated with phenelzine on an outpatient basis. After 3 weeks at a dose of 90 mg/day, she reported no longer feeling depressed and having lost the urge to binge and vomit. . . . During 10 months of phenelzine treatment she binged and vomited only 3 times, felt consistently less depressed, and was less sensitive to others' reaction to her. For example, during this period she lost a job because of financial cutbacks, binged and vomited once, and withdrew from her friends for 1 week. However, she then quickly resumed other activities and began to look for new work. This contrasts with previous situations, in which she had been incapacitated for several months and binged and vomited several times a day. In spite of her obvious improvement, Ms. A has continued to have difficulty getting along with superiors and developing close personal relationships and has relatively few friends.

Since the time of this report, Walsh's group has continued to report success with monoamine oxidase inhibitors in a majority of bulimic outpatients.[6,7] Similarly, our own group has published a preliminary report on six patients treated with monoamine oxidase inhibitors; five experienced a complete disappearance of their binges within a matter of a few weeks.[8] Two other reports, one from Pennsylvania[9] and one from Maryland and California,[10] have similarly described success with some bulimic patients treated with antidepressants.

However, we must emphasize strongly that all of these five studies are open to the same criticisms that we have leveled at previous studies of bulimia: They are retrospective, uncontrolled, and nonblind. In other words, we cannot be certain whether these patients improved because of the medications, because of the placebo effect, or by chance alone.

In response to this, we need a placebo-controlled double-blind study, similar to those described in Chapter 7, in order to rule out the possibilities of spontaneous remission and/or the power of suggestion. Two have now been published.

The first, conducted in England, compared the drug mianserin to a placebo in bulimia.[11] Mianserin is not approved by the Food and Drug Administration for use in the United States, but it has been available in Europe for many years. In this study, surprisingly, *both* the patients on mianserin *and* those taking a placebo improved dramatically on a number of indices, including ratings of anxiety, depression, eating attitudes, and a "bulimia rating scale." In spite of this improvement, neither group of patients reported a decrease in frequency of binge eating.

What are we to make of these results? The first question is why the placebo group improved so markedly. The authors explain that their contact with all patients was brief, and that they never employed any formal psychotherapy. Nevertheless, they suggest that the placebo patients' improvement may have been due to this transient professional contact. This impression stands in contrast to the experience of a number of other researchers, including ours: Bulimic patients often describe repeated and unsuccessful courses of prior therapy; they would seem unlikely to respond to a few brief professional contacts. Therefore, the patients in the mianserin study may have been more suggestible, less severely ill, or otherwise different from the patients with bulimia whom we typically see.

Second, given that both the mianserin and the placebo patients improved on many measures, why was there no change in the frequency of binges? There are several possible explanations. First, the dose of mianserin used in the British study was only 60 mg a day, a dose below that required for an antidepressant effect in some other studies. For example, a recent study in New York reported that 150 mg a day was required to treat depression in some patients.[12] Second, even if we assume that 60 mg is adequate, we do not know how much of the drug may have been lost by the study patients through vomiting or laxative abuse. The only way to test this would be to measure blood levels of mianserin in each patient, and this was not performed. Third, allowing, for the moment, that the patients were taking—and retaining—enough mianserin, it may be that mianserin is simply not effective for bulimia. The only way to distinguish among these various possibilities would be to do a new study, using higher doses of mianserin, with some safeguard (such as blood levels) to ensure that patients were not purging the drug, and taking care to choose study subjects with chronic and refractory cases of bulimia—subjects who would not respond merely to a few professional contacts and a supply of placebo capsules. Until such a study is performed, it would probably be unfair to draw conclusions for or against mianserin in the treatment of bulimia.

In some sense, this discussion is academic for American readers, since mianserin is not available in the United States; the Food and Drug Administration is presumably still awaiting further data on its safety or effectiveness. However, our group has just published a placebo-controlled double-blind study of the treatment of bulimia with imipramine, a drug with a twenty-five-year record of safety and effectiveness, widely used throughout the United States.[13] Since this study has direct implications for American readers, we will describe it in detail. The following pages are more technical, but if you are still skeptical about antidepressants, you will want to read them carefully.

We began by recruiting subjects who unquestionably met the full *DSM*-III criteria for bulimia, and who had severe and chronic symptoms. For admission to the study, we required that subjects had experienced at least two binges per week during the past month, with each binge followed by self-induced vomiting or laxative abuse; and that the bulimia had been present for at least one year. These were only minimum criteria; our twenty-two subjects actually averaged about 1.4 binges per *day*, and some binged three or four times every day. The average duration of illness among the subjects was more than seven years; several had been binging almost continuously for twelve, fourteen, or even sixteen years.

We recruited the subjects from three sources. The first was an advertisement in the monthly newsletter of the Anorexia Nervosa Aid Society, a self-help organization in the Boston area with several hundred members with bulimia. This yielded sixteen subjects. Second, we placed a small advertisement in the *Boston Phoenix*, a weekly newspaper with a circulation of 134,000, stating simply that we were seeking "subjects with uncontrollable eating binges" for a treatment study. We received more than forty telephone calls from this small advertisement, but screened out all but five subjects. The others either did not meet the full *DSM*-III criteria for bulimia, did not display sufficiently chronic symptoms, or did not binge often enough to meet our requirements for severity. Finally, we obtained one more subject from Feeding Ourselves, a local organization for the treatment of eating disorders.

By obtaining subjects from these diverse sources, and by accepting every subject who met the full study criteria, we obtained a diverse sample of subjects, unlikely to be biased in any particular direction. In other words, the odds are remote that we could have "stacked the deck" in order to produce a group of subjects who were particularly likely to respond to antidepressants.

As it turned out, all twenty-two subjects were women, although there were several men who barely missed meeting our study criteria. As mentioned above, these women had displayed very chronic symptoms of bulimia, lasting two to sixteen years. Many of them had received extensive psychotherapy, behavior therapy, group therapy, and even hospital treatment for their eating-disorder symptoms—all with no lasting effect. Several had tried so many therapies that they had reached complete despair, convinced they were incurable. In short, we had collected a group of veteran bulimic patients: people who would not be likely to get better out of mere enthusiasm or from a series of brief professional contacts. A treatment that could help these patients would have to be genuinely effective.

All the subjects received a physical examination and various laboratory tests. All signed a consent form acknowledging that they would be participating in a placebo-controlled, double-blind study, and that they would not know whether they were receiving the genuine antidepressant pills or the placebo.

We chose to use the antidepressant drug imipramine (Tofranil). Imipramine is the grandfather of true antidepressants, the first to be discovered, used since the 1950s. Since it was the first antidepressant, imipramine is often considered the prototype—the standard against which others are judged, much in the manner that penicillin is one of the prototypes of antibiotics. Also, since imipramine is the oldest antidepressant, it has been used by millions of people over nearly thirty years; it is a tried and tested drug with an established record of long-term safety. Finally, imipramine has few side effects. Many people notice only some dry mouth, light-headedness on standing up (which usually goes away after a week or two), and sleepiness. The sleepiness is rarely a problem, because the drug is taken just once a day, at bedtime, when one is going to sleep anyway. For all these reasons, imipramine seemed the logical choice.

The imipramine was packed in yellow capsules, each containing 50 milligrams of the drug. We also made up a batch of exactly identical yellow placebo capsules, containing lactose, a white powder which has no psychiatric effects at all.

The subjects were assigned on a random basis to receive either the imipramine or placebo. A code was prepared, identifying which subjects were receiving the drug and which were receiving the placebo. The code was sealed in an envelope, and neither the subjects nor those of us who were following them were allowed to know whether they were receiving the genuine pills or the false ones. A research assistant who rated the subjects' progress was also kept blind as to which treatment was being received by which subject.

The subjects were seen on initial evaluation and at the end of two, four, and six weeks by both the treating physician and the research assistant. The physicians monitored the subjects for side effects or medical problems, but performed no ratings themselves. The research assistant deliberately did not ask the subjects about side effects (to avoid any possibility that she might guess whether or not the subject was receiving the genuine medication), but recorded the frequency of binges during the preceding two weeks and asked about the presence of certain depressive symptoms. The subjects rated themselves on three subjective indices—intensity of binges, preoccupation with food, and self-control with relation to food—using a scale from 0 (none) to 5 (maximum). They also rated their subjective overall improvement on a scale of − 1 (worse), 0 (unchanged), 1 (slight), 2 (moderate), and 3 (marked). We used these several scales to test whether the antidepressant would be effective for the whole syndrome of bulimia and its associated symptoms, and not just for the binges themselves.

During the six weeks of the study, we had to exclude three of the twenty-two subjects. Two developed rashes and itchiness. We immediately stopped their pills and broke their codes to find out what they were receiving. Not surprisingly, both were on imipramine; allergic reactions to imipramine do occasionally occur. Such reactions are usually mild, and sometimes even go away simply with changing to a different brand of imipramine. But for the purposes of the study, at least, these two subjects had to be excluded. We continued to treat them, but with other antidepressants on a nonblind basis, separate from the study. The third subject had a different problem—her pills didn't seem to be helping her bulimia at all. She became so frustrated that she impulsively took an overdose of them. Nothing happened. Not surprisingly, when we broke the code, she turned out to have been on placebo. We immediately removed her from the study, and arranged for her to see a local physician so she could be carefully treated on a nonstudy basis.

The remaining nineteen subjects completed the full six weeks of the study. At the end, we broke the codes for all subjects, revealing to ourselves and to them who had received imipramine and who had received the placebo. Of course, some of the subjects had already guessed, because their urge to binge had declined dramatically. Others felt no better at all, and correctly guessed that they had been taking the placebo. But some had guessed wrong: Two women complained of annoying dry mouth, light-headedness, and sleepiness, and were convinced that they were receiving imipramine. However, neither of them experienced any decrease in their binges. When we broke the code, they were surprised to find that they had both been on the placebo all along.

The results are shown in the six graphs in Fig. 3 (p. 151). The average scores of the nine imipramine subjects are represented by a solid line, and the average of the ten placebo subjects by a dotted line. As you will see, the imipramine subjects averaged a 70% reduction in binge-eating frequency by the sixth week; there was essentially no change in the placebo group. On the Hamilton Rating Scale, which measures symptoms of depression, the imipramine subjects were almost 50% better by the sixth week, and again the placebo group showed no difference. By statistical tests, we were able to show that such differences were "statistically significant": The probabilities that these differences could have occurred by chance are less than 1 in 100 and less than 1 in 50, respectively.

Looking at the four smaller graphs, we see that imipramine was superior to the placebo on all the subjective indices as well, particularly on subjective global improvement. The great majority of the imipramine subjects rated themselves as feeling markedly better overall, whereas the placebo subjects rated themselves as feeling virtually the same as when they started. In statistical terms, the difference between imipramine and placebo on this index was the most striking: The odds are less than 1 in 1,000 that it could have been due to chance. Even on the graphs showing more modest differences, such as "Intensity of Binging" and "Preoccupation with Food," imipramine is still superior to the placebo, with a probability of 20 to 1 or better.

Finally, as long as we are quoting statistics, here is one more: Of the nine imipramine subjects, four reported a marked (greater than 75%) decrease in binging, four reported a moderate decrease (greater than 50%), and one was unchanged. Among the ten placebo subjects, one was moderately improved, eight showed no change at all, and one was worse. When we compare the number of subjects with a moderate or marked improvement in the two groups, using a statistical technique called Fisher's exact test, the odds are 500 to 1 against imipramine's superiority being due to chance alone.

The most important aspect of this data is not the strength of the statistics but the fact that the imipramine subjects improved on a broad range of measures. Imipramine not only reduced the frequency of their binges, but, more important, it decreased their preoccupation with food and the intensity of binges, improved their feelings of self-control with regard to food, decreased their depressive symptoms, and improved their overall sense of well-being. As one subject put it, "It's not just that the binges have gone away. The *real* difference is that I don't even think about it anymore. That constant, nagging preoccupation with food, that I've had every day for so many years—it's just vanished!"

Comments like these cannot be reduced to a graph or a statistical calculation, but in some ways they were the most telling responses of all: They suggest that the imipramine was not just suppressing binges but actually going to the source of the problem. And if our theory is correct—namely that bulimia is closely related to major affective disorder—this is just what one would predict: Imipramine seems to treat the underlying major affective disorder, and the bulimia, together with its many associated symptoms, goes away automatically.

Of course, an important further test of these findings is the long-term follow-up. At the end of the six-week study period, most of the imipramine subjects remained on imipramine. The others were switched to different antidepressant drugs in order to try to achieve even better effects or reduce side effects. The placebo subjects were all offered a trial of imipramine, with the same option of switching to a different antidepressant, if desired, in order to obtain fewer side effects or improved protection against their bulimic symptoms.

The results of follow-up are shown in Table 5. The table shows the name of each antidepressant used (imipramine, desipramine, trazodone, tranylcypromine, etc.) and the response of each subject. For example, subject 1 in the imipramine group experienced a dramatic reduction in her binging during the six-week blind phase of the study. Thereafter, the imipramine continued to work well, but she was annoyed by the side effects of

FIGURE 3:
Changes on Various Ratings Over the Course of 6 Weeks in Bulimia Patients Treated with Imipramine (N = 9) or Placebo (N = 10)

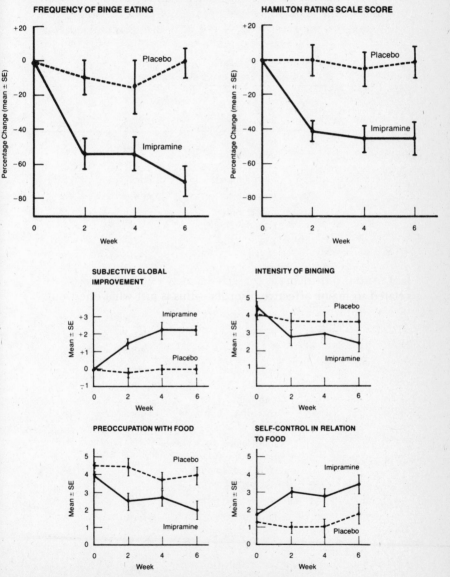

Reprinted by permission of the American Psychiatric Association, from H.G. Pope, Jr., J.I. Hudson, J.M. Jonas, and D. Yurgelun-Todd, American Journal of Psychiatry *140 (1983):554–58.*

dry mouth and constipation. Therefore, she switched to desipramine, a very similar antidepressant, with less tendency to cause dry mouth or constipation. At the time the table was initially written, eight months had elapsed, and she had remained free of the urge to binge, free of her former preoccupations with food, and—to her great relief—free of depression. Subject 5 in

TABLE 5
Follow-up Data on Study Patients

	Subject	Medication	Response[a]	Follow-up Interval (months)[b]
IMIPRAMINE GROUP	1	imipramine desipramine	remission	8
	2	imipramine	marked	6
	3	imipramine	marked	5[c]
	4	imipramine trazodone	marked	2[c]
	5	imipramine tranylcypromine	none remission	5
	6	imipramine trazodone phenelzine	moderate	6
	7	imipramine	remission	5[d]
	8	imipramine	marked	2[c]
	9	imipramine	moderate	4[d]
PLACEBO GROUP	1	imipramine	marked	3[c]
	2	imipramine trazodone + lithium buproprion	none	6
	3	imipramine trazodone tranylcypromine phenelzine	none	6
	4	tranylcypromine	remission	3
	5	imipramine	remission	6[d]
	6	imipramine desipramine	moderate	2[c]
	7	trazodone phenelzine	marked	4
	8	imipramine	remission	5

	Subject	Medication	Response[a]	Follow-up Interval (months)[b]
	9	(declined treatment)		
	10	imipramine	moderate	1[c]
SUBJECTS	1	tranylcypromine	remission	7
EXCLUDED		phenelzine	remission	
DURING	2	(declined treatment)		
THE STUDY	3	nortriptyline	moderate	7
PERIOD				
(SEE TEXT)				

Reprinted by permission of the American Psychiatric Association from H. G. Pope, Jr., J. I. Hudson, J. M. Jonas, and D. Yurgelun-Todd, *American Journal of Psychiatry* 140 (1983):554–58.

[a]Responses: *none:* less than 50% decrease in binge frequency; *moderate:* more than 50% decrease in binge frequency; *marked:* more than 75% decrease in binge frequency; *remission:* complete remission of binges for one month or more.

[b]Follow-up interval represents time that response has been maintained or time until patient was lost to follow-up.

[c]Lost to follow-up.

[d]The three subjects marked "d" recently experimented with stopping their imipramine for various reasons. They relapsed to original levels of binge eating within 1–12 weeks, and have all chosen to resume imipramine.

the imipramine group, on the other hand, experienced no benefit from imipramine at all. Therefore, when the study was over, she tried an entirely different type of antidepressant— tranylcypromine. Her binging promptly disappeared with the new drug, and she had remained free of binges for five months at the time the table was constructed. At the time of this writing, these subjects have both maintained their improvement— though each with one brief relapse—for more than a year.

Let us hasten to point out that not every story is as easy as this. With two of the subjects (placebo group numbers 2 and 3), we have tried a number of different antidepressants over the course of six months, with no success. Actually, both these patients did feel better on one or another of the antidepressants, and they even binged slightly less. But since we required at least a 50% reduction in binging to score any response at all, they are scored as "none" in the table.

Adding it all up, then, of the twenty subjects who received a full trial of at least one antidepressant medication (either during the blind phase of the study or subsequently), 90% experienced at least a 50% decrease in binging, and more than a third of the subjects experienced a complete remission of their binges. In order to score a remission, we required that the subject experience no binges for at least one month. In fact, at the time the follow-up data were tabulated, the subjects had maintained their response for periods of up to eight months. At the time of this writing, we have followed many of them for more than one year, observing continued success.

More recently, we expanded our tabulation to include the first sixty-five bulimic patients treated in our center, including the twenty from the placebo-controlled study.[14] The findings agree closely with those shown in Table 5: After one or more trials of antidepressants, 33.8% of the sixty-five patients displayed a remission of their binge eating for one month or more; 38.5% reported at least a 75% reduction in binges; 18.5% reported at least a 50% reduction; and 9.2% did not respond at all.

We would be the first to point out that these figures are hardly spectacular: Turning around and looking from the negative side, we failed to completely eliminate binging in almost two-thirds of the patients, and in 10% we accomplished almost nothing. But it must be remembered that we are examining an extremely ill, very chronic group of patients. When we consider that they had been binge eating for as many as sixteen years, and that many of them had tried three, four, or five courses of psychotherapy or behavior therapy without success, it would have been impressive if even a few of them had improved. Thus, a 90% rate of at least partial improvement, often in the space of a few weeks, is gratifying.

In conclusion, let us allow two of the imipramine study subjects to speak for themselves. Again, we must point out that *a personal account is not scientific evidence*, but it may be of interest for the reader to hear a firsthand description of what the effect was like. Subject number 1 in the imipramine group wrote a letter to the Anorexia Nervosa Aid Society, describing her experience:

Dear Friends:
    This is one of those thank you letters that is so profoundly felt that words seem too awkward to convey my gratitude.
    Your January newsletter saved my life. That's really the crux of it. . . . With the correction of my chemical imbalance, by a drug called imipramine, my 12-year hell of bulimia has completely been eradicated. I mean, it's absolutely gone. No more fear of food. No more frenzying through my kitchen cupboards to eat any and everything in an hour-long passionate stuffing of food. No more getting out of bed, dressing in a coat and driving to the grocery to buy cake mix, ice

cream, coffee cakes and milk to eat the second my house door slammed behind me. No more embarrassment at grocery checkouts. No more shame. No more hiding. And most especially, no more retching. My face had become permanently swollen. My nose red from that daily pressure. My spirit broken because I thought I was a living lie.

I had tried OA [Overeaters Anonymous]. I had gone to therapy. And, I attended one of your groups and even went through the "team" approach at [a local hospital] last year. All of these things helped, but I knew I wasn't getting to the real source of it. Or, I knew I was failing at everything. . . .

The imipramine has not only eliminated my desire to binge, it has eliminated the incessant thinking about it. And better than that, my whole perception of the world is so changed. I mean, I'm *really* happy. I'm not struggling, not finding things to feel miserable about—I'm just enjoying being alive.

And I'm ever grateful to you. I realize that there are different answers to this complex behavior—but for those of us whose chemistry is unbalanced, there is truly a merciful solution for them in imipramine.

I just wish all my sisters could know the freedom, and the joy, that's now mine.

Another woman had a very different experience with imipramine. She was one of the two subjects who developed a rash, and, as a result, we took her off the study and treated her with tranylcypromine. Her binging of thirteen years' duration, was gone in three weeks. Later, she read a Boston newspaper article about bulimia, which mentioned nothing about antidepressant treatment. So she wrote a letter to the editor:

Your article on bulimia fails to mention the work done by the Anorexia Nervosa Aid Society (ANAS) or the research currently underway at McLean Hospital in Belmont.

Thanks to . . . the antidepressant medication prescribed, after thirteen years I now have "that monkey off my back."

. . . I spent thirteen years talking about bulimia with a psychologist, a psychiatrist, and a group leader with a self-help group. I even tried hypnosis. All of these hourly sessions accomplished nothing but to give me a sense of futility.

What a wonderful freedom I now have.

These two letters, of course, are from people who had good results from antidepressants. We have many other such patients, but we must reiterate—lest the reader get a biased message—that a fair percentage of patients do *not* experience such dramatic relief as described by the two women above. Antidepressant drug therapy is far from perfect, and there is no way to know in advance whether one will experience a complete disappearance of the symptoms, a moderate improvement, or no change at all.

Cross-Examination

If you remain unimpressed by personal testimonials and insist on rigorous scientific technique, you may still have reservations. In an attempt to respond to those who remain dissatisfied with the evidence that antidepressant drugs are effective for bulimia, let us subject the double-blind study to cross-examination. Listed below are nine questions we have frequently been asked about the study, followed by our answers.

1. How can you say the study was truly "blind"? Surely the people who were on imipramine could tell that they were receiving a drug, because of the side effects. Maybe, once they recognized the side effects, they stopped binging just because they so desperately wanted *the drug to work. In other words, it might have been just the power of suggestion.*

There are several responses to this. First, a number of the subjects guessed wrong. In particular, two of the placebo subjects developed numerous "side effects" and were convinced that they were receiving the genuine drug. But their binging did not decrease at all. If the power of suggestion had been operating, these subjects should have gotten better too.

Second, several of the subjects were convinced that the drugs would not work. Some of them were quite invested in other forms of therapy and were reluctant to believe that their bulimia could be treated by a pill. For them, the power of suggestion, if anything, might have operated in reverse.

Third, our subjects had endured an average of seven years of chronic bulimia, refractory to many previous treatments. Since these previous treatments had little "power of suggestion" effect on them, it seems unlikely their symptoms would go away after a few weeks in our study simply because they recognized some side effects and wanted to think they would get better.

Fourth, even allowing that some subjects did correctly guess that they were on imipramine and did improve due to the power of suggestion, how does one explain the fact that they have remained better for many months? If they were reacting merely to the power of suggestion, the first blush of enthusiasm would soon have worn off, and the bulimia would have returned in spite of the drug. But this did not happen.

In summary, although suggestion might have had some influence at some time in some subjects, it cannot explain the full magnitude of the results.

2. How do you know that the subjects were telling the truth? Maybe the subjects on imipramine were denying the true frequency of their binges and exaggerating how good they felt.

This would be extremely unlikely. After all, the placebo subjects described virtually no improvement. If all the imipramine subjects were lying, how did the placebo subjects know *not* to lie? Furthermore, if some of the subjects were only pretending to get better, they would not have continued to come back for refills of their medication for many months. If the subjects were merely fabricating their improvement, they would be unlikely to have continued in treatment for so long.

3. How do you know it was the medication that made the subjects better? Maybe it was the fact that you were showing them such care and attention.

If improvement was due merely to our care and attention, why did the placebo subjects *fail* to get better? This is the whole point of doing a placebo-controlled study. We treated all the patients identically in every respect except one: Half of them got the real medication and half did not. Therefore, the *only* variable that can explain the large difference in outcome between the imipramine group and the placebo group is the effect of the drug itself.

4. Granted that the imipramine actually did work to reduce binges, you still weren't helping the whole person. Weren't you just suppressing their eating with a pill?

Untrue. In fact, as shown by the letters quoted above, what we found was just the opposite. The subjects were impressed by the fact that they felt globally better. Not only the binging but their preoccupation with food, their obsessions, and their depressive symptoms all declined. The striking difference on the scale of "subjective global improvement" in Figure 3 testifies to this.

5. How do you know that imipramine is necessarily better than any other sedative or tranquilizer?

You have missed the point! Imipramine, and the other anti-depressant drugs used, are *not* sedatives or tranquilizers. If an ordinary person takes imipramine, he or she feels nothing but a dry mouth, light-headedness, and a few other side effects—no tranquilization at all. Imipramine appears to be correcting the cause of the bulimia, not putting individuals into a drug-induced, sedated state. If bulimia could be cured with tran-quilizers, patients with bulimia would long since have gotten better just by taking Valium or an equivalent drug.

6. How can you prove that it is the antidepressant *effect of im-ipramine that makes bulimia better? Maybe the improvement is due to some other property of imipramine.*

This question deserves a careful answer. There are four main reasons for believing that bulimia is responding to the anti-depressant effects of imipramine, rather than to some novel property of the drug. First, the reduction in frequency of bing-ing and the reduction in Hamilton Rating Scale scores for de-pression were closely correlated. (In technical terms, the Spearman rank correlation coefficient for these two variables was 0.65; there is less than 1 chance in 200 that such a correla-tion could have occurred just by accident.) In nontechnical lan-guage, what this means is that in people whose depression improved, the binging decreased; in people whose depression did not improve, the binging did not decrease. This suggests that the antidepressant effects and the antibulimic effects of imip-ramine are one and the same.

Second, the time it took for bulimia to respond to imipramine was about the same as the time that it takes for imipramine to work for depression—about two to four weeks.

Third, the percentage of bulimic patients who improve with imipramine is about 70% to 80%. This is in the same range as the percentage of depressed patients who respond to imipramine. Once again, these observations suggest that what we are seeing in the bulimic patients is an antidepressant effect.

Fourth, bulimia clearly responds to a range of other antidepres-sants, including trazodone, phenelzine, and tranylcypromine. These drugs are chemically different from imipramine; the main feature they have in common with it is their antidepressant effect. Thus, the fact that they all work for bulimia is most likely due to their mutual antidepressant effect, rather than to some other novel property they happen to share.

In summary, although we cannot prove that it is the antidepressant effect of imipramine which works for bulimia, we would have to stretch credibility to construct any other explanation that would fit all of the four observations listed above. In scientific language, we would say that the most parsimonious (i.e., straightforward and economical) explanation is that imipramine works for bulimia simply because it is working as an antidepressant.

7. But this raises another question. How do you know that your sample of bulimic subjects wasn't biased in some way to include an unusual number of severely depressed patients?

Another very reasonable question, to which we again have several responses.

First, our sample was recruited from three separate sources, and we accepted all eligible subjects from each source without regard to the presence or absence of depressive symtomatology. In other words, our sample was as random as we could make it.

Second, our study criteria excluded people who had received prior antidepressant treatment and those with serious suicidal ideation. If anything, this may have tended to bias the sample *away* from bulimic subjects with concomitant major depression.

Third, our subjects were similar, both in their demographic characteristics (age, age at onset of symptoms, etc.) and in their prevalence of depressive symptomatology, to other unselected (random) samples of bulimic patients reported by us in two other studies, as well as the three largest series reported in the literature by others.

Fourth, as mentioned earlier, we have continued to have a comparable success rate in treating dozens of other bulimic patients since the double-blind study was completed. Thus, there is nothing to suggest that the study sample was particularly unusual or differed in some way from other bulimic individuals seeking treatment.

8. How do you know that people need to stay on imipramine over the long term? Once they respond to imipramine, maybe you could stop the drug after a couple of weeks and they would continue to be fine.

This is not likely. With subjects who have been binge eating for an average of seven years, it would be unrealistic to stop the drug as soon as they were better and expect them to remain better. A period of six to twelve months on antidepressants would be more reasonable before attempting to discontinue them.

After the study, one of our subjects deliberately tapered off her imipramine after a couple of months because she wanted to become pregnant and didn't want to risk harming the baby—a perfectly appropriate thing to do. Unfortunately, her bulimia returned to its original level within a week. Another woman stayed on imipramine for about four months, then tried stopping it. She went for more than two months without a recurrence of binging, but then it reappeared. There have been several other patients, not associated with the study, in whom we have stopped one antidepressant prior to starting another, more promising one. In virtually all these cases, once the protection of the antidepressant was lifted, the symptoms returned. When protection was restored, the symptoms remitted again.

This does not mean that people with bulimia must take antidepressants for life. But if someone has had bulimia for many years, it is only reasonable to expect that he or she may have to take the medication for a year, two years, or more, to keep the symptoms in check. In each patient, we deliberately try to discontinue the medication at least once a year. If the symptoms do not reappear, we continue without medication; if they do reappear, we can resume the medication quickly and continue until we and the patient next want to try stopping it.

1985 Update: In the fourteen months since our book was published, new scientific studies have strongly underscored our conclusion that antidepressants are effective in the treatment of bulimia. These include three new placebo-controlled double-blind studies.

Using the antidepressant phenelzine in a sample of twenty-five subjects, Dr. Timothy Walsh and his colleagues at Columbia University found highly significant differences between phenelzine and placebo, with many subjects experiencing a complete remission of their bulimic symptoms within a few weeks of starting treatment. However, the authors noted that side effects posed a problem for some patients, so that not all were able to take the drug in adequate doses.

In a second study at the Mayo Clinic, Dr. Patrick Hughes and his colleagues used desipramine. Again, desipramine proved markedly superior to placebo: of the twenty-two subjects in this study ultimately treated with desipramine, fifteen, or 68%, experienced a complete remission of their bulimia within ten weeks. Measures of associated symptoms of eating disorder and depression also revealed striking improvement. As in the Columbia study, this improvement occurred with medication alone; no concomitant psychotherapy was administered.

Underscoring the need for testing the blood levels of antidepressant medication to be sure that the dose was adequate, the study showed ten of the Mayo Clinic subjects had desipramine levels below the therapeutic range. In six of these subjects, dosage was adjusted upward, and four then experienced a remission of their binge eating.

The third study, performed by Drs. James Mitchell and Ronald Groat at the University of Minnesota, used the antidepressant amitriptyline. Blood levels were tested on eight of the sixteen patients receiving the active medication. Of these, one had a level of zero (in other words, she may not have been taking her pills at all) and three others had levels which were probably below the therapeutic range for amitriptyline. Since these levels were measured near the end of the study, it was too late for the researchers to correct the dosage in the manner of the Mayo Clinic study just described. Yet, despite this potentially important drawback, amitriptyline still was found to be significantly superior to placebo on a measure of depression, and moderately superior to placebo on all four measures of eating behavior.

The results of these three new methodologically sound, carefully performed studies, combined with our own, add up to a powerful scientific case for the effectiveness of antidepressants in bulimia.

One new uncontrolled study, however, by Brotman and colleagues at Massachusetts General Hospital, has yielded disappointing results with antidepressants in bulimia: only 23% of the subjects showed lasting improvement. This study has been cited as evidence against the effectiveness of antidepressant treatment. Yet, not only was this study retrospective and uncontrolled, but it frequently used inadequate doses of antidepressants, failed to measure blood levels of antidepressants in any patient, often failed to try a second antidepressant if the first was unsuccessful, and based many of its impressions on differences which were statistically nonsignificant. This accumulation of methodological shortcomings renders the findings almost unusable for scientific purposes—and certainly no match for the many well-controlled studies described above.

Do antidepressants continue to work well over the long term? Does the effect deteriorate or disappear in some patients as time passes? Of the patients treated in our original placebo-controlled double-blind study with imipramine, eleven have been followed for two years or more. Of these, eight—or 73%—are free of bulimic symptoms. None has received any form of therapy other than medication during the follow-up interval. Three of the eight have been able to stop their antidepressants without a recurrence of bulimia—one after six and a half months, one after nine months, and one after twenty-three months. The others are still on medication. Of the remaining three subjects followed for two years, one is now markedly improved, one moderately improved, and one unchanged. Interestingly, this last subject is the only individual who stopped antidepressants against our advice; her bulimia returned to its original level and has not improved since.

Looking at the total group of twenty (including the nine additional subjects from our original study who were lost to follow-up at some time during the two-year interval), and rating their symptoms at the time of last follow-up, we find that ten (50%) were in remission, nine (45%) were partially improved, and only one (5%)—the subject described above—was unchanged.

The subjects also improved in depression. When we administered the Hamilton Depression Rating Scale to the subjects followed two years or more, we found that they continued to experience a highly significant decrease in their depressive symptoms.

These several new studies strongly reinforce the scientific foundation of this chapter: Under blind and controlled conditions, antidepressants have repeatedly been shown to be effective in bulimic patients. This benefit is maintained, or even improves, over the long term. And most important, antidepressants do not just treat the symptom of binge eating; they produce a global benefit for the whole patient, reflected in markedly decreased depressive symptoms, decreased preoccupation with food, and in other measures of eating behavior.

9

HOW TO GET GOOD TREATMENT

We finally come to the information that readers with bulimia have been waiting for: the details of getting competent treatment.

Of course, no one treatment or combination of treatments is best for everyone. Therefore, we can provide only general guidelines on how to find good treatment—and good treatment-providers. Once you have taken these initial steps, you will be in a position to work out a specific treatment program tailored to your needs.

If you have experienced severe and unremitting symptoms of bulimia, and especially if previous therapies have not worked, we feel that your first priority should be to consider treatment with antidepressant medication from a psychiatrist who is knowledgeable in this area. There are three reasons that we recommend consideration of an antidepressant medication. First, antidepressant medication is thus far the only treatment that has been demonstrated in a controlled study to be highly effective for both bulimia *and* its associated symptoms. Second, antidepressants work quickly, often in three to four weeks. Other forms of therapy, such as group therapy, behavior therapy, or individual psychotherapy, if they are effective, may require several months, or sometimes even years. Third, antidepressant treatment is often much less expensive than other forms of treatment.

Once you have addressed the question of medication, you should then decide how much nonmedication therapy you need.

Some bulimic patients, who have relatively few problems other than their bulimia, and who have an excellent response to antidepressants, may not want or need much additional therapy at all. A larger number of patients, even many who improve greatly with antidepressants, find that they want at least some concomitant nonpharmacological treatment—either meetings with a self-help group for individuals with eating disorders (such as Overeaters Anonymous), group psychotherapy, or individual treatment with an experienced psychotherapist. Patients who have numerous problems unrelated to bulimia, or experience a poor response to antidepressants, should invest most or all of their time in seeking nonmedical therapy, both psychological and behavioral.

Therefore, we shall first discuss antidepressant treatment in detail, and then provide suggestions for treatment with other therapeutic modalities.

Choosing a Psychopharmacologist

Not all psychiatrists are specially trained in psychopharmacology—the use of psychiatric medications. Thus, your first step is to find someone who uses antidepressant medications frequently and is familiar with their effects. If you live in or near a city with a medical school and an academically affiliated hospital, you can probably obtain the names of several psychopharmacologically oriented psychiatrists simply by calling the department of psychiatry at the hospital and explaining your purpose. You don't necessarily have to find someone who specializes in eating disorders. Many such specialists, as we have seen, are more familiar with other forms of treatment, such as psychotherapy, behavior therapy, or group therapy. Although there is no harm in this, chances are they will be correspondingly less familiar with the use of antidepressants. Therefore, if you see someone known for the treatment of eating disorders, make sure that he or she is also thoroughly experienced with using medications.

At the other end of the spectrum, you may find someone who is an excellent psychopharmacologist but has never seen anyone with bulimia. Chances of this happening are becoming rarer as bulimia comes out of the closet. But even if your psychiatrist confesses that he has seen few bulimic patients, don't despair.

You might want to show him the source notes of this book so that he can look up some of the scientific articles referenced, if he is not already familiar with them.

Finally, don't be afraid to interview more than one psychiatrist to find one who seems knowledgeable. You may be surprised at how easily you can select one over the others. We have always been impressed at how often patients can distinguish a good psychiatrist. So, after going through all available channels to get the best possible referrals, see one or more psychiatrists and trust your instincts.

Choosing an Antidepressant

You will begin by having one or more interviews with your psychiatrist. He or she will want to be certain that you truly have bulimia and will want to find out if you have any medical problems that might complicate your taking an antidepressant. An example of this would be if you have anorexia nervosa in conjunction with bulimia and are severely underweight, or have severe electrolyte abnormalities (see Chapter 2).

Assuming there are no complications and the two of you have decided that antidepressants are worth a try, which one do you choose?

Only your doctor can tell you which medication or sequence of medications to try, and his or her instructions should always take precedence over anything you read in this book. Since your doctor knows you personally, he or she may be aware of important individual factors that we could not anticipate when writing this chapter. Therefore, we will offer only general suggestions; you and your doctor can work out the details together.

Three types of antidepressants are commonly used in this country: tricyclics, monoamine oxidase inhibitors, and trazodone (see Table 6, p. 166).[1] The tricyclics have been marketed since the 1950s and are the most popular, as evidenced by the wide range now available. The monoamine oxidase inhibitors have been used for about the same length of time, but fell out of favor for a while, and only in recent years have regained popularity. Trazodone is new; although it has been used in Europe for years—and has a fine safety record—the Food and Drug Administration did not approve its use in this country until 1982.

TABLE 6
Commonly Used Antidepressants

TRICYCLIC ANTIDEPRESSANTS (AND THEIR RELATIVES)

imipramine (Tofranil, SK-Pramine, etc.)
amitriptyline (Elavil, Endep, etc.)
desipramine (Norpramin, Pertofrane)
protriptyline (Vivactyl)
trimipramine (Surmontil)
doxepin (Sinequan, Adapin)
nortriptyline (Aventyl, Pamelor)
maprotiline (Ludiomil)
amoxapine (Asendin)

MONOAMINE OXIDASE INHIBITORS

phenelzine (Nardil)
tranylcypromine (Parnate)
isocarboxazid (Marplan)

TRIAZOLOPYRIDINES

trazodone (Desyrel)

Note: Chemical or generic names are listed first; brand names are shown in parentheses.

Each of the three classes of antidepressants appears to work in a large percentage of bulimic patients. Some patients probably would respond to any of these medications. Others might receive no benefit from one class of antidepressants but respond beautifully to a drug from another class. For example, a fair number of patients experience little or no benefit from a tricyclic, but then respond dramatically to a monoamine oxidase inhibitor. This was the case with subject 5 in the imipramine group in Table 5 (p. 152): Her binging got no better at all with imipramine (a tricyclic), but vanished entirely with tranylcypromine (a monoamine oxidase inhibitor).

Unfortunately, there is really no way to tell in advance which medication will work for you and which will not. In the future, tests may be devised that allow us to predict which drug will be most effective; for the present, the best you can do is try a medication from one of the three classes and, if it fails, try a medication from one of the other classes. Such experimentation may be tedious, but you may be greatly rewarded for your perseverance.

Speaking of tests, you may remember the dexamethasone suppression test (DST) described in Chapter 6. Should you get a DST? And if it is positive, does that improve the odds that you will respond to antidepressants?

In our experience, it does not make much difference. The 50% or so of bulimic patients who do *not* have positive DST's seem to respond to medication about as well as those who do. In short, although the DST is an interesting theoretical tool, one that may contribute evidence to our hypothesis that bulimia is related to major affective disorder, it is not of great practical value; even if you do not have a positive DST, we would still recommend antidepressants and still predict good odds of success. So you can take the DST if you like, but if it comes back negative, you should not assume that medications will fail for you.

In summary, even if your doctor has obtained your own history, your family history, your DST results, and other data, he or she still will not know whether antidepressants will work until you actually try them. Assuming you decide to go ahead, let us give you some idea of what to expect with each of the three classes of medications.

The tricyclics, as mentioned earlier in our discussion of imipramine, have a long track record of efficacy and safety. Their main side effects are so-called anticholinergic side effects, such as dry mouth, constipation, and, less commonly, blurred vision, urinary hesitancy, and forgetfulness. Some tricyclics, such as desipramine and nortriptyline, have very mild anticholinergic side effects; imipramine usually has somewhat more, and amitriptyline usually the most. As a result, we rarely use amitriptyline. Sleepiness is another side effect—often quite pronounced with amitriptyline, less with imipramine, and still less with desipramine and nortriptyline. Light-headedness is common with all tricyclics, but it usually is not annoying if one starts with a low dose and gradually works up, so as to allow the body to become acclimatized to the drug. Many people find that the light-headedness disappears almost entirely after a few weeks. There is one major exception: If you have anorexia nervosa in conjunction with bulimia, the light-headedness and other side effects may be magnified. In fact, in our hands, tricyclics have been the least satisfactory of the three classes of antidepressants for bulimic patients who are well below ideal body weight.

Of course, tricyclics may have other occasional or rare side effects that are more serious. When you consider that these drugs have been used by millions of people in the last thirty years, you can guess that practically every side effect imaginable has happened to somebody at some time. But then, almost all medications produce serious side effects in rare cases. When you balance the odds of benefit against the very small odds of a serious side effect, the ratio is strongly in your favor.

Another advantage: There are essentially no known long-term medical dangers from taking tricyclics, or, for that matter, either of the other two classes of antidepressants. Even taken daily for years and years, they appear to do no harm to the body. In the last thirty years, so many people have taken the drugs for such long blocks of time that long-term medical complications, even rare ones, would likely have shown up by now if they existed.

On the matter of long-term effects, let us try to put you at ease on one more point. If you read any literature on the tricyclics, or either of the other two classes of antidepressants, you will notice that they have been reported to increase the appetite. Some of our bulimic patients have become terrified when they heard this. How could we be so sadistic as to give them a drug that would actually increase appetite?

The answer is simple: Bulimia is not an illness in which one simply has too much of an appetite; the urge to binge is very different from ordinary hunger. And although tricyclics do increase the appetite in some people, they greatly decrease the urge to binge, which is a different type of symptom entirely. As a result, many of our bulimic patients—particularly those who binge but do not purge—actually manage to lose weight after being treated with tricyclics, because they are no longer ingesting thousands of calories during binges. We have had few bulimic patients complain of being too hungry or gaining weight with tricyclics or other antidepressants; once relieved of the urge to binge, they seem to have little problem keeping their weight under control.

Again, if you have anorexia nervosa—even a tendency toward it—in conjunction with bulimia, the above paragraph may provide you with scant reassurance. The very prospect of taking a drug that has even a *chance* of making you gain weight may make you panic. But remember one thing, and keep it in mind as you read this chapter: You can stop taking an antidepressant whenever you wish. Starting the drug does not commit you to taking it for the next six months! If everything we say is wrong and you actually do gain weight and you can't stand it, just tell your doctor and he will taper off the medication.

By now, we hope we have convinced you that trying a tricyclic antidepressant, in the hands of an experienced psychiatrist, is straightforward and safe. Next let us consider a few of the fine points.

If you look back again at Table 5—the follow-up data from the double-blind study—you will notice that we used only three tricyclics: imipramine, desipramine, and nortriptyline. The reason for this is that it is now possible to obtain laboratory tests of the blood levels of these drugs, and careful studies have been done to find out what level should be in the bloodstream for optimum effect. For example, with imipramine, the total level of imipramine plus its metabolite (which happens to be desipramine) should probably be above 240 nanograms per milliliter in order to be certain that the level is in the therapeutic range. With desipramine, we shoot for a level of over 160 nanograms per milliliter; whereas with nortriptyline, several studies suggest that the level should be in a therapeutic "window" between about 50 and 140 nanograms per milliliter. If your level is below 50 or above 140, the drug may be less likely to work.[2]

Blood levels are available for the other tricyclics too, but there is not such good agreement among scientific studies as to what constitutes an optimum level. With amitriptyline (Elavil), for example, some studies find good results with low blood levels, others only at high levels, and others only at intermediate levels, with poor results at both low and high levels. Thus, even if you go to the laboratory and get a blood level while taking amitriptyline, you cannot be as certain that you are in the optimum range. With imipramine, desipramine, and nortriptyline, studies agree fairly well on the levels that we should try to obtain.

In general, then, we might start a typical bulimic patient with 50 mg of imipramine at bedtime, and increase the dose by 25 mg every day (or 50 mg every other day) until we reach 3.5 mg per kilogram of body weight. In other words, if you weigh 132 pounds, or 60 kilograms, we would go up to 210 mg (3.5 x 60) at bedtime. In actual practice, imipramine is usually taken in multiples of 25 mg, so we would probably go, in such a case, to 225. If you felt particularly light-headed or developed other annoying side effects as you increased the dose, we would tell you to increase the dose more gradually—say, 25 mg every other day—or even to stop at a lower plateau.

Once you had attained a full dose, we would wait a few days and measure the blood level. The blood level must be measured twelve hours after the last dose; in other words, you could take the drug at 9:00 P.M. and show up at the laboratory at 9:00 A.M. the following day. If you took the drug at 9:00 P.M. but had the test later on the following day, your level might appear unrealistically low, since it was measured too long after taking the last dose.

A good laboratory can have the blood-level results by the following day. If your level turned out to be below 240 nanograms per milliliter (for imipramine and desipramine combined), we would increase your dose further and get a new blood level a week or so later. On the other hand, if your level was well above 240, we might be able to cut down on your dose and still have the level in the therapeutic range.

Some people complain that 200 mg or so "sounds like an awful lot of drug." But imipramine is a fairly weak compound: If you took 10 mg a day, or even 75 mg a day, chances are it would do absolutely nothing. Besides, you probably wouldn't hesitate to take two aspirin, and that comes to 650 mg.

Perhaps some people make these assumptions because they have heard of doctors treating patients with, say, 25 mg of imipramine twice a day. In fact, you yourself may have been treated with low doses of some antidepressant. Unfortunately, this is a common mistake among doctors who are inexperienced with antidepressant medications: They use too low a dose, the patient fails to get better, and then both patient and doctor erroneously conclude that antidepressants don't work. If this has happened to you, take heart. Antidepressants may work beautifully for you. You have just never been treated with a proper dose of them.

This is why we make a point about the antidepressant blood levels. Although they are not perfect, they take much of the guesswork out of choosing the dose. You don't have to decide whether the dose "seems like a lot" or not; you can test it.

Returning to our example: You have started imipramine, reached the full dose, and a blood test has confirmed that you are in the therapeutic range. You notice some dry mouth, a bit of constipation, and maybe a few moments of forgetfulness—perhaps you're looking for your car keys, which you *know* you put down just two minutes ago, somewhere. The imipramine makes you feel a bit sleepy in the morning, but a cup of coffee seems to solve that problem. You still notice some light-headedness as you walk up stairs, but this is disappearing. Now you have been on the drug for more than two weeks, but you notice absolutely *no beneficial effect*. The urge to binge is as bad as ever.

Don't worry—this is entirely normal. There is always a lag time, usually about three to four weeks, before tricyclic antidepressants begin to produce an effect. If you are not forewarned, you're likely to get very discouraged because you will have been taking the medication faithfully and getting nothing in return. But beginning in the third week, start looking for something to happen.

What most of our patients describe is a remarkable "lifting" of the urge to binge. They gradually begin to notice that they are no longer thinking constantly about food, and that the obsessions no longer dominate them. And they often report that they are beginning to feel more "normal" in other respects too: They are sleeping better, feeling more energy, feeling less anxious. A number of patients report that, for the first time in years, they are truly liberated from their many symptoms.

But remember: Imipramine and its relatives work for only a certain percentage of patients. On the basis of our experience, the chances are—very roughly—40% that you will feel the dramatic improvement just described, 40% that you will feel definitely better but far from "cured," and 20% that you will feel essentially no change at all, despite all your time and trouble. Obviously, if you are lucky and fall into the first 40%, your only remaining problem is the side effects: If imipramine has abolished the bulimia but gives you an intolerably dry mouth, or makes you terribly forgetful, you might want to switch to desipramine. Desipramine may give you equally good antidepressant and antibulimic protection, but, in our experience, produces fewer anticholinergic side effects. Or you can stay on imipramine and take a second medication, bethanechol, which counteracts the dry mouth and most other anticholinergic side effects (but not the forgetfulness). Taking two different pills, however, can be a nuisance.

But suppose that tricyclic antidepressants simply prove unsatisfactory. What next? In such a situation, some psychophar-macologists would try trazodone, because it is a chemically different substance and has remarkably few side effects. In most people, trazodone produces practically no dry mouth, constipation, blurred vision, or forgetfulness. It does cause sleepiness—but again, this is not much of a problem since the drug is usually taken only at bedtime and the sleepiness wears off by morning; most of our patients don't notice "hangovers" from trazodone. It takes the same three or four weeks to work, and its odds of working are about the same as with the tricyclics, at least in our experience.

Of all the antidepressants, however, we have obtained the most impressive results with the monoamine oxidase inhibitors (MAO inhibitors), phenelzine and tranylcypromine. Our experience, in agreement with the New York study cited in Chapter 8, is that more bulimic patients experience more thorough remissions of their symptoms with MAO inhibitors than with any other medication. Therefore, assuming there is no medical problem with your taking an MAO inhibitor, we would be quick to try one if tricyclics and/or trazodone seem less than satisfactory.

If MAO inhibitors are so good, why don't we start off with them right at the beginning? Because, unlike imipramine and trazodone, they present a peculiar problem: You cannot eat certain foods—such as aged cheeses, beer, Chianti wine, pickled herring, chicken livers, sour cream, and broad-bean pods—when taking MAO inhibitors. If you do, you may get an attack of high blood pressure, come down with a splitting headache, and perhaps have to visit your local emergency room to receive an antidote to bring your blood pressure back down. There have even been some rare reports of people having had a stroke from the effects of high blood pressure after eating something like a large amount of cheddar cheese while they were taking an MAO inhibitor.

Why such a strange list of forbidden foods? It turns out that these foods contain tyramine or (in the case of broad-bean pods) dopamine, substances that cause high blood pressure. Normally, we can consume all the cheddar cheese we like, because our bodies contain an enzyme—monoamine oxidase—that "detoxifies" the tyramine and makes it harmless. But MAO inhibitor, remember, stands for "monoamine oxidase inhibitor." The MAO inhibitor drugs decrease the body's level of monoamine oxidase, and therefore reduce its ability to detoxify tyramine. Hence the high blood pressure.

The same applies to certain medications, such as decongestants. Many decongestants are also detoxified by monoamine oxidase; thus, if you are taking an MAO inhibitor and you swallow a decongestant cold pill, you may feel as though you ingested ten cold pills instead of just one. Of course, most medications, such as aspirin and most antibiotics, can be used perfectly safely in conjunction with MAO inhibitors. But you must always check with your psychiatrist before taking any new medication in conjunction with these particular antidepressants.

We don't mean to scare you; obviously, countless people taking MAO inhibitors have accidentally (or even deliberately) eaten cheese, drunk beer, or taken a cold pill without anything happening to them at all. But we would strongly urge you to follow the rules and not "cheat" by eating something you shouldn't if you are taking MAO inhibitors. Go over the instructions thoroughly with your psychiatrist and be sure you understand them before starting.

Many people have asked us if it is not dangerous to give MAO inhibitors to bulimic patients. What if they go out and binge on one of the dangerous foods? Well, for one thing, we don't see many bulimic patients who prefer to binge on aged cheeses, pickled herring, sour cream, chicken livers, or broad-bean pods. Most binge on carbohydrates—and you can munch on doughnuts all day without the slightest problem on MAO inhibitors. Of course, if you binged on pizza made with certain types of cheese, you could induce a reaction. Therefore, before starting an MAO inhibitor, you and your doctor must be convinced that you can restrict your binges—even when they're at their peak—to safe foods.

Finally, remember one other thing: If the MAO inhibitors work well, your binges will largely disappear, and there will be a much reduced risk that you would impulsively eat a great deal of cheese. And if the MAO inhibitors don't work, you and your doctor will throw them away, in which case you can go out and feast on all the pickled herring and chicken liver you want, washed down with Chianti.

With these caveats, then, let us return to our example.

Before starting an MAO inhibitor, we would first make sure that any previous drugs you were taking were completely out of your system. Then, just before starting the medication, we would get another type of lab test, called a platelet monoamine oxidase level. Having determined your base-line level, you would start taking phenelzine or tranylcypromine and build up to a full dose in the same manner as with the tricyclics. Phenelzine has moderate anticholinergic side effects, like imipramine. It can also cause light-headedness. But unlike imipramine, the light-headedness usually *doesn't* go away. If you're too light-headed, you may have to lower the dose.

Tranylcypromine causes almost no anticholinergic side effects—which is very nice indeed—but it, too, can cause chronic light-headedness if the dose is too high. Tranylcypromine (and, less frequently, phenelzine) can also have a stimulant effect, as though you had too many cups of coffee. Some people like this feeling, but it can be a problem if it gives you insomnia. Again, there are various tricks for dealing with these side effects. A good psychopharmacologist can usually work things out so that you won't have too many difficulties.

After you have been at full doses of the MAO inhibitor for about ten days, we would get a second platelet monoamine oxidase level. Since MAO inhibitors *inhibit* the enzyme monoamine oxidase, your platelet MAO should be greatly *reduced*. Ideally, it should drop to only about 10% of the base-line level. Using your percentage of platelet monoamine oxidase reduction as a guide, we can adjust your dose up or down as needed to optimize the level. As with the tricyclics and trazodone, there is usually a lag time before MAO inhibitors work—sometimes as long as three to four weeks, but occasionally as short as one week. Again, if the drug works, the effect should be obvious to you: There should be an unequivocal reduction, if not a complete disappearance, of the urge to binge, the obsessions with food, and associated symptoms.

Using tricyclics, trazodone, and the MAO inhibitors, we have had partial or complete success in better than 80% of our first 100 patients. Not every patient experiences a total disappearance of his or her bulimia—although many do—but the urge to binge often becomes sufficiently minor to be no longer a significant problem. For example, many of our patients on antidepressants, who formerly binged five to ten times a week for a number of years, now binge once every month or two. Typically these patients go for long periods with no binges, then encounter a period of unusual anxiety or stress, binge once or twice, and return to another long binge-free interval after the stress is resolved.

Perhaps even more impressive is the number of patients who remark that they suddenly feel better in other ways as well: Many note that they feel less depressed; others cease to have panic attacks; a few feel less agoraphobic; and a number report that their obsessive-compulsive symptoms have declined. This is what might be predicted on the basis of our hypothesis: If bulimia, and all of the several bulimia-associated syndromes, are related to major affective disorder, then a drug that works for major affective disorder should improve not only the symptoms of eating disorders but the associated syndromes as well.

Misconceptions

Some common misconceptions about antidepressants make many of our bulimic patients hesitant to try them. We have already discussed one of these misconceptions—the notion that antidepressants are "happy pills" that make one feel artificially good. They are not, and they don't.

A second misconception is that antidepressants are addictive—that one can get hooked on them and not be able to get off.

The fact is that none of the antidepressants we have described is addictive. You could take a group of ordinary people and give them imipramine or trazodone for a year, then taper the drug off over the course of a week or two, and they would feel the same as before they had started. The body does not develop a *need* for the antidepressant in any way. Of course, if you were to take high doses of an antidepressant and then stop it abruptly, you would notice some withdrawal sensations. But that is not because the drug is addictive; the body simply is reacclimatizing itself to a sudden chemical change.

Now, if you have a depressive illness and/or bulimia, and you get better with antidepressants, it is perfectly possible that your symptoms will come back if you stop taking the drug. This is not a drug-withdrawal symptom; it's just your original illness resurfacing after the protection of the antidepressant has been removed. If you have had bulimia for only a short time, and then respond to antidepressants, there is a fair chance that your symptoms will not recur if you try tapering off the antidepressants after a few months. On the other hand, if you have had chronic bulimia for many years, and you stop your antidepressants after a few months, there is a good chance that your symptoms will recur. This is not the fault of the antidepressant; it's the fault of your illness, so to speak. Chronic illnesses do not go away as fast as acute illnesses, as we have emphasized before.

A third misconception is that using antidepressants is just switching one's dependence on food for dependence on a pill. In other words, taking a pill isn't a real solution to the problem; one has to lick the bulimia by oneself without resorting to some artificial aid.

This is the saddest misconception of all. It is based on the notion that getting over an illness by yourself is better than getting over it with therapeutic assistance. If you had pneumonia, would you insist on licking it yourself, rather than "depending" on penicillin? If you had epilepsy, would it be somehow healthier or more honorable to try to control the seizures by yourself, rather than resorting to some artificial aid like Dilantin? Of course not. So why would you be reluctant to take a medication to try to correct bulimia, which is also well demonstrated to be a biologic disorder?

Lurking in the heart of this misconception, we suspect, is the good old Puritan ethic. The peculiar philosophy of the people who landed on Plymouth Rock was that if something hurt, it must be good for you, and that a reward obtained through hard work was better than the same thing obtained the easy way. Now, 350 years later, some patients still secretly feel that a cure obtained through long pain and suffering is somehow better, or more thorough, than one obtained through prompt and effective treatment.

In the final analysis, you can debate this question endlessly, but if you have not even tried an antidepressant, you're hardly in a position to come to an unbiased conclusion. If you take an antidepressant and your bulimia goes away, you can then decide whether or not you are being "too dependent on an artificial aid." If you feel you are, you're welcome to stop the antidepressant at any point.

In actual practice, this rarely happens. Many of our bulimic patients vacillate a good deal about whether or not to try an antidepressant. But if they take the plunge, try the medication, and derive a good effect, they often kick themselves for having waited so long.

If Antidepressants Fail

Now we come to the tough question: What if you are one of the 10%–20% of patients for whom antidepressants don't work? Or what if a given antidepressant does work, but you develop a rare or unusual side effect and your doctor has to stop it? Or what if you have some medical condition (such as severe weight loss from anorexia nervosa) and your doctor is reluctant to try antidepressants at all? Or—to pose the most common question— what if antidepressants clearly help, but they give you only partial control of the bulimic symptoms?

First of all, if your psychiatrist is a good psychopharmacologist, and you are willing to continue, he won't throw in the towel. There are many alternate medications for people who do not improve with the common drugs. In addition to the routine drug therapies outlined above, we've had luck with a combination of MAO inhibitors plus L-tryptophan; tricyclics plus lithium carbonate; lithium carbonate alone; lithium plus carbamazepine; and other combined therapies. With a certain amount of experimentation (which can be quite time-consuming), we have been able to make a considerable dent in the number of patients who are "nonresponders." Of course, we've also tried other medications without success—notably phenytoin. Certainly phenytoin may work in some instances, but we haven't yet encountered such a case.

Suppose, however, that after considerable experimentation with a wide range of antidepressant drugs and their relatives, you experience no effect or only a partial effect. You are convinced that your doctor is knowledgeable and has thoroughly explored the possibilities, but without success. Where now?

Well, to begin with, you're no worse off than when you started. You've spent some money and experienced some side effects, but unless you were extremely unfortunate and experienced some particularly unusual side effect, you probably will not feel wrong for having at least tried. And you can take some comfort in one thing: Bulimia is an illness that can spontaneously remit at any time; you're not doomed to have it for the rest of your life.

But clearly that consolation is not enough. If you have not done so already, you should start investigating other forms of therapy.

Other Therapies

If your bulimic symptoms have failed to improve, or have improved only partially on antidepressant medications, you may want to examine other therapeutic alternatives extensively. In fact, even if antidepressants have worked nicely, you may still profit greatly from other therapies.

In the final analysis, only you can decide what other therapies to investigate, and how much additional therapy you may need. Since there are few published studies of other therapies (as we have seen in Chapter 7), we cannot offer you advice that is as specific and as factual as that offered for antidepressants. But we can offer a number of guidelines with regard to the three other therapies most commonly available: self-help groups, behavior therapy, and psychodynamic psychotherapy.

Self-help groups—such as Overeaters Anonymous, or groups run by local organizations for people with eating disorders (listed on page 229–30)—we mention first because we can recommend them almost without qualification. Our patients—even those who have responded beautifully to antidepressants—have consistently told us that these groups were an indispensable source of empathy and support. Often these groups stood with them at times when others—family, friends, and professionals— had seemed to abandon them. If you contact any organization that helps individuals with eating disorders in your area, you should be able to obtain a list of groups that are available. Most of these are not formal psychotherapy groups (of the type led by a professional psychotherapist), but rather self-help groups run by individuals who may have had an eating disorder, or who have had extensive experience with them.

Also, you should be aware of the new developments with more formal group treatment programs, such as those described by Dr. Lacey and Dr. Johnson in the studies reviewed in Chapter 7. If you are aware of such a group treatment program in your area, it certainly deserves investigation.

If group support is not enough, and if in addition you are in the minority of patients who derive little or no benefit from antidepressants, then we would suggest that you next investigate the opportunities for behavior therapy in your area. Admittedly, as we said in Chapter 5, we can cite only one published study of behavior therapy for bulimia as of the middle of 1983—and thus we have only minimal scientific evidence to justify this recommendation. Nevertheless, our experience suggests that behavior therapy is helpful in a certain percentage of patients. It is, of course, often more expensive than antidepressants or self-help groups, but if the first two treatments are inadequate, you would do well to seek a consultation from a behavior-therapy expert in your area.

The longest (and most expensive) treatment is psychodynamic psychotherapy. As we have mentioned, a wide range of psychodynamic techniques may be employed in the treatment of eating disorders, including several forms of individual therapy, group therapy, and family therapy. Such diversity is partly due to the fact that there is no *specific* theory, based on scientific studies, to support the superiority of any one particular psychodynamic treatment as compared to another. It is therefore difficult for us to offer more than general suggestions as to which treatment, or which therapist, to select.

If you find the self-help-group experience stimulating, but lacking in intensity and depth, you may wish to consider psychodynamic group therapy, which has the possibility of offering a richer experience. If, however, you find group interactions inhibiting, or feel that your particular difficulties are not adequately addressed by this approach, you may wish to consider individual psychotherapy. As we have mentioned, experts disagree on these points. Drs. Marlene Boskind-White and William White advocate group therapy because of the powerful experience created by this technique. On the other hand, Dr. Christopher Fairburn has written that he is skeptical about group therapy's ability to deal adequately with each individual's difficulties with bulimia. Others might argue that neither group nor individual therapy is best, and would recommend family therapy.

Here, again, we cannot offer any scientific evidence, pro or con, since there are no formal studies of family therapy in bulimia. However, our impression is that it can be particularly helpful for younger patients with bulimia who are living at home with their families. Since one ill family member disrupts the entire family system, other family members, particularly parents, often have a difficult time. Family therapy may be especially helpful in sorting out each individual's feelings about the situation, and in resolving family conflicts surrounding the patient's eating-disorder symptoms.

We have listed psychodynamic therapy after behavior therapy in the above discussion for one main reason: Behavior therapy, when it is successful, is usually quicker and less expensive, since it focuses directly on the binge-eating behavior itself. But we reiterate that there is practically no scientific evidence yet available on the relative merits of these two techniques, nor is there a consensus among experts. For example, Dr. Hilde Bruch has written of the dangers of behavior therapy in anorexia nervosa, arguing that the patient may be worse off when deprived of a behavior that is serving an important psychological purpose. Behavior therapists, on the other hand, have argued that psychodynamic therapists spend too much time exploring individual concerns, and don't address the major problem—the binge eating. Our own patients have described positive and negative experiences with both types of treatment. Given these conflicting opinions and the lack of clear scientific evidence, only you can decide which approach is best for you.

Choosing a Psychotherapist

Because of the variety of psychodynamic treatments offered, as well as their length and expense, you will want to be particularly careful in selecting a psychotherapist. Just as the correct choice of a psychopharmacologist will often determine whether you are given optimal treatment with medications, the proper choice of psychotherapist can make the difference between an enormously valuable and rewarding experience and one that may leave you feeling no better—or even worse—than when you started.

Earlier in this chapter, we were able to offer rather detailed advice on what to look for in a psychopharmacologist. This is because much is known about what should and should not be done in the use of antidepressant medications. As we have mentioned, less is known about what constitutes optimal psychotherapeutic treatment. Furthermore, psychotherapy is a much more subtle and sensitive technique; the qualities that make for a gifted psychotherapist cannot be as easily reduced to a set of criteria. But we can suggest a few things to look for, as well as a few things to avoid; just as there are inexperienced or incompetent psychopharmacologists, there are also inexperienced or even harmful psychotherapists. Here are three qualities we look for in recommending a psychotherapist:

Empathy. A good therapist is someone who has the capacity to understand you and your particular difficulties, someone you can trust and feel comfortable with. Therapeutic styles vary, however. A therapist need not be informal or talk a lot during the session; an emotional display of concern may actually be superficial and lacking in true understanding. On the other hand, a therapist with a more distant, detached approach should not be hiding a cold or a condescending attitude; his or her warmth should show through.

Acceptance. A good therapist should be able to accept you for what you are, and see your difficulties as a series of problems to work on together. There should be a sense of mutuality in the therapeutic relationship. If you are having a difficult time in the course of treatment, both you and your therapist may need to work harder together. You should not get the sense that you are being *blamed* for your bulimia or, if progress is slow, for your overall lack of success in treatment.

Unfortunately, some therapists subtly assign blame for eating-disorder symptoms to the patient or the family, especially when things are not going well. This may say more about the therapist's own insecurity in dealing with a difficult situation than it does about the cause of the patient's problems. Since there is good evidence of a biologic component to bulimia, it is particularly irresponsible to blame a patient for something he or she did not cause and may be genuinely unable to control. We have seen many patients and family members—particularly parents— who were victimized by accusatory therapists.

This is not to say that a good therapist should always agree with you, or "take your side" in any conflict you may have. A good therapist will often help you to challenge your own assumptions in order to see things in a larger perspective. Nonetheless, you should still feel that you are working together, not against each other.

Open-mindedness. Just as a good psychopharmacologist should know under what circumstances psychotherapy or other therapies may be useful, so should a good psychotherapist know when medication treatment, or behavior therapy, or family therapy, is appropriate. These various forms of treatment are not mutually exclusive; a combination of treatments is often better than one treatment alone. A good psychotherapist will recognize this, and be secure enough not to be threatened by other forms of treatment.

These are three rather general qualities to look for in a psychotherapist. Since it is difficult to give you more specific advice, let us tell two stories from among many we have heard, to illustrate first, a very bad and, second, a very good therapeutic experience.

Ellen had been involved with a local chapter of Overeaters Anonymous for several months. Although the group meetings provided much-needed support, she continued to binge daily, and decided to try individual psychotherapy. Because one of the bulimic women in the group had been helped by antidepressant medications, she was also interested in exploring pharmacologic treatment. She went to see a psychiatrist and later told us this story:

My experience with Dr. ——— was really horrible. I went to see him primarily for psychotherapy, but told him that I was also interested in trying antidepressant medications. He laughed at me and said that I was foolish to think I could change my life just by taking a little pill. Besides, he said, I wasn't depressed, just angry. In fact, he said that I was so angry that my inner fantasy was to go out and murder someone.

That caught me completely unawares. I started to cry. While I was crying, he asked about my sex life and I said I had sex only infrequently with my husband. He told me he was certain that my husband was being unfaithful to me, because "what red-blooded American male would tolerate that?"

I told my husband later about that remark and he was furious! I was feeling so badly at the time, though, that I didn't know what to say. Dr. ——— was so suave and talked so smoothly. He said I needed psychotherapy and that only he could help me. So I scheduled a second appointment. I went home in a daze, and then went to my OA group that evening. Only then did I realize how outrageous it was—many of the group members told me of similar experiences. I don't know what would have happened without them to talk to.

I think I could have seen him, out of guilt, for many sessions before I came to my senses.

Joan, a secretary in her late twenties with mild bulimic symptoms, had been seeing a social worker specializing in psychotherapy.

One night, the day before I had to have an important meeting with my boss, I went on a terrible binge, eating everything in the house. I took too many laxatives afterward and I felt sick and drained the following morning. Fortunately, I had an appointment with my therapist before work.

I felt uncharacteristically anxious as I went into her office. I told her about the binge and about the upcoming meeting with my boss, but still the anxiety wouldn't go away. "Something is bothering you, it seems," she said.

"I'm sorry," I said, "I'm really sorry, but I just can't seem to pull myself out of this."

"But why are you being so apologetic to me? Do you have the feeling that I am upset with you or blaming you?"

"No, I don't think so," I said. But then for some reason I felt like crying.

"Are you sure?" she asked.

Then I realized she might be right—I was expecting her to berate me for my misbehavior. "You're right," I said, "I *was* expecting you to be mad at me."

"And yet I didn't show any anger at all. It's as if you expect people—your boss, perhaps—to think you're a bad person, just because you binged."

"But it's silly—my boss couldn't possibly know I had binged. But I still seem to be worried about it."

"Well, when you were a small child, your parents must have seemed to have ways to tell when you had been naughty, even when you tried to hide it. Maybe you still fantasize that your boss could somehow tell that you were bad, no matter how much you tried to disguise it."

With the realization that she was right, I felt relieved. Somehow the boss didn't seem so frightening anymore, and somehow I was no longer the bad little girl.

When I left the office, a weight seemed lifted from my shoulders. That's what I liked about seeing her—she almost instinctively knew how to help me put things in perspective.

As these examples illustrate, if you choose to have psychotherapy, the proper choice of therapist is crucial. Try to get several recommendations, perhaps by consulting with the members of a local self-help organization. As with selecting a psycho-pharmacologist, don't be reluctant to interview more than one therapist. You may have radically different experiences with different therapists, and you can probably tell quickly whether or not you will be able to work with someone. Once again, trust your own judgment—it's better than you might think. And even if you are well into therapy and feel that it has not been productive, don't hesitate to get a second opinion, or perhaps start again with someone new. Although such changes are difficult, you may be well rewarded.

1985 Update: The last fourteen months have seen no new studies of individual psychotherapy or behavior therapy in bulimia. However, the literature on group therapy continues to expand. In May 1984, at the Annual Meeting of the American Psychiatric Association, Dr. Richard Pyle summarized the results of six group therapy studies performed to date. The first three of these—by Boskind-Lodahl, White, and Lacey—have already been summarized in Chapter 7. The other three—by Craig Johnson, James Mitchell, Phyllis Phelan, and their respective associates—are new. In these studies, between 8% and 39% of patients demonstrated a remission of bulimic symptoms on follow-up; of the remainder, a majority displayed at least a partial decline in their frequency of binge eating.

These recent studies are all uncontrolled; none employed a placebo group to test what rate of spontaneous improvement might be expected in a comparable population of bulimic subjects. Also, the single measure of frequency of binge eating may not accurately reflect the status of the patient as a whole: As we have seen in the Lacey study, described in Chapter 7, binge eating declined dramatically with group therapy, but depression ratings actually rose with treatment. Thus, although group therapy clearly reduces the symptoms of binge eating per se, it is not clear how often it relieves the associated depression and other symptoms.

Despite these reservations, we continue to recommend strongly that anyone with bulimia investigate the possibilities for group therapy in his or her area. It is important to remember, in this regard, that antidepressant therapy and group therapy are not contradictory or competing treatments; many people will profit from both together.

10

THE TWENTY MOST-ASKED QUESTIONS

Now that we've finished, you may still be left with items that puzzle you. So let us conclude by opening the floor to questions, as it were. We've chosen twenty of the questions we hear most frequently from patients or from lecture audiences. We hope to have anticipated some of yours.

1. I don't think I meet the full criteria you describe for bulimia. I've never made myself vomit or used laxatives. But I'm still convinced that my eating binges are worse than those of an ordinary person. What should I do?

The real question here is whether or not your problem might respond to treatment—particularly antidepressant treatment—in the manner that "true" bulimia does. To start with, take the Binge Eating Quiz at the beginning of Chapter 2. We designed this quiz to give some guidelines to people who have less-than-definite cases of bulimia. Next, take the Bulimia-Associated-Disorders Quiz at the beginning of Chapter 4, and read carefully the description of any disorder you think you may have. If you score 8 or above on the Binge Eating Quiz, and/or if you suspect that you have any of the bulimia-associated disorders, we think it is worth your time and money to at least go for a consultation with a psychiatrist. After a complete interview, he or she should be able to give you a detailed opinion of whether or not you should pursue treatment.

Don't feel that you have to be satisfied with one opinion, however. If the first psychiatrist promptly tries to persuade you to start on medications, feel free to get a second opinion before you make a decision. Even if your first consultant tells you that you're perfectly normal, you may want to hear the same thing from a second person.

If you think you may have an eating disorder or a related syndrome, the only real mistake would be not looking into the problem at all. We frequently see patients, with eating disorders and with other syndromes, who have suffered from their symptoms for years without ever consulting a professional. Often these symptoms prove quite routine to treat with medications, and we find ourselves thinking it tragic that this suffering was allowed to persist for so long when it could have been arrested in the early stages.

2. We're convinced that our daughter has bulimia, but we can't get her to talk about it with us or go with us to see a psychiatrist. What should we do?

If your daughter had migraine headaches, you would probably have little trouble persuading her to see an internist or a neurologist. Therefore the question is: What is different, in her mind, about bulimia as compared to an ordinary medical illness? Possibly she believes that it is not an illness at all, but merely her own fault. She may be embarrassed to talk about it to a psychiatrist, or she may have misconceptions about what the psychiatrist might say to her or tell her to do. It's also possible that she might be willing to seek help, but only on her own, with you out of the picture.

In any event, you can hardly force your daughter to see a psychiatrist, but you can help her to overcome her possible misconceptions—by giving her this book or perhaps by steering her toward one of the self-help organizations in your area. If you read this book yourselves, you may well be able to guess what her misconceptions—or yours—may be, and respond to them directly.

3. Has bulimia always been as common as you say it is now? How come the news media have only started talking about it in the last few years?

Bulimia may currently be increasing in prevalence, but to date, the only hard evidence favoring this (to our knowledge) is our shopping-mall study, discussed in Chapter 3. It may be that the number of people with bulimia was substantial a decade or two ago, but that such people are much more frequently coming to doctors now, or otherwise admitting their illness. Perhaps most notable is the fact that several celebrities have recently confessed that they suffered from bulimia; this may have contributed to the increased media coverage. Therefore, although the incidence of bulimia might be increasing, much of what we're seeing may be simply the result of greatly increased public awareness of the problem. This is a desirable thing; it may alert many secret sufferers to the fact that they have a common and treatable illness.

4. How common is bulimia in other countries?

Again, there are no hard data. Good scientific studies of bulimia have regularly emerged in the British literature; we have found studies in the Swedish and Japanese literature; and since we began publishing our studies on bulimia, we have received requests for reprints from more than twenty countries in Europe, Asia, and North America. Surely bulimia is present in these countries, as well as many others around the world. It is believed to be uncommon in less-developed areas, where food is not so readily available, but even this belief is untested; for all we know, binge eating may be common in such areas, except that bulimic individuals may devour breadfruit or nuts or honey instead of ice cream and doughnuts.

5. In line with what you say about other countries, I'm convinced that bulimia has a lot to do with the fast-food and refined-carbohydrate diets that we eat in "developed" countries. If we had more natural diets, don't you think bulimia would be very rare?

We can't disprove that theory, but there is no evidence to support it, either. There is no particular physiological reason why fast food or refined sugar should be any more "addictive" than natural sweets. Of course, it's easier to binge in a society where you can go to the corner supermarket and buy anything you want. So we might guess that bulimia would be more common in places where food is more *accessible,* but we doubt that it makes much difference whether the food is more *natural* or not. We have yet to see a bulimic patient who was cured just by switching to a more natural diet.

After all, bulimia is an illness with an apparent hereditary basis; it is not caused by refined foods any more than, say, alcoholism is caused by distilled liquor. Stiff regulations on the availability of alcoholic beverages—as in many Northern European countries—do precious little to reduce the prevalence of alcoholism; similarly, we suspect that you could take all the refined foods off the supermarket shelves and it would not greatly change the prevalence of bulimia.

6. When I binge eat and then vomit, I know I lose a lot of vitamins. Doesn't that contribute to the problem?

Apparently not. Although bulimia has a number of medical complications, as we described in Chapter 2, vitamin-deficiency diseases are probably uncommon, although one recent study has described this problem.[1] If you have severe anorexia nervosa in conjunction with bulimia, it seems more likely that vitamin deficiencies might occur, but the deficiencies of calories and protein in anorexia nervosa are immediate problems that long precede any problems with vitamins.

Certainly you should not be misled into believing that vitamin deficiencies could *cause* your bulimic symptoms. If that were true, bulimic patients would get better just by taking vitamin pills. They don't.

7. I'm skeptical of your allegations that bulimia is a biochemical disorder. I know my own story. My binges stem from my desire, as a child, to be a perfect girl. As an adult, I still live under that pressure to be perfect, which includes being good-looking and slim. Isn't it obvious that that's where my bulimia comes from?

Practically everybody comes to us with a theory of why he or she developed bulimia. Often the theory is quite logical and sounds perfectly plausible. But remember, it's human nature to construct such theories. No one wants to believe that his or her illness occurred at random, out of the blue. It is far more comforting to construct an explanation of one's symptoms, a theory of why they evolved.

Although we do not question that psychological factors play a role in bulimia, we find that detailed psychological theorizing is often attractive to bulimic patients because it offers the feeling of some sort of control in an otherwise uncontrollable situation. As a result of this, we find that our patients often become angry when we suggest that their theories may perhaps be unnecessary to explain their conditions, and that they are merely ordinary people with a bad illness. At first, this thought is frightening, but ultimately it is liberating. As patients finally dare to relinquish their psychological theories, they realize that they haven't failed, that they're not to blame for the persistence of their strange symptoms. And this can be a tremendous relief.

8. I'm a counselor who has worked with many bulimic women, and I'm a former bulimic myself. Both from my own experience and from that of the other women I've talked to, it's obvious that they are responding a great deal to the social—and sexual—pressures our society imposes upon them. Now surely you're not going to claim that that is a biochemical problem?

Again, this is a reasonable and attractive theory, and—as discussed in Chapter 5—we now even have some data to support it. Certainly, social and perhaps even sexual pressures contribute to bulimia, but there is abundant evidence, as we have presented, that they do not *cause* the syndrome in and of themselves.

There may be exceptions to this. Some people may temporarily develop bulimic behavior simply because they have learned it from others. Girls in a college dorm may try binging and vomiting because someone else has described it to them, or boys on a wrestling team may deliberately vomit in order to keep their weight under the limit. Obviously, such cases of "bulimia" are in response to social learning or social pressures; we suspect that they are usually transient, "copycat" cases, rather than the true disease. But in people with the full-blown, chronic syndrome—with unremitting obsessions about food, an uncontrollable urge to binge, and an inability to stop their compulsion even though they want to—the evidence suggests that societal or sexual pressures do not play a major role in comparison to the biochemical ones.

9. I'm not surprised that your patients with bulimia are depressed. I'm bulimic, and I can tell you that you'd be depressed, too, if you had such an awful addiction. Therefore, why do you claim that depression causes bulimia? I think that the bulimia causes the depression.

We discussed this in Chapter 6, but we'll go over it again because it is important. Of course bulimia causes depression as a secondary phenomenon. But how would you explain the fact that 48% of our bulimic patients developed depressive symptoms a year or more *prior* to the onset of their bulimia, and that an additional number displayed periods of depression at later times when bulimic symptoms were absent? How would you explain the fact that bulimic patients have strongly positive family histories of depressive illness? These and many other pieces of data presented earlier in this book, especially in Chapter 6, simply do not support the theory that bulimia, by itself, causes the depressive symptoms.

The idea that the depression causes the bulimia fits the data much better, but it is still a bit of an oversimplification. You don't necessarily have to experience active depressive symptoms in order to develop bulimic symptoms. But the evidence strongly suggests that major depression and bulimia are closely related. A patient may experience major depression at one point, bulimia at another point, or, very often, both at the same time.

10. I was intrigued when you said that many patients with bulimia had a family history of psychiatric illnesses such as depression. My mother had a nervous breakdown in her forties and started thinking that people were poisoning her coffee. They diagnosed her as schizophrenic, gave her shock therapy, and she got better. Do you think my mother and I have different forms of the same *illness?*

Yes, we do. First of all, we would strongly suspect that your mother did not have schizophrenia. Schizophrenia is a chronic disorder that begins early in life and probably never gets completely better. What your mother had was probably an episode of major depression with psychotic symptoms (such as the delusion that she was being poisoned). Someone misdiagnosed her as schizophrenic, based on the erroneous belief that a patient who has psychotic symptoms must have schizophrenia. In fact, psychotic symptoms occur commonly in episodes of major depression, particularly in older people.

Of course, your bulimia and your mother's psychotic depression are not precisely the same illness, for the symptoms are very different. But both illnesses appear to be expressions of the same underlying disorder. We know this because bulimia and major depression (with or without psychotic symptoms) run in the same families together, appear at different times (or even at the same time) in the same patient, share laboratory features, and respond to the same medications.

We don't mean to scare you, but if you have bulimia, and particularly if you have bulimia plus a family history of psychotic depression, you have a greater than average chance of developing a psychotic depression yourself someday. But remember, if you find an antidepressant that works for your bulimia now, the chances are very good that the same drug would work for you years from now if you ever did develop a psychotic depression. In such a situation, you would probably have to add a small amount of an antipsychotic drug to your antidepressant, but you would be unlikely to have to resort to shock therapy as your mother did.

11. If it's really true that bulimia has a biochemical basis and a hereditary component, why does it not begin until adolescence? If you inherit it, shouldn't you have it from the time you're born?

Many hereditary disorders appear long after birth. As you probably know, there's a hereditary component in high blood pressure, heart attacks, and various forms of cancer. But you're not born suffering from these problems—they strike only at a later age, when they're programmed to occur, as it were.

Many of the hereditary psychiatric disorders are similarly programmed to start in a given age range—usually in the teens or twenties. Bulimia is one of them. Some disorders, such as severe obsessive-compulsive disorder, may start at the age of four or five; whereas others, such as major depression, may strike for the first time anywhere between childhood and age ninety. What determines this timing is unknown.

12. If bulimia, major depression, and other forms of major affective disorder run together in family trees, does that mean my children might get these illnesses?

We would be misleading you if we told you otherwise. If you have major depression and bulimia, each of your children will have a higher chance than a random individual of developing major affective disorder and/or an eating disorder. To get some idea of the odds—and this is only a rough idea—we can extrapolate from the data in our family-history study. If you have bulimia and your spouse has no psychiatric disorder, the chances are somewhere around 30% that a given child of yours will develop at least one episode of major affective disorder at some point in the course of life. If you have a female child, the chances are somewhere around 8% that she will develop an episode of bulimia and/or anorexia nervosa. For a male child, the chances of an eating disorder are much less.

These may sound like frighteningly high figures, but remember several things. First, they are very rough estimates, based on our experience with just one sample of patients. Only when there are several other studies in the literature will we be able to estimate these figures more reliably.

Second, the probability that your child will develop a severe or protracted case of major affective disorder, or of an eating disorder, is obviously much less than the 30% and 8% figures quoted here. In our family study, we were scoring first-degree relatives who had displayed any episode of illness, even a mild or short one.

Third, remember that these episodes are treatable. Even if your child does develop an episode of major depression or bulimia, chances are good that it will respond quickly to anti-depressants.

Fourth, if you have not had children yet and are considering having a child, remember that it will be the twenty-first century before that child is old enough to develop one of these disorders. By then, treatment will be even better and even easier than it is now. It's even possible that by then, major affective disorder will have been "cracked" entirely, and that some vastly superior treatment will have been invented.

Adding all these factors together, we don't feel that you should worry excessively about whether or not your child will develop a psychiatric syndrome. There is only one thing that you might do differently: As your children reach their teens and twenties, keep an eye out, just to be sure that they're not developing any suspicious symptoms. If they do, you should be a little quicker than the average parent to get them to an experienced psychiatrist who is knowledgeable about psychopharmacology.

13. With all this biochemical and hereditary stuff, you're still ducking the question of why bulimia is twenty times more common in women than in men.

We would again point to analogies from medicine. Cancer of the breast is at least twenty times more common in women, whereas lung cancer has always been more common in men. The former differential is due to biological differences between the sexes, whereas the latter seems to be due to environmental factors, such as cigarette smoking.

In bulimia, we simply do not know why women are more frequently afflicted than men. It may be due to biologic factors (perhaps the female hypothalamus, or some other brain structure, is more vulnerable in some way) or potentiated by social or environmental factors, as other theories suggest. If anyone tells you with certainty why bulimia is more common in women, don't believe it. At this stage of scientific research, no one can responsibly claim to know for sure.

14. I'll buy that some cases of bulimia are related, as you claim, to major affective disorder. But this "chemical imbalance" may apply to only a small fraction of cases. What makes you think it applies to a majority of cases?

A fair question. Among patients who meet the full *DSM*-III criteria for bulimia, and who have chronic symptoms, such as the patients in our studies, several lines of evidence suggest that a large majority of their cases are closely related to major affective disorder. First, nearly 80% of them have actually had an episode of major affective disorder during their lives. Second, more than 80% of them respond to antidepressant medications, a figure that compares closely with that obtained in pure samples of patients with major depression. Third, bulimic patients show essentially the same prevalence of familial major affective disorder as reference samples of patients with clear-cut cases of major affective disorder. Fourth—but much more tentative—is the endocrine data cited in Chapter 6.

Now if, say, only half of bulimic patients actually had cases related to major affective disorder, and the other half had some nonbiologic form of bulimia, none of the above findings would be expected. A much smaller percentage of any given sample of bulimic patients would be observed to have displayed a lifetime history of major affective disorder, far fewer would be likely to respond to antidepressants, and the familial prevalence of major affective disorder would likely be well below that observed in samples of patients with major depression. Therefore, although we are certainly not claiming that 100% of cases of bulimia are related to major affective disorder, the percentage must be high.

We should remind you that we're talking about people with

chronic and severe symptoms which meet the *DSM*-III criteria for bulimia. Obviously, if you include people who only transiently experiment with bulimia, or other "copycat" cases, as described in the answer to question 8, the percentage of cases related to major affective disorder may drop considerably.

15. Other experts have entirely different theories about the causes of bulimia. What makes you so sure your theory is necessarily the right one?

It's simply a matter of the scientific data. If you hear anyone argue a psychological, social, nutritional, or other theory of bulimia, ask what well-controlled, methodologically sound scientific studies form the basis for his or her opinion. In Chapter 5, we reviewed extensively the scientific literature on both bulimia and anorexia nervosa, and as you can see, dependable studies are few indeed. On the other hand, our affective-disorder theory of bulimia now rests on a foundation of many quantitative studies, from several different centers, all of which agree closely with one another. So don't be misled if someone sounds authoritative. Judge the facts for yourself.

16. I read your book and then discussed it with the counselor I'm seeing. He says that if I go away simply believing that my bulimia is a chemical imbalance, I'm going to cover up all my important feelings. Whom should I believe?

Again, it's a matter of the scientific facts. Ask your counselor if he is familiar with the scientific literature on bulimia, and what methodological arguments he can advance to refute the biological studies we have reviewed.

We would suggest that the problem with your counselor's position is his implication that taking antidepressants and exploring your feelings are mutually exclusive activities. In fact, if an antidepressant works, it will probably *help* you to uncover your feelings. Depression—and bulimia, for that matter—can make you numb to many of your emotions. With successful antidepressant treatment, you may suddenly get back the richness of those feelings, and thus work far *more* effectively in your therapy with your counselor. Several research studies have specifically noted that antidepressants can enhance the benefits of psychotherapy in depressed patients.[2]

17. I've had bulimia for several years and I can easily believe that it may be a biological disease, because I simply have no control over my binges. But my husband still acts as though it's all psychological—he just can't understand my inability to control it. What can I do?

This can be a real difficulty for anyone with bulimia, not only in dealing with husbands but in dealing with almost anyone else who knows of your problem. In fact, probably the only person who can fully understand what it's really like is another person with bulimia, or perhaps a treatment specialist who has had very extensive experience with the illness. Therefore, your husband is not being pigheaded; he's just like everyone else. It seems unbelievable to him that someone could not just "turn off" such bizarre behavior.

Maybe you could illustrate it to him by the analogy of a phobia (particularly if he has any phobia himself). Explain to him that asking you to "turn off" the bulimia would be like asking someone with claustrophobia (fear of closed-in spaces) to ride in an elevator with the lights off, or asking someone afraid of heights to stand at the edge of a cliff. Phobias are similar to eating binges in that the sufferer knows perfectly well that they're abnormal and undesirable, but can't eradicate them by a simple act of will. In that respect, they're the best analogy that we can think of.

If your husband listens to your arguments, reads this book, and still remains skeptical, don't exhaust yourself trying to convince him. But do see an experienced psychiatrist and try an antidepressant. If it works, that may be the most convincing thing of all. He can't argue with success—we hope!

18. I have bulimia and I was previously treated with two different tranquilizers and then with an antidepressant by my former psychiatrist. The tranquilizers made me feel like a zombie, and the antidepressants did nothing at all. I'm reluctant to go back and try pills again—I don't think they'll work. Do you?

Your previous psychiatrist may have been inexperienced with medications. First, there is no evidence that "tranquilizers" are of any value for bulimia, and they may make things worse. In fact, if they gave you a "zombie" feeling, we suspect that what you received was an antipsychotic drug. Antipsychotic drugs—such as Thorazine, Mellaril, Trilafon, Stelazine, Haldol, and many others—aren't really tranquilizers at all; they are drugs that counteract psychotic symptoms, such as delusions and hallucinations. Unfortunately, they are often inappropriately prescribed as "tranquilizers." Rarely will they make you feel any better; and they may give you numerous undesirable side effects, such as dystonia (muscle stiffness), akathisia (a bizarre restless feeling, as though you need to get up and pace), akinesia (a slowed-down sensation), and sometimes pronounced sedation. They are unlikely to relieve bulimia.

As for the antidepressant you tried, there's a good chance that you were on too low a dose (did your psychiatrist check your blood level?) or took the drug for too short a time—less than four weeks or so. And even if you're sure you were treated with an adequate amount for a long enough period, you should still not despair. As you may remember from our results in Chapter 8, many of our patients experienced little or no response to one antidepressant but improved rapidly on another.

19. I have anorexia nervosa and bulimia. Will antidepressants work for me?

Antidepressant medications may not be as effective for the anorexic component of your illness as they are for bulimia—the scientific evidence is not yet clear on this point. But as long as you have a knowledgeable psychiatrist who takes your low weight into account and uses antidepressants carefully in order to minimize the side effects for you, we think you should try.

You will probably find that you'll have more trouble than a normal-weight patient in reaching an adequate dose of antidepressants, because you will be more likely to experience lightheadedness and other side effects. You might find the side effects of tricyclics, in particular, too bothersome, and have better luck with medications such as tranylcypromine or trazodone. But if you work closely with an experienced psychopharmacologist, there's a fair chance you will benefit.

The bulimic symptoms will almost certainly be quicker to go away than the anorexic ones. But if you're lucky, you may eventually experience improvement in both syndromes. Several of our patients experienced a prompt decline in their bulimia, and then gradually, over the course of several months, lost their fear of eating and of gaining weight, and emerged from their anorexia as well. But remember, we're generalizing on the basis of a small sample of cases, so these impressions *must* be regarded as tentative.

20. I'm the mother of a teen-age bulimic daughter. We're having lots of family problems, and my daughter's bulimia seems to get worse every time there's a period of family stress. Wouldn't family therapy be more helpful than medication?

It's not an either/or situation. You should consider *both* family therapy and medication—neither of these therapies contradicts the other. If you're fortunate enough to find a psychiatrist who is knowledgeable in both areas, he or she can handle the entire treatment. Otherwise, your daughter might begin by seeing someone knowledgeable in psychopharmacology, and then, once she has been treated with antidepressants, you can be referred to someone who can see you as a family.

It is very important to remember this point: Biological treatment and psychological treatment do not preclude one another; and for a majority of patients, the best treatment is a combination of both.

21. Throughout this book, you imply that bulimia is caused primarily by a biological abnormality; you almost ridicule the idea that bulimia is a multidimensional disorder, caused by the interplay of many forces. I think you're being dangerously oversimplistic.

We have suggested, in chapters 4 and 6, that bulimia is part of a family of disorders which all appear related to major affective disorder. Within this family, we would grant, psychological, social, cultural, and nutritional factors may influence which symptoms a given patient may experience—be they bulimia, anorexia, alcoholism, agoraphobia, simple depression, or a combination. But we will not retreat from our "simplistic" suggestion that the primary cause of this family of disorders is biological: There is just not enough sound scientific evidence that other factors play a major causal role.

Stated another way, if bulimia were a multidimensional disorder, we would expect antidepressant medications to benefit only part of the syndrome, or to affect only a specific subgroup of patients. But this is not the case: Repeatedly, in placebo-controlled double-blind studies (reviewed in Chapter 8), a majority of bulimic patients have been found to respond to antidepressants—in the absence of any concomitant therapy—and many have experienced a complete remission of the entire syndrome. Anyone proposing a complex, "multiaxial" theory of bulimia must explain why most bulimic patients respond to a single, "simplistic" treatment.

11

EPILOGUE

The last several chapters of this book have of necessity been technical, in order to present as thoroughly as possible the available scientific evidence on the causes and treatment of bulimia. But let us end by returning to the human side of this illness, and particularly to those of you reading this book who are now suffering from bulimic symptoms.

Impressive though the scientific evidence may be, and as much as you may have learned from this book, it still may be difficult for you to go out and seek treatment. If you have endured your symptoms alone for months or years, confiding in only a few, or in no one, it may take much courage to "come out of the closet." We see this with countless patients who visit our offices: It is no easy task for them to summon the resolve to see a professional. At first, many find it awkward and embarrassing to discuss their secret symptoms with strangers. Only a minority of our patients are comfortable enough to describe their symptoms in the initial interview as openly as Sally did in Chapter 1. Most are apprehensive about telling their stories, fearing that they will appear disgusting, or weak-willed—or incurable.

So if you have never before sought treatment, or if you have had a negative experience with treatment in the past, we can easily understand that you may feel hesitant, even scared, to go out and seek help.

But you have already taken the first step: You have read this book, and made it all the way through the technical chapters to these final paragraphs. You have heard virtually all that has been published about bulimia, and you know that knowledgeable help is available to you. So do not lose your momentum—seek that help as soon as you can.

We leave you with our best wishes for success in your endeavor.

Source Notes

CHAPTER 2: WHAT IS BULIMIA?

1. Janet, P. 1903. *Les Obsessions et la Psychasthénie*. Paris: Felix Alcan.

2. The American Psychiatric Association. 1980. *Diagnostic and Statistical Manual of Mental Disorders*, Third Edition, Washington, D.C., APA. Used with permission. This book contains not only diagnostic criteria for the entire range of psychiatric disorders, but a wealth of descriptive material as well. For further examples of cases, see American Psychiatric Association, 1982, *DSM-III Case Book*, Washington, D.C., American Psychiatric Association, 1982. Both may be ordered through the American Psychiatric Association, 1400 K St. N.W., Washington, D.C. 20005.

3. Mitchell, J. E., R. L. Pyle, and E. D. Eckert. 1981. Frequency and duration of binge-eating episodes in patients with bulimia. *American Journal of Psychiatry* 138:835–36.

For further descriptions of the experience of binge eating, see:

Abraham, S. F., and P. J. V. Beaumont. 1982. How patients describe bulimia or binge-eating. *Psychological Medicine* 12:625–35.

Johnson, C., and R. Larson. 1982. Bulimia: An analysis of moods and behavior. *Psychosomatic Medicine* 44:341–50.

4. Stunkard, A. J. 1959. Eating patterns and obesity. *Psychiatric Quarterly* 33:284–95.

5. Loro, A. D., and C. S. Orleans. 1981. Binge eating in obesity—preliminary findings and guidelines for behavioral analysis and treatment. *Addictive Behaviors* 6:155–66.

6. Gormally, J., S. Black, and S. Daston. 1982. The assessment of binge-

eating severity among obese persons. *Addictive Behaviors* 7:47–55.

7. Mitchell, J. E., and J. P. Bantle. 1983. Metabolic and endocrine investigations in women of normal weight with the bulimia syndrome. *Biological Psychiatry* 18:355–65.

8. On the medical complications of self-induced vomiting, see:

Wallace, M., P. Richard, E. Chester, et al. 1963. Persistent alkalosis and hypokalemia caused by surreptitious vomiting. *Quarterly Journal of Medicine* 37:577–88.

Levin, P. A., J. M. Falko, and K. Dixon. 1980. Benign parotid enlargement in bulimia. *Annals of Internal Medicine* 93:827–29.

Mitchell, J. E., R. L. Pyle, E. D. Eckert, et al. 1983, in press. Electrolyte and other physiological abnormalities in patients with bulimia. *Psychological Medicine.*

9. NIMH shaken by death of research volunteer. 25 July 1980. *Science* 209:475 ff.

10. For complications related to laxatives and diuretics, see:

Gilman, A. G., L. S. Goodman, and A. Gilman, eds. 1980. *The Pharmacologic Basis of Therapeutics.* 6th ed. New York: Macmillan.

Oster, J. R., B. J. Materson, and A. I. Rogers. 1980. Laxative abuse syndrome. *American Journal of Gastroenterology* 74:451–58.

11. Niiya, K., T. Kitagawa, M. Fujishita, et al. 1983. Bulimia nervosa complicated by deficiency of vitamin K–dependent coagulation factors. *Journal of the American Medical Association* 250:792–793.

12. For complications of bulimia in the patient with diabetes, see:

Hudson, J. I., M. S. Hudson, and S. M. Wentworth. 1983. Self-induced glycosuria: A novel method of purging in bulimia. *Journal of the American Medical Association* 249:2501.

Hudson, M. S., J. I. Hudson, and S. M. Wentworth. 1983. Eating disorders and diabetic control (abstract). *Diabetes* 42 (suppl. 1):82A.

Hudson, M. S., J. I. Hudson, and S. M. Wentworth. 1983. Bulimia and diabetes. *New England Journal of Medicine* 309:431–32.

Szmukler, G. I., and G. F. M. Russell. 1983. Diabetes mellitus, anorexia nervosa, and bulimia. *British Journal of Psychiatry* 142:305–308.

Hillard, J. R., M. C. Lobo, and R. P. Keeling. 1983. Bulimia and diabetes: A potentially life-threatening combination. *Psychosomatics* 24: 292–95.

CHAPTER 3: THE 1980s: BULIMIA COMES OUT OF THE CLOSET

1. Wermuth, B. M., K. L. Davis, L. E. Hollister, et al. 1977. Phenytoin treatment of the binge-eating syndrome. *American Journal of Psychiatry* 134:1249–53.

2. Russell, G. F. M. 1979. Bulimia nervosa: An ominous variant of anorexia nervosa. *Psychological Medicine* 9:429–48.

3. A sampling of recent articles in the popular press is as follows:

Boskind-Lodahl, M., and J. Sirlin. March 1977. The gorging-purging syndrome. *Psychology Today,* 50 ff.

Young, N. September 1979. Full stomachs and empty lives: Why thousands of women secretly binge and purge. *Glamour,* 204 ff.

Brenner, M. June 1980. Bulimarexia: The eating disorder of the perfectionistic woman. *Savvy,* 49–55.

Weber, M. October 1980. Slim overeater's disease. *Vogue,* 205.

Neil, J. November 1980. Eating their cake and heaving it too. *MacLean's,* 51–52.

Eating binges: Anorexia's sister ailment. 17 November 1980. *Time,* 94.

Stein, M. B. August 1981. The eating disorder women don't talk about. *McCall's,* 42.

Squire, S. October 1981. Why thousands of women don't know how to eat normally anymore. *Glamour,* 244–45.

Lance, K., and J. Barrile. November 1981. How to control binge eating. *Ladies' Home Journal,* 48 ff.

Langway, L., et al. 2 November 1981. The binge-purge syndrome. *Newsweek,* 60 ff.

Stein, B. 21 December 1981. Dangerous eat-and-purge disorder called bulimia strikes young women. *People,* 47–48.

Fischer, A. January 1982. Do you stuff yourself one moment and starve yourself the next? *Seventeen,* 106–107.

Bulimia: The new danger in dieting. March 1982. *Harper's Bazaar,* 148 ff.

Schildkraut, M. L. April 1982. Bulimia: The secret dieter's disease. *Good Housekeeping,* 239.

Bulima and young women. June 1982. *USA Today,* 6.

Seligmann, J., et al. 7 March 1983. A deadly feast and famine. *Newsweek,* 59–60.

4. Stangler, R. S., and A. M. Printz. 1980. *DSM*-III: Psychiatric diagnosis in a university population. *American Journal of Psychiatry* 137: 937–40.

5. Halmi, K. A., J. R. Falk, and E. Schwartz. 1981. Binge-eating and vomiting: A survey of a college population. *Psychological Medicine* 11:697–706.

6. Pyle, R. L., J. E. Mitchell, E. D. Eckert, et al. 1983. The incidence of bulimia in freshman college students. *International Journal of Eating Disorders* 2:75–85.

7. Pope, H. G., Jr., J. I. Hudson, D. Yurgelun-Todd, et al. 1984. Prevalence of anorexia nervosa and bulimia in three student populations. *International Journal of Eating Disorders 3:* 45–51.

8. Pope, H. G., Jr., J. I. Hudson, and D. Yurgelun-Todd. 1984. Prevalence of anorexia nervosa and bulimia among 300 suburban women shoppers. *American Journal of Psychiatry* 141:292–94.

9. Cooper, P. J., and C. G. Fairburn. 1983. Binge-eating and self-induced vomiting in the community. *British Journal of Psychiatry* 142:139–44.

Other estimates of the prevalence of bulimia, based on less specific data, can be found in the following:

Hawkins, R. C., and P. F. Clement. 1980. Development and construct validation of a self-report measure of binge-eating tendencies. *Addictive Behaviors* 5:219–26.

Crisp, A. H. 1981. Anorexia nervosa at normal body weight: The abnormal/normal weight control syndrome. *International Journal of Psychiatry in Medicine* 11:203–33.

Fairburn, C. G., and P. J. Cooper. 1982. Self-induced vomiting and bulimia nervosa: An undetected problem. *British Medical Journal* 284:1153–55.

For data on the prevalence of anorexia nervosa, see the papers cited above by Stangler and Printz, Crisp, and both papers by Pope et al.; as well as the following:

Bruch, H. 1966. Anorexia nervosa and its differential diagnosis. *Journal of Nervous and Mental Disease* 141:555–56.

Theander, S. 1970. Anorexia nervosa. *Acta Psychiatrica Scandinavica* (suppl. 214).

Kendall, R. E., D. J. Hall, A. Hailey, et al. 1973. The epidemiology of anorexia nervosa. *Psychological Medicine* 3:200–203.

Duddle, M. 1973. An increase of anorexia nervosa in a university population. *British Journal of Psychiatry* 123:711–12.

Halmi, K. A. 1974. Anorexia nervosa: Demographic and clinical features in 94 cases. *Psychosomatic Medicine* 36:18–26.

Crisp, A. H., R. L. Palmer, and R. S. Kalucy. 1976. How common is anorexia nervosa? A prevalence study. *British Journal of Psychiatry* 128:549–54.

Kalucy, R. S., A. H. Crisp, J. H. Lacey, et al. 1977. Prevalence and prognosis of anorexia nervosa. *Australian and New Zealand Journal of Psychiatry* 11:251–57.

Jones, D. J., M. M. Fox, H. M. Babigian, et al. 1980. Epidemiology of anorexia nervosa in Monroe County, New York: 1960–1976. *Psychosomatic Medicine* 42:551–58.

Ballot, N. S., N. E. Delaney, P. J. Erskine, et al. 1981. Anorexia nervosa—a prevalence study. *South African Medical Journal* 59:992–93.

Button, E. J., and A. Whitehouse. 1981. Subclinical anorexia nervosa. *Psychological Medicine* 11:509–16.

Joseph, A., I. K. Wood, and S. C. Goldberg. 1982. Determining populations at risk for developing anorexia nervosa based on selection of college major. *Psychiatry Research* 7:53–58.

CHAPTER 4: EIGHT BULIMIA-ASSOCIATED DISORDERS

1. The National Institute of Mental Health Diagnostic Interview Schedule can be obtained from Dr. John Helzer, Washington University School of Medicine, Department of Psychiatry, 4940 Audubon Ave., St. Louis, MO 63110.

For information on the reliability and use of this interview see:

Helzer, J. E., L. N. Robins, M. Taibleson, et al. 1977. Reliability of psychiatric diagnosis. I: A methodological review. *Archives of General Psychiatry* 34:129–33.

Helzer, J. E., P. J. Clayton, R. Pambakian, et al. 1977. Reliability of psychiatric diagnosis. II: The test/retest reliability of diagnostic classification. *Archives of General Psychiatry* 34:136–41.

Robins, L. H., J. E. Helzer, J. Croughan, et al. 1981. National Institute of Mental Health Diagnostic Interview Schedule: Its history, characteristics, and validity. *Archives of General Psychiatry* 38:381–89.

2. Weissman, M. M., and J. K. Myers. 1978. Affective disorders in a United States urban community: The use of Research Diagnostic Criteria in an epidemiological survey. *Archives of General Psychiatry* 35:1304–11.

3. Vernon, S. W., and R. E. Roberts. 1982. Use of the SADS-RDC in a tri-ethnic community survey. *Archives of General Psychiatry* 39:47–52.

4. Hudson, J. I., H. G. Pope, Jr., J. M. Jonas, et al. In press, 1983. Phenomenologie relationship of eating disorders to major affective disorder. *Psychiatry Research*.

5. Pope, H. G., Jr., J. I. Hudson, D. Yurgelun-Todd, et al. Submitted for publication 1983. Prevalence of anorexia nervosa and bulimia in three student populations.

For information on any of the bulimia-associated disorders, perhaps the best place to start is *DSM*-III (see note 2, Chapter 2). For other general references, see:

Feighner, J. P., E. Robins, S. B. Guze, et al. 1972. Diagnostic criteria for use in psychiatric research. *Archives of General Psychiatry* 26:57–63. The forerunner of *DSM*-III.

Woodruff, R. A., D. W. Goodwin, and S. B. Guze, eds. 1974. *Psychiatric Diagnosis*. New York: Oxford University Press. Particularly recommended for the lay reader.

Akiskal, H. S., and W. L. Webb, eds. 1978. *Psychiatric Diagnosis: Exploration of Biological Predictors*. Jamaica, N.Y.: Spectrum. A more technical discussion of diagnosis in general.

See also any of the leading textbooks of psychiatry:

Arieti, S., ed. 1974. *American Handbook of Psychiatry*. 2d ed. New York: Basic Books.

Noyes, A. P., and L. C. Kolb. 1977. *Modern Clinical Psychiatry*. 9th ed. Philadelphia: W. B. Saunders.

Freedman, A. M., and H. I. Kaplan, eds. 1980. *Comprehensive Textbook of Psychiatry*. 3rd ed. Baltimore: Williams & Wilkins.

Make sure you're reading the *most recent edition* of any of these textbooks. Anything more than ten years old is liable to be seriously out of date. Even the editions listed here are beginning to get out of date in many places.

6. For further information on anorexia nervosa, see the following scientific and popular references:

SCIENTIFIC

Thoma, H. 1967. *Anorexia Nervosa*. New York: International Universities Press.

Bruch, H. 1970. Psychotherapy in primary anorexia nervosa. *Journal of Nervous and Mental Disease* 150:51–67. A clear presentation of the psychodynamic approach to treatment.

Crisp, A. H., and D. A. Toms. 1972. Primary anorexia nervosa or weight phobia in the male: Report on 13 cases. *British Medical Journal* 1:334–38.

Morgan, H. G., and G. F. M. Russell. 1975. Value of family background and clinical features as predictors of long-term outcome in anorexia nervosa: Four-year follow-up study of 41 patients. *Psychological Medicine* 5:355–71.

Vigersky, R. A., ed. 1977. *Anorexia Nervosa*. New York: Raven Press. A collection of a large number of scientific papers covering many topics.

Halmi, K. A. 1978. Anorexia nervosa: Recent investigations. *Annual Review of Medicine* 29:137–48.

Hsu, L. K. G., A. H. Crisp, and B. Harding. 1979. Outcome of anorexia nervosa. *Lancet* 1:61–65. One of the best outcome studies of anorexia nervosa.

Dally, P., and J. Gomez. 1979. *Anorexia Nervosa*. London: Heinemann.

Crisp, A. H., L. K. G. Hsu, B. Harding, et al. 1980. Clinical features of anorexia nervosa: A study of a consecutive series of 102 female patients. *Journal of Psychosomatic Research* 24:179–91.

Halmi, K. A. Anorexia nervosa. In *Comprehensive Textbook of Psychiatry*. 3rd ed. Edited by A. M. Freedman and H. I. Kaplan. 1980. Baltimore: Williams & Wilkins, pp. 1882–91. A good review of studies up to 1979.

Strober, J. 1980. Personality and symptomatological features in young, nonchronic anorexia nervosa students. *Journal of Psychosomatic Research* 24:353–59. Suggests that bulimic and nonbulimic patients with anorexia nervosa have different personality profiles.

Lucas, A. R. 1981. Toward the understanding of anorexia nervosa as a disease entity. *Mayo Clinic Proceedings* 56:254–64. A short review with 204 references.

Sours, J. A. 1981. Depression and the anorexia nervosa syndrome. *Psychiatric Clinics of North America* 4:145–58. Depression and anorexia nervosa related to psychodynamic theory.

Crisp, A. H., and A. V. Bhat. 1982. "Personality" and anorexia nervosa—the phobic avoidance stance: Its origins and symptomatology. *Psychotherapy and Psychosomatics* 38:178–200. A largely psychodynamic paper.

Darby, P. L., P. E. Garfinkel, D. M. Garner, et al., eds. In press. *Anorexia Nervosa*. New York: Alan Liss.

See also the prevalence studies of anorexia nervosa cited under note 9, Chapter 3, particularly those of Halmi and of Kalucy and colleagues.

POPULAR

Bruch, H. 1973. *Eating Disorders: Obesity, Anorexia Nervosa, and the Person Within*. New York: © 1973, Basic Books, Inc. A classic work written from a psychodynamic perspective.

Bruch, H. 1978. *The Golden Cage: The Enigma of Anorexia Nervosa*. Cambridge, Mass.: Harvard University Press. A more popularized version of Dr. Bruch's view of anorexia nervosa

Levenkron, S. 1979. *The Best Little Girl in the World*. New York: Warner Books. A novel about anorexia nervosa.

Crisp, A. H. 1980. *Anorexia Nervosa: Let Me Be*. London: Academic Press. A leading British researcher on eating disorders presents a readable description of the illness and details of his treatment approach.

Palmer, R. L. 1980. *Anorexia Nervosa: A Guide for Sufferers and Their*

Families. New York: Penguin Books. A balanced, simple, straightforward presentation.

Levenkron, S. 1982. *Treating and Overcoming Anorexia Nervosa.* New York: Scribner's. Focuses primarily on Dr. Levenkron's "nurturant-authoritative" technique of psychotherapy in anorexia nervosa.

O'Neill, C. B. 1982. *Starving for Attention.* New York: Continuum. A vivid personal account of anorexia and bulimia, written by the daughter of entertainer Pat Boone.

There have recently been a number of articles on anorexia nervosa in popular magazines. Although these are far less sophisticated than the books cited above, a few examples are:

Woods, J. May 1981. I was starving myself to death: A story of anorexia nervosa. *Mademoiselle,* 200–201.

Starving amid plenty. July 1981. *Science Digest,* 56.

My daughter was starving herself to death. May 1982. *Good Housekeeping,* 32 ff.

McCoy, K. July 1982. Are you obsessed with your weight? *Seventeen,* 80–81.

Anorexia nervosa: The starving disease epidemic. 30 August 1982. *U.S. News and World Report,* 47–48.

7. Russell, G. F. M. 1979. Bulimia nervosa: An ominous variant of anorexia nervosa. *Psychological Medicine* 9:429–48.

8. Pyle, R. L., J. E. Mitchell, and E. D. Eckert. 1981. Bulimia: A report of 34 cases. *Journal of Clinical Psychiatry* 42:60–64.

9. Nogami, Y., and F. Yabana. 1977. On kibarashi-gui (binge eating). *Folia Psychiatrica et Neurologica Japonica* 31:159–66.

10. Walsh, B. T., S. P. Roose, A. H. Glassman, et al. 4 May 1983. Depression and eating disorders. Presented at the Annual Meeting, American Psychiatric Association.

11. Herzog, D. A., and F. J. Osuna. 4 May 1983. Depression and eating disorders. Presented at the Annual Meeting, American Psychiatric Association.

12. Hudson, J. I., H. G. Pope, Jr., J. M. Jonas, et al. 1983. Family history study of anorexia nervosa and bulimia. *British Journal of Psychiatry* 142:133–38.

13. For further information on major depression, see the following scientific and popular references:

SCIENTIFIC

Paykel, E. S., ed. 1982. *Handbook of Affective Disorders.* New York:

Guilford Press. Includes material about both major depression and manic-depressive illness.

Clayton, P. J., and J. E. Barrett, eds. 1982. *Treatment of Depression: Old Controversies and New Approaches.* New York: Raven Press.

POPULAR

Plath, S. 1971. *The Bell Jar.* New York: Harper & Row. An autobiographical novel by a woman with major depression.

Winokur, G. 1981. *Depression: The Facts.* New York: Oxford University Press. An authoritative discussion by a national authority on diagnosis, epidemiology, and genetics.

Wender, P. H., and D. F. Klein. 1981. *Mind, Mood, and Medicine: A Guide to the New Biological Psychiatry.* New York: Farrar, Straus & Giroux.

14. For further information on manic-depressive illness, see the following scientific and popular references:

SCIENTIFIC

Clayton, P., R. H. Pitts, Jr., and G. Winokur. 1965. Affective Disorder. IV: Mania. *Comprehensive Psychiatry* 6:313–22.

Winokur, G., P. J. Clayton, and T. Reich. 1969. *Manic Depressive Illness.* St. Louis: C. V. Mosby. Unfortunately, out of print.

Taylor, M. A., and R. Abrams. 1973. The phenomenology of mania: A new look at some old patients. *Archives of General Psychiatry* 29:520–22.

Taylor, M. A., and R. Abrams. 1975. Acute mania: Clinical and genetic study of responders and nonresponders to treatments. *Archives of General Psychiatry* 32:863–65.

Pope, H. G., Jr., and J. F. Lipinski. 1978. Diagnosis in schizophrenia and manic-depressive illness: A reassessment of the specificity of "schizophrenic" symptoms in the light of current research. *Archives of General Psychiatry* 35:811–28. A detailed review that discusses the problem of misdiagnosis of manic-depressive illness as schizophrenia.

Pope, H. G., Jr., J. F. Lipinski, B. M. Cohen, et al. 1980. "Schizoaffective disorder": An invalid diagnosis? A comparison of schizoaffective disorder, schizophrenia, and affective disorder. *American Journal of Psychiatry* 137:921–27. Further information on misdiagnosis.

Abrams, R., and M. A. Taylor. 1981. Importance of schizophrenic symptoms in the diagnosis of mania. *American Journal of Psychiatry* 138:658–61. Similar to the Pope et al. study.

Pope, H. G., Jr., 1983. Misdiagnosis of affective disorder as schizophrenia in clinical practice: A review and illustrations. *Hospital and Community Psychiatry* 34:322–28.

Most of the above articles are focused on the *diagnosis* of manic-depressive illness. For material on the biology, genetics, and treatment of manic-depressive illness, see references for Chapter 6.

POPULAR

Fieve, R. 1975. *Moodswing.* New York: William Morrow.

Vonnegut, M. 1975. *The Eden Express.* New York: Praeger. An autobiographical account of manic-depressive illness. (Although the author was diagnosed as having schizophrenia, he almost unquestionably had manic-depressive illness with psychotic features.)

15. For further information on alcohol abuse, see the following scientific and popular references:

SCIENTIFIC

Behar, D., and G. Winokur. Research in alcoholism and depression: A two-way street. In *Psychiatric Factors in Drug Abuse.* Edited by R. W. Pickens and L. L. Heston. 1979. New York: Grune & Stratton. 125–52.

Goodwin, D. W., and C. K. Erickson, eds. 1979. *Alcoholism and Affective Disorders: Clinical, Genetic, and Biochemical Studies with Emphasis on Alcohol-Lithium Interaction.* New York: Spectrum.

Frances, R. J., S. Timm, and S. Bucky. 1980. Studies of familial and nonfamilial alcoholism. I: Demographic studies. *Archives of General Psychiatry* 37:564–66.

Cloninger, C. R., M. Bohman, and S. Sigvardsson. 1981. Inheritance of alcohol abuse: Cross-fostering analysis of adopted men. *Archives of General Psychiatry* 38:861–68.

Bohman, M., S. Sigvardsson, and R. Cloninger. 1981. Maternal inheritance of alcohol abuse: Cross-fostering analysis of adopted women. *Archives of General Psychiatry* 38:965–69.

POPULAR

Goodwin, D. W. 1981. *Alcoholism: The Facts.* New York: Oxford University Press. An authoritative popular book by a noted researcher.

A few recent magazine articles specifically address the problem of alcohol abuse in women:

Zabolasi-Cxekme. August 1981. Alcohol and women. *World Health,* 8–11.

Closet alcoholism. September 1981. *Harper's Bazaar,* 312 ff.

Lake, A. June 1982. Alcoholism: Suddenly it's a young woman's problem. *Redbook,* 77 ff.

Could you be an alcoholic? September 1982. *Harper's Bazaar*, 159 ff.

16. For further information on panic disorder and agoraphobia, see the following scientific and popular references:

SCIENTIFIC

Klein, D. F., C. M. Zitrin, and M. G. Woerner. Antidepressants, anxiety, panic, and phobia. In *Psychopharmacology: A Generation of Progress*. Edited by M. A. Lipton, A. DiMascio, and L. F. Killiam. 1978. New York: Raven Press, pp. 1401–10.

Bowen, R. C., and J. Kohout. 1979. The relationship between agoraphobia and primary affective disorders. *Canadian Journal of Psychiatry* 24:314–21.

Crowe, R. R., D. L. Pauls, D. J. Slymen, et al. 1980. A family study of anxiety neurosis: Morbidity risk in families of patients with and without mitral valve prolapse. *Archives of General Psychiatry* 37:77–79. A family study suggesting anxiety disorders run in families but are *not* related to major affective disorder.

Sheehan, D. V., J. Ballenger, and G. Jacobsen. 1980. Treatment of endogenous anxiety with phobic, hysterical and hypochondriacal symptoms. *Archives of General Psychiatry* 37:51–59.

Liebowitz, M. R., and D. F. Klein. 1981. Differential diagnosis and treatment of panic attacks and phobic states. *Annual Review of Medicine* 32:583–99.

Munjack, D. J., and H. B. Moss. 1981. Affective disorder and alcoholism in families of agoraphobics. *Archives of General Psychiatry* 38:869–71. A family study suggesting that agoraphobia is related to major affective disorder.

Curtis, G. C., O. G. Cameron, and R. M. Nesse. 1982. The dexamethasone suppression test in panic disorder and agoraphobia. *American Journal of Psychiatry* 139:1043–46.

Zitrin, C. M., D. F. Klein, M. G. Woerner, et al. 1983. Treatment of phobias. I: Comparison of imipramine hydrochloride and placebo. *Archives of General Psychiatry* 40:125–38.

Klein, D. F., C. M. Zitrin, M. G. Woerner, et al. 1983. Treatment of phobias. II: Behavior therapy and supportive psychotherapy: Are there any specific ingredients? *Archives of General Psychiatry* 40:139–45. This and the preceding study present data suggesting these disorders have a biological basis.

Marks, I. M., S. Gray, D. Cohen, et al. 1983. Imipramine and brief therapist-aided exposure in agoraphobics having self-exposure homework. *Archives of General Psychiatry* 40:153–62. This paper presents data that support a strong behavioral basis of agoraphobia.

POPULAR

Marks, I. M. *Fears and Phobias*. 1969. New York: Academic Press. *Living with Fear*. 1980: New York: McGraw-Hill. *Cure and Care of Neuroses*. 1981. New York: John Wiley. Dr. Marks, a world expert in the area of agoraphobia and related disorders, places particular emphasis on techniques of behavior therapy.

Mathews, A. M., M. G. Gelder, and D. W. Johnston. 1981. *Agoraphobia, Nature and Treatment*. New York: Guilford Press.

Here are two recent magazine articles:

Patrick, J. G. May 1981. Agoraphobia: When the familiar becomes frightening. *Mademoiselle*, 109–10.

Finch, M. October 1981. My fight against fear. *Ladies' Home Journal*, 48 ff.

17. For further information on obsessive-compulsive disorder, see the following scientific references:

Goodwin, D. W., S. B. Guze, and E. Robins. 1969. Follow-up studies in obsessional neurosis. *Archives of General Psychiatry* 20:182–87.

Kendell, R. E., and W. J. DiScipio. 1970. Obsessional symptoms and obsessional personality traits in patients with depressive illness. *Psychological Medicine* 1:65–72.

Beech, H. R. 1974. *Obsessional States*. London: Methuen.

Welner, A., T. Reich, E. Robins, et al. 1976. Obsessive-compulsive disorder: Record, follow-up, and family studies. *Comprehensive Psychiatry* 17:527–39.

Dowson, J. H. 1977. The phenomenology of severe obsessive-compulsive neurosis. *British Journal of Psychiatry* 131:75–78.

Marks, I. M., R. S. Stern, D. Mawson, et al. 1980. Clomipramine and exposure for obsessive-compulsive rituals. I: *British Journal of Psychiatry* 136:1–25.

Thoren, P., M. Asberg, B. Cronholm, et al. 1980. Clomipramine treatment of obsessive-compulsive disorder. I: A controlled clinical trial. *Archives of General Psychiatry* 37:1281–85.

Insel, T. R., and D. L. Murphy. 1981. The psychopharmacological treatment of obsessive-compulsive disorder: A review. *Journal of Clinical Psychopharmacology* 1:304–11. A particularly good review of available studies to date.

Coryell, W. 1981. Obsessive-compulsive disorder and primary unipolar depression. Comparisons of background, family history, course, and mortality. *Journal of Nervous and Mental Disease* 169:220–24.

Salzman, L., and F. H. Thaler. 1981. Obsessive-compulsive disorders: A review of the literature. *American Journal of Psychiatry* 138:286–96.

Insel, T. R., N. H. Kalin, and L. B. Guttmacher. 1982. The dexamethasone suppression test in patients with primary obsessive-compulsive disorder. *Psychiatry Research* 6:153–60.

18. Casper, R. C., E. D. Eckert, K. A. Halmi, et al. 1980. Bulimia: Its incidence and clinical importance in patients with anorexia nervosa. *Archives of General Psychiatry* 37:1030–35.

19. Garfinkel, P. E., H. Moldofsky, and D. M. Garner. 1980. The heterogeneity of anorexia nervosa: Bulimia as a distinct subgroup. *Archives of General Psychiatry* 37:1036–40.

20. For further information on kleptomania and other impulse-control disorders, see the following scientific and popular references:

SCIENTIFIC

Wihels, F. 1942. Kleptomania and other psychopathic crimes. *Journal of Criminal Psychopathology* 4:205–16.

Lewis, N. D. C., and H. Yarnell. 1951. *Pathological Firesetting.* Monograph No. 82. New York: Nervous and Mental Diseases.

Bolen, D. W., and W. H. Boyd. 1968. Gambling and the gambler. *Archives of General Psychiatry* 18:617–30.

Möller, H. J. 1977. Psychopathologie von Stehlhandlungen ohne (wesentliche) Bereicherungstendenz. *Archiv für Psychiatrie und Nervenkrankheiten* 223:323–36.

Singer, B. A. 1978. A case of kleptomania. *Bulletin of the American Academy of Psychiatry and the Law* 6:414–22.

Ramelli, E., and G. Mapelli. 1979. Du vol mélancolique. *Acta Psychiatrica Belgica* 79:56–74.

Lesieur, H. R. 1979. The compulsive gambler's spiral of options and involvement. *Psychiatry* 42:79–87.

Gruber, A. R., E. T. Heck, and E. Mintzer. 1981. Children who set fires: Some background and behavioral characteristics. *American Journal of Orthopsychiatry* 51:484–88.

Crisp, A. H., L. K. G. Hsu, and B. Harding. 1980. The starving hoarder and voracious spender: Stealing in anorexia nervosa. *Journal of Psychosomatic Research* 24:225–31.

POPULAR

Pilfering urges: Is shoplifting an illness? November 17, 1980. *Time*, 94.

Taylor, L. B. January 1982. Shoplifting: When honest women steal. *Ladies' Home Journal*, 88 ff.

CHAPTER 5: WHAT CAUSES BULIMIA?

1. For notes on the history of bulimia, see Ziolko, H. U. 1982. Hyper-phage Esstörungen. Münchener Medizinische Wachenschrift 124: 685–88.

Also of historical interest are:

Friedländer, L. 1968. *Roman Life and Manners Under the Early Empire.* Translated by J. H. Freese and L. A. Magnus. New York: Barnes & Noble.

Morton, R. 1720. *Phthisiologia: or a Treatise of Consumptions.* London: W. and J. Innys.

Laycock, T. 1840. *A Treatise on the Nervous Diseases of Women.* London: Langman, Orme, Brown, Green & Longmans.

The first two clinical descriptions of anorexia nervosa, which appeared almost simultaneously, are:

Lasègue, C. 1873. L'Anorexie hystérique. *Archives Générales de Médecine* 21:385–403. Essentially the same article appears in English as Lasègue, C. 1873. On hysterical anorexia. *Medical Times and Gazette* 2:265–66, 367–69.

Gull, W. W. 1874. Anorexia nervosa. *Transactions of the Clinical Society* (London) 7:22–28.

2. Whytt, R. 1765. *Observations on the Nature, Causes, and Cure of Those Disorders which have been Commonly Called Nervous, Hypochondriac or Hysteric.* Edinburgh: Balfour.

3. Briquet, P. 1859. *Traité Clinique et Thérapeutique de l'Hystérie.* Paris: Baillière et Fils.

4. Janet, P. 1903. *Les Obsessions et la Psychasthénie.* Paris: Felix Alcan.

5. Binswanger, L. The case of Ellen West. In May, R. 1957. *Existence.* New York: Basic Books.

6. Freud, S. 1954. *The Origins of Psychoanalysis: Letters to Wilhelm Fliess, Drafts and Notes: 1887–1902.* Edited by M. Bonaparte, A. Freud, and E. Kris. Translated by E. Mosbacher and J. Strachey. New York: Basic Books.

7. Waller, J. V., M. R. Kaufman, and F. Deutsch. 1940. Anorexia nervosa: A psychosomatic entity. *Psychosomatic Medicine* 1:3–16.

8. Bruch, H. 1970. Psychotherapy in primary anorexia nervosa. *Journal of Nervous and Mental Disease* 150:51–67. © 1970 The Williams & Wilkins Co., Baltimore.

9. Bruch, H. 1973. *Eating Disorders: Obesity, Anorexia Nervosa, and the Person Within*. New York: Basic Books.

For other examples of psychoanalytic theories of the eating disorders, see:

Ballet, G. 1907. L'anorexie mentale. *Journal des Practiciens* 21:293–94.

Bartlett, W. M. 1928. An analysis of anorexia. *American Journal of Diseases of the Child* 35:26–35.

Alexander, F. 1935. Uber den Einfluss psychischer Faktoren auf gastrointestinale Störungen. *Internationale Zeitschrift für Psychoanalyse* 21:188–219.

Berlin, I. N., M. J. Boatman, S. L. Shelmo, et al. 1951. Adolescent alternation of anorexia and obesity. *American Journal of Orthopsychiatry* 21:387–419. This is one of the few articles to discuss bulimia as well as anorexia nervosa.

Guiora, A. Z. 1967. Dysorexia: A psychopathological study of anorexia nervosa and bulimia. *American Journal of Psychiatry* 124:147–49.

10. Yager, J. 1982. Family issues in the pathogenesis of anorexia nervosa. *Psychosomatic Medicine* 44:43–59.

Some of the family studies (including those whose results are cited in Chapter 5) are:

Cobb, S. 1943. *Borderlands of Psychiatry*. London: Oxford University Press.

Taipale, V., O. Tuomi, and M. Aukee. 1971. Anorexia nervosa: An illness of two generations: *Acta Paedopsychiatrica* 38:31–35.

Wald, P. 1973. Family structure in three cases of anorexia nervosa: The role of the father. *American Journal of Psychiatry* 130:1394–97.

Kalucy, R. S., A. H. Crisp, and B. Harding. 1977. A study of 56 families with anorexia nervosa. *British Journal of Medical Psychology* 50:381–95.

Hall, A. 1978. Family structure and relationship of 50 female anorexia nervosa patients. *Australian and New Zealand Journal of Psychiatry* 12:263–68.

Norris, D. L., and E. Jones. 1979. Anorexia nervosa: A clinical study of ten patients and their family systems. *Journal of Adolescence* 2:101–11.

Strober, M. 1981. The significance of bulimia in juvenile anorexia nervosa: An exploration of possible etiologic factors. *International Journal of Eating Disorders* 1:28–43. An article that distinguishes bulimic from nonbulimic anorexic patients.

See also Dally and Gomez; Crisp, Hsu, and Harding, under note 6, Chapter 4.

11. For a general discussion of behavior theory, see:

Agras, W. S., ed. 1978. *Behavior Modification: Principles and Clinical Applications*. 2d ed. Boston: Little, Brown.

Goldfried, M. R. 1976. *Clinical Behavior Therapy.* New York: Holt, Rinehart & Winston.

For specific discussions of behavior therapy in anorexia nervosa and bulimia, see the notes for Chapter 7.

12. Boskind-Lodahl, M., and W. C. White. Oct. 1978. The definition and treatment of bulimarexia in college women—a pilot study. *Journal of American College Health Association* 27:85, a publication of the Helen Dwight Reid Educational Foundation.

For other feminist perspectives on binge eating, see:

White, W., and M. Boskind-White. 1981. An experiential behavioral approach to the treatment of bulimarexia. *Psychotherapy: Theory, Research, and Practice* 4:501—507.

Orbach, S. 1978. *Fat Is a Feminist Issue.* London: Paddington Press. Discusses binge eating primarily in the context of obesity.

Orbach, S. 1982. *Fat Is a Feminist Issue II: A Program to Conquer Compulsive Eating.* New York: Berkley. Holds out great promise, but delivers no evidence to support its claims.

Boskind-White, M., and W. C. White. 1983. *Bulimarexia: The Binge-Purge Cycle.* New York: W. W. Norton.

13. Garner, D. M., P. E. Garfinkel, D. Schwartz, et al. 1980. Cultural expectations of thinness in women. *Psychological Reports* 47:483–91.

14. For an excellent popular review of this theory, see Bennett, W., and J. Gurin. 1983. *The Dieter's Dilemma.* New York: Basic Books.

15. For a review of this data, and evidence for suppression of carbohydrate craving with serotonin agonists, see:

Wurtman, J. J., and R. J. Wurtman. 1979. Drugs that enhance central serotonergic transmission diminish elective carbohydrate consumption by rats. *Life Science* 24:895–904.

Wurtman, J. J., R. J. Wurtman, J. H. Growdon, et al. 1981. Carbohydrate craving in obese people: Suppression by treatments affecting serotonergic transmission. *International Journal of Eating Disorders* 1:12–15.

16. Some of the early endocrinological studies of anorexia nervosa and of medical syndromes involving weight loss are as follows:

Simmonds, M. 1914. Über Hypophysisschwund mit tödlichem Ausgang. *Deutsche Medizinische Wochenschrift* 40:322–23.

Schur, M., and C. V. Medvei. 1937. Uber Hypophysenvorderlappeninsuffizienz. *Weiner Archiv für Innerermedizin* 31:67–98.

Bliss, E. L., and C. J. Migeon. 1957. Endocrinology of anorexia nervosa. *Journal of Endocrinology and Metabolism* 17:766–76.

17. Recent studies assessing the role of hypothalamic dysfunction in the eating disorders are:

Boyar, R. M., L. D. Hellman, H. P. Roffwarg, et al. 1977. Cortisol secretion and metabolism in anorexia nervosa. *New England Journal of Medicine* 296:190–93.

Walsh, B. T. 1980. The endocrinology of anorexia nervosa. *Psychiatric Clinics of North America* 3:299–312.

Luck, P., and A. Wakeling. 1980. Altered thresholds for thermoregulatory sweating and vasodilatation in anorexia nervosa. *British Medical Journal* 281:906–908.

Walsh, B. T., J. L. Katz, J. Levin, et al. 1981. The production rate of cortisol declines during recovery from anorexia nervosa. *Journal of Clinical Endocrinology and Metabolism* 53:203–205.

Gerner, R. H., and H. E. Gwirtsman. 1981. Abnormalities of dexamethasone suppression test and urinary MHPG in anorexia nervosa. *American Journal of Psychiatry* 138:651–53.

Beaumont, P. J. V., and S. F. Abraham. 1981. Continuous infusion of luteinizing hormone releasing hormone (LHRH) in patients with anorexia nervosa. *Psychological Medicine* 11:477–84.

18. Hudson, J. I., P. S. Laffer, and H. G. Pope, Jr. 1982. Bulimia related to affective disorder by family history and response to the dexamethasone suppression test. *American Journal of Psychiatry* 139:695–98.

See also: Hudson, J. I., H. G. Pope, Jr., J. M. Jonas, et al. 1983. Hypothalamic-pituitary-adrenal axis hyperactivity in bulimia. *Psychiatry Research* 8:111–17.

19. Gwirtsman, H. E., P. Roy-Byrne, J. Yager, et al. 1983. Neuroendocrine abnormalities in bulimia. *American Journal of Psychiatry* 140:559–63.

The theory that bulimia might be a form of seizure disorder is presented in the following series of studies:

Green, R. S., and J. H. Rau. 1974. Treatment of compulsive eating disturbances with anticonvulsant medication. *American Journal of Psychiatry* 131:428–32.

Rau, J. H., and R. S. Green. 1975. Compulsive eating: A neuropsychologic approach to certain eating disorders. *Comprehensive Psychiatry* 16:223–31.

20. Green, R. S., and J. H. Rau. The use of diphenylhydantoin in compulsive eating disorder: Further studies. In *Anorexia Nervosa*. Edited by R. A. Vigersky. 1977. New York: Raven Press.

Rau, J. H., and R. S. Green. 1978. Soft neurological correlates of compulsive eating. *Journal of Nervous and Mental Disease* 166:435–37.

Rau, J. H., F. A. Struve, and R. S. Green. 1979. Electroencephalographic correlates of compulsive eating. *Clinical Electroencephalography* 10:180–88.

Moore, S. L., and S. M. Rakes. 1982. Binge eating—therapeutic response to diphenylhydantoin: Case report. *Journal of Clinical Psychiatry* 43:385–86.

21. Wermuth, B. M., K. L. Davis, L. E. Hollister, et al. 1977. Phenytoin treatment of the binge-eating syndrome. *American Journal of Psychiatry* 134:1249–53.

CHAPTER 6: BULIMIA AND MAJOR AFFECTIVE DISORDER

1. For a synopsis of some of the biological studies of major affective disorder, and evidence concerning specific chemical abnormalities in the brain, see the references under notes 13 and 14 in Chapter 4, and also:

Coppen, A. 1967. The biochemistry of affective disorders. *British Journal of Psychiatry* 113:1237–64.

Charney, D. S., D. B. Menkes, and G. R. Heninger. 1981. Receptor sensitivity and the mechanism of action of antidepressant treatment: Implications for the etiology and therapy of depression. *Archives of General Psychiatry* 38:1160–80.

2. Some studies of laboratory tests are as follows:

DEXAMETHASONE SUPPRESSION TEST

Schlesser, M. A., G. Winokur, and B. M. Sherman. 1980. Hypothalamic-pituitary-adrenal axis activity in depressive illness. *Archives of General Psychiatry* 37:737–43.

Carroll, B. J., M. Feinberg, J. F. Greden, et al. 1981. A specific laboratory test for the diagnosis of melancholia: Standardization, validation, and clinical utility. *Archives of General Psychiatry* 38:15–22.

Carroll, B. J. 1982. The dexamethasone suppression test for melancholia. *British Journal of Psychiatry* 140:292–304.

Targum, S. D., A. C. Sullivan, and S. M. Byrnes. 1982. Neuroendocrine interrelationships in major depressive disorder. *American Journal of Psychiatry* 139:282–86.

Amsterdam, J. D., A. Winokur, S. N. Caroff, et al. 1982. The dexamethasone suppression test in outpatients with primary affective disorder and healthy control subjects. *American Journal of Psychiatry* 139:287–91.

Rothschild, A. J., A. F. Schatzberg, A. H. Rosenbaum, et al. 1982. The dexamethasone suppression test as a discriminator among subtypes of psychotic patients. *British Journal of Psychiatry* 141:471–74.

Schatzberg, A. F., A. J. Rothschild, J. B. Stahl, et al. 1983. The dexamethasone suppression test: Identification of subtypes of depression. *American Journal of Psychiatry* 140:88–91.

Also see the study by Insel and colleagues cited in note 17, Chapter 4; and notes 17 and 18, Chapter 5.

See also the entire May 1983 issue of *Archives of General Psychiatry*, which contains many articles on this topic.

TRH STIMULATION TEST

Loosen, P. T., and A. J. Prange. 1980. Thyrotropin releasing hormone (TRH): A useful tool for psychoneuroendocrine investigation. *Psychoneuroendocrinology* 5:63–80.

Gold, M. S., A. L. C. Pottash, R. Ryan, et al. 1980. TRH-induced TSH response in unipolar, bipolar, and secondary depression: Possible utility in clinical assessment and differential diagnosis. *Psychoneuroendocrinology* 5:147–55.

Kirkegaard, C. 1981. The thyrotropin response to thyrotropin-releasing hormone in endogenous depression. *Psychoneuroendocrinology*, 6:189–212.

TYRAMINE EXCRETION STUDIES

Carter, S. M., M. A. Reveley, M. Sandler, et al. 1980. Decreased urinary output of conjugated tyramine is associated with lifetime vulnerability to depressive illness. *Psychiatry Research* 3:13–21.

Sandler, M., S. M. Carter, M. A. Reveley, et al. 1980. Further light on the tyramine test in depression. *Canadian Journal of Neurological Science* 7:265–66.

This may be a hot area of research in the next few years. Several other research groups have studies that will be forthcoming in the near future in various psychiatric journals.

STUDIES OF REM LATENCY

Kupfer, D. J., F. G. Foster, P. Coble, et al. 1978. The application of EEG sleep for the differential diagnosis of affective disorders. *American Journal of Psychiatry* 135:69–74.

Feinberg, M., J. C. Gillin, B. J. Carroll, et al. 1982. EEG studies of sleep in the diagnosis of depression. *Biological Psychiatry* 17:305–10.

3. Reviews and studies of the genetics of major affective disorder include the following:

Zerbin-Rüdin, E. Endogene Psychosen. In *Humangenetik, ein Kurzes Handbuck*. Vol. 2. Edited by P. E. Becker. 1967. Stuttgart, West Germany: Thieme. An exhaustive review of studies through the mid-1960s.

Slater, E., and V. Cowie. 1971. *The Genetics of Mental Disorders.* London: Oxford University Press. Similar to Zerbin-Rüdin, but in English.

Winokur, G., J. Morrison, J. Clancy, et al. 1972. The Iowa 500. II: A blind family history comparison of mania, depression, and schizophrenia. *Archives of General Psychiatry* 27:462–64.

Tsuang, M. T. Genetics of affective disorder. In *The Psychobiology of Depression.* Edited by J. Muendels. 1975. New York: Spectrum, pp. 85–100.

Johnson, G. F. S., and M. M. Leeman. 1977. Analysis of familial factors in bipolar affective illness. *Archives of General Psychiatry* 34:1074–83.

Baron, M., J. Klotz, J. Mendlewicz, et al. 1981. Multiple-threshold transmission of affective disorders. *Archives of General Psychiatry* 38:79–83.

Nurnberger, J. I., and E. S. Gershon. Genetics. In *Handbook of Affective Disorders.* Edited by E. S. Paykel. 1982. New York: Guilford Press, 126–45. The most up-to-date review available.

Gershon, E. S., J. Hamovit, J. J. Guroff, et al. 1982. A family study of schizoaffective, bipolar I, bipolar II, unipolar, and normal control probands. *Archives of General Psychiatry* 39:1157–67.

Weissman, M. M., K. K. Kidd, and B. A. Prusoff. In press. Variability in the rates of affective disorders in the relatives of severe and mild nonbipolar depressives and normals. *Archives of General Psychiatry*

4. Mendlewicz, J., and J. Rainer. 1977. Adoption study supporting genetic transmission in manic-depressive illness. *Nature* 268:327–29.

5. Some general references on medical treatment of major affective disorder are as follows:

Hollister, L. E. 1973. *Clinical Use of Psychotherapeutic Drugs.* Springfield, Ill.: Thomas.

Baldessarini, R. J. 1977. *Chemotherapy in Psychiatry.* Cambridge, Mass.: Harvard University Press.

Klein, D. F., R. Gittelman, F. Quitkin, et al. 1980. *Diagnosis and Drug Treatment of Psychiatric Disorders: Adults and Children.* 2d ed. Baltimore: Williams & Wilkins.

See also popular works such as *Moodswing; Depression: The Facts;* and *Mind, Mood, and Medicine: A Guide to the New Biological Psychiatry,* cited in the notes for Chapter 4.

Another popular book on drug treatment of major affective disorder is:

Kline, N. S. 1981. *From Sad to Glad.* New York: Ballantine Books.

For scientific reviews of antidepressant studies, see relevant chapters in the textbooks cited above as well as:

Glassman, A. H., J. M. Perel, M. Shostak, et al. 1977. Clinical implications of imipramine plasma levels for depressive illness. *Archives of General Psychiatry* 34:197–204.

Quitkin, F., A. Rifkin, and D. F. Klein. 1979. Monoamine oxidase inhibitors: A review of antidepressant effectiveness. *Archives of General Psychiatry* 36:749–60.

For articles on trazodone, see the special supplemental issue of the *Journal of Clinical Psychopharmacology*, Vol. 1. 1981.

Books and papers on lithium therapy include:

Johnson, F. N., ed. 1975. *Lithium and Therapy*. London: Academic Press.

Davis, J. M. 1976. Overview: Maintenance therapy in psychiatry. II: Affective disorders. *American Journal of Psychiatry* 133:1–13.

Goodwin, F. K., ed. 1976. The lithium ion. Impact on treatment and research. *Archives of General Psychiatry* 36:833–916.

Jefferson, J. W., and J. H. Greist. 1977. *Primer of Lithium Therapy*. Baltimore: Williams & Wilkins.

Studies of carbamazepine treatment of affective disorders are mostly quite recent:

Ballenger, J. C., and R. M. Post. 1980. Carbamazepine in manic-depressive illness: A new treatment. *American Journal of Psychiatry* 1317:782–90.

Okuma, T., K. Inanaga, S. Otsuki, et al. 1981. A preliminary double-blind study on the efficacy of carbamazepine in prophylaxis of manic-depressive illness. *Psychopharmacology* 73:95–96.

Lipinski, J. F., and H. G. Pope, Jr. 1982. Possible synergistic action between carbamazepine and lithium carbonate: A report of three cases. *American Journal of Psychiatry* 139:948–49.

6. Reviews of electroconvulsive therapy include:

Fink, J., S. S. Kety, J. McGaugh, et al., eds. 1974. *The Psychobiology of Convulsive Therapy*. Washington, D.C.: V. H. Winston & Sons.

Weiner, R. D. 1979. The psychiatric use of electrically induced seizures. *American Journal of Psychiatry* 136:1507–17.

7. Studies of lecithin and L-tryptophan include:

Cohen, B. M., A. L. Miller, J. F. Lipinski, et al. 1980. Lecithin in mania: A preliminary report. *American Journal of Psychiatry* 137:242–43.

Cohen, B. M., J. F. Lipinski, and R. I. Altesman. 1982. Lecithin in the treatment of mania: Double-blind, placebo-controlled trials. *American Journal of Psychiatry* 139:1162–64.

Cole, J. O., E. Hartmann, and P. Brigham. 1980. L-tryptophan: Clinical studies. *McLean Hospital Journal* 5:37–71.

Thomson, J., H. Rankin, G. W. Ashcroft, et al. 1982. The treatment of depression in general practice: A comparison of L-tryptophan, amitriptyline, and a combination of L-tryptophan and amitriptyline with placebo. *Psychological Medicine* 12:741–51.

8. On the use of different "validating indices" to test the validity of a psychiatric diagnosis, see the following examples:

Robins, E., and S. Guze. 1970. Establishment of diagnostic validity in psychiatric illness: Its application to schizophrenia. *American Journal of Psychiatry* 126:983–87.

Rosenthal, N. E., N. L. Rosenthal, F. Stallone, et al. 1980. Toward the validation of RDC schizoaffective disorder. *Archives of General Psychiatry* 37:804–10.

Fogelson, D. L., B. M. Cohen, and H. G. Pope, Jr. 1982. A study of the validity of *DSM*-III schizophreniform disorder. *American Journal of Psychiatry* 139:128–185.

Pope, H. G., Jr., J. M. Jonas, and B. Jones. 1982. Factitious psychosis: Phenomenology, family history, and long-term outcome of the nine cases. *American Journal of Psychiatry* 139:1480–83.

Pope, H. G., Jr., J. M. Jonas, J. I. Hudson, et al. 1983. Borderline personality disorder: A phenomenologic, family history, treatment response, and long-term follow-up study. *Archives of General Psychiatry* 40:23–30.

See also the studies by Pope and Lipinski (1978) and Pope et al. (1980), cited under note 14, Chapter 4.

9. Hudson, J. I., H. G. Pope, Jr., J. M. Jonas, et al. 1983. Phenomenologic relationship of eating disorders to major affective disorder. *Psychiatry Research* 9:345–54.

10. Herzog, D. A., and F. J. Osuna. 4 May 1983. Depression and eating disorders. Presented at the Annual Meeting, American Psychiatric Association.

11. Walsh, B. T., S. P. Roose, A. H. Glassman, et al. 4 May 1983. Depression and eating disorders. Presented at the Annual Meeting, American Psychiatric Association.

12. Pyle, R. L., J. E. Mitchell, and E. D. Eckert. 1981. Bulimia: A report of 34 cases. *Journal of Clinical Psychiatry* 42:60–64.

13. Russell, G. F. M. 1979. Bulimia nervosa: An ominous variant of anorexia nervosa. *Psychological Medicine* 9:429–48.

14. Nogami, Y., and F. Yabana. 1977. On kibarashi-gui (binge eating). *Folia Psychiatrica et Neurologica Japonica* 31:159–66.

15. Hudson, J. I., P. S. Laffer, and H. G. Pope, Jr. 1982. Bulimia related to affective disorder by family history and response to the dexamethasone suppression test. *American Journal of Psychiatry* 137:695–98.

16. Hudson, J. I., H. G. Pope, Jr., J. M. Jonas, et al. 1983. Family history study of anorexia nervosa and bulimia. *British Journal of Psychiatry* 142:133–38.

17. Cantwell, D. P., S. Sturzenberger, J. Burroughs, et al. 1977. Anorexia Nervosa: An affective disorder? *Archives of General Psychiatry* 34:1087–93.

18. Winokur, A., V. March, and J. Mendels. 1980. Primary affective disorder in relatives of patients with anorexia nervosa. *American Journal of Psychiatry* 137:695–98.

19. Gershon, E. S., J. R. Hamovit, J. L. Schreiber, et al. 2 May 1983. Affective and eating disorders in anorexic families. Presented at the Annual Meeting, American Psychiatric Association.

For an earlier report of this study see:

Gershon, E. S., J. R. Hamovit, J. L. Schreiber, et al. Anorexia nervosa and major affective disorders associated in families: A preliminary report. In *Childhood Psychopathology and Development*. Edited by S. B. Guze, F. J. Earls, and J. E. Barrett. 1983. New York: Raven Press, 279–86.

20. Strober, M. 4 May 1983. Familial depression in anorexia nervosa. Presented at the Annual Meeting, American Psychiatric Association.

21. Hudson, J. I., H. G. Pope, Jr., J. M. Jonas, et al. 1983. Hypothalamic-pituitary-adrenal axis hyperactivity in bulimia. *Psychiatry Research* 8:111–17.

22. Gwirtsman, H. E., P. Roy-Byrne, J. Yager, et al. 1983. Neuroendocrine abnormalities in bulimia. *American Journal of Psychiatry* 140:559–63.

CHAPTER 7: THE TREATMENT OF BULIMIA: PREVIOUS APPROACHES

1. Teuber, N. L., and E. Powers. 1953. Evaluating therapy in a delinquency prevention program. *Proceedings of the Association for Research in Nervous and Mental Disease* 31:138–47.

2. Strupp, H. H., and S. W. Hadley. 1979. Specific vs. nonspecific factors in psychotherapy: A controlled study of outcome. *Archives of General Psychiatry* 36:1125–36.

For further reading on psychotherapy, see:

American Psychiatric Association Commission on Psychotherapies 1982. *Psychotherapy Research: Methodological and Efficacy Issues.* Washington, D.C.: American Psychiatric Association.

3. For reports favoring the use of long-term psychoanalytic psychotherapy in anorexia nervosa or bulimia, see references in the notes for Chapter 5, as well as:

Deutsch, H. 1981. Anorexia nervosa. *Bulletin of the Menninger Clinic* 45:502–11. This describes a patient with both anorexia nervosa and bulimia.

Stunkard, A. J. 1976. *The Pain of Obesity*. Palo Alto, Cal.: Bull Press. Describes successful treatment with psychotherapy of bulimia associated with obesity.

4. Bruch, H. 1970. Psychotherapy in primary anorexia nervosa. *Journal of Nervous and Mental Disease* 150:51–67.

5. Rollins, N., and A. Blackwell. 1968. The treatment of anorexia nervosa in children and adolescents: Stage 1. *Journal of Child Psychology and Psychiatry* 9:81–91.

6. Frazier, S. H. 1965. Anorexia nervosa. *Diseases of the Nervous System* 26:155–59.

For reports on the course of anorexia nervosa using various forms of standard hospital and outpatient treatment, see the following two recent reviews:

Hsu, L. K. G. 1980. Outcome of anorexia nervosa: A review of the literature (1954 to 1978). *Archives of General Psychiatry* 37:1041–46. A detailed review of major studies that have followed patients at least two years.

Swift, W. J. 1982. The long-term outcome of early-onset anorexia nervosa: A critical review. *Journal of the American Academy of Child Psychiatry* 21:38–46.

For important individual studies, see Morgan and Russell; Hsu, Crisp, and Harding (both cited in note 6, Chapter 4); Cantwell, et al. (note 17, Chapter 6); as well as:

Sturzenberger, S., D. P. Cantwell, J. Burroughs, et al. 1977. A follow-up study of adolescent psychiatric inpatients with anorexia nervosa. I: The assessment of outcome. *Journal of the American Academy of Child Psychiatry* 16:703–15.

Bassøe, H. H., and I. Eskeland. 1982. A prospective study of 133 patients with anorexia nervosa: Treatment and outcome. *Acta Psychiatrica Scandinavica* 65:127–33.

Other reports on general hospital treatment of anorexia nervosa include (among many others):

Crisp, A. H. 1965. A treatment regime for anorexia nervosa. *British Journal of Psychiatry* 112:505–12.

Silverman, J. A. 1974. Anorexia nervosa: Clinical observations in a successful treatment plan. *Journal of Pediatrics* 84:68–73.

Lucas, A. R., J. W. Duncan, and V. Piens. 1976. The treatment of anorexia nervosa. *American Journal of Psychiatry* 133:1034–38.

Russell, G. F. M, 1981. The current treatment of anorexia nervosa. *British Journal of Psychiatry* 138:164–66.

Pierloot, R., W. Vandereycken, and S. Verhaest. 1982. An inpatient treatment program for anorexia nervosa patients. *Acta Psychiatrica Scandinavica* 66:1–8.

7. For a critical evaluation of treatment studies of anorexia nervosa from 1930 to 1980, see:

Agras, W. S., and H. Kraemer. Anorexia nervosa: Treatment and outcome. In *Eating and Its Disorders.* Edited by A. J. Stunkard and E. Stellar. 1983, in press. New York: Raven Press. The authors conclude that there has been *no* major advance in the treatment of anorexia nervosa in the past fifty years!

8. Reports of the family study by Minuchin and colleagues are as follows:

Liebman, R., S. Minuchin, and L. Baker. 1974. An integrated treatment program for anorexia nervosa. *American Journal of Psychiatry* 131:432–36.

Rosman, B. L., S. Minuchin, L. Baker, et al. A family approach to anorexia nervosa: Study, treatment, and outcome. In *Anorexia Nervosa.* Edited by R. A. Vigersky. 1977. New York: Raven Press, 341–48.

Minuchin, S., B. L. Rosman, and L. Baker. 1978. *Psychosomatic Families: Anorexia Nervosa in Context.* Cambridge, Mass.: Harvard University Press.

9. For reviews of behavior therapy in anorexia nervosa, see:

Stunkard, A. J. 1972. New therapies for the eating disorders: Behavior modification of obesity and anorexia nervosa. *Archives of General Psychiatry* 26:391–98.

Bhanji, S., and J. Thompson. 1974. Operant conditioning in the treatment of anorexia nervosa: A review and retrospective study of 11 cases. *British Journal of Psychiatry* 124:166–72.

10. Wulliemier, F., F. Rossel, and K. Sinclair. 1975. La thérapie comportementale de l'anorexie nervose. *Journal of Psychosomatic Research* 19:267–72.

11. Eckert, E. D., S. C. Goldberg, K. Λ. Halmi, et al. 1979. Behavior therapy in anorexia nervosa. *British Journal of Psychiatry* 134:55–59.

12. Pertschuk. M. J. Behavior therapy: Extended follow-up. In *Anorexia Nervosa.* Edited by R. A. Vigersky. 1977. New York: Raven Press, 305–14.

13. Garfinkel, P. E., H. Moldofsky, and D. M. Garner. The outcome of anorexia nervosa: Significance of clinical features, body image, and behavior modification. In *Anorexia Nervosa*. Edited by R. A. Vigersky. 1977. New York: Raven Press, 315–29.

14. Fairburn, C. G. 1981. A cognitive behavioural approach to the management of bulimia. *Psychological Medicine* 11:707–11.

15. For more on cognitive therapy techniques, see:

Beck, A. T. 1976. *Cognitive Therapy and the Emotional Disorders*. New York: International Universities Press.

Beck, A. T., A. J. Rush, B. F. Shaw, et al. 1979. *Cognitive Therapy of Depression*. New York: Guilford Press.

16. For a counterpoint on behavior therapy, see:

Bruch, H. 1974. Perils of behavior modification in treatment of anorexia nervosa. *Journal of the American Medical Association* 230: 1419–22.

17. Boskind-Lodahl, M., and W. C. White. Oct. 1978. The definition and treatment of bulimarexia in college women—a pilot study. *Journal of the American College Health Association* 27:85–86, a publication of the Helen Dwight Reid Educational Foundation.

18. White, W. C., and M. Boskind-White. 1981. An experiential-behavioral approach to the treatment of bulimarexia. *Psychotherapy: Theory, Research, and Practice* 4:501–507.

19. Lacey, J. H. 1983. Bulimia nervosa, binge eating, and psychogenic vomiting: A controlled treatment study and long-term outcome. *British Medical Journal* 286:1609–13.

20. Johnson, C. L., and M. C. Connors. 4 May 1983. Short-term group therapy of bulimia. Presented at the Annual Meeting, American Psychiatric Association.

21. Zubiate, T. N. 1970. Tratamiento de la anorexia nervosa con una associacion cyproheptadina-vitaminas. *Revista Médica de la Caja Nacional de Segura Social* 19:147–53.

22. Vigersky, R. A., and D. L. Loriaux. The effect of cyproheptadine in anorexia nervosa: A double-blind trial. In *Anorexia Nervosa*. Edited by R. A. Vigersky. 1977. New York: Raven Press, 349–56.

23. Goldberg, S. C., K. A. Halmi, E. D. Eckert, et al. 1979. Cyproheptadine in anorexia nervosa. *British Journal of Psychiatry* 134:67–70.

24. Halmi, K. A. 1982. Cyproheptadine for anorexia nervosa. *Lancet* 1:1357–58.

25. Halmi, K. A., E. D. Eckert, and J. R. Falk. 1983. Cyproheptadine,

an antidepressant and weight-inducing drug for anorexia nervosa. *Psychopharmacology Bulletin* 19:103–105.

26. Eckert, E. D., K. A. Halmi, and J. R. Falk. 4 May 1983. A new antidepressant for anorexia nervosa. Presented at the Annual Meeting, American Psychiatric Association.

27. Gross, H., M. H. Ebert, V. B. Faden, et al. 1983. A double-blind trial of Δ^9-tetrahydrocannabinol in primary anorexia nervosa. *Journal of Clinical Psychopharmacology* 3:165–71.

28. For studies of chlorpromazine in anorexia nervosa, see:

Dally, P. J., and W. Sargant. 1960. A new treatment of anorexia nervosa. *British Medical Journal* 1:1770–71.
Crisp, A. H. 1965. A treatment regime for anorexia nervosa. *British Journal of Psychiatry* 112:505–12.

See also the book by Dally and Gomez, cited under note 6, Chapter 4.

29. Vandereycken, W., and R. Pierloot. 1982. Pimozide combined with behavior therapy in the short-term treatment of anorexia nervosa: A double-blind placebo-controlled cross-over study. *Acta Psychiatrica Scandinavica* 60:446–51.

30. Moore, R., I. H. Mills, and A. Forster. 1981. Naloxone in the treatment of anorexia nervosa: Effect on weight gain and lipolysis. *Journal of the Royal Society of Medicine* 74:129–31.

31. Uncontrolled studies of antidepressants in anorexia nervosa include:

Mills, I. H. 1973. Endocrine and social factors in self-starvation amenorrhea. Royal College of Physicians of Edinburgh Publication No. 42.
Needleman, H. L., and D. Waber. 1976. Amitriptyline therapy in patients with anorexia nervosa. *Lancet* 2:580.
Mills, I. H. 1976. Amitriptyline therapy in anorexia nervosa. *Lancet* 2:687.
Moore, D. C. 1977. Amitriptyline therapy in anorexia nervosa. *American Journal of Psychiatry* 134:1303–04.
Needleman, H. L., and D. Waber. Amitriptyline in anorexia nervosa. In *Anorexia Nervosa.* Edited by R. A. Vigersky. 1977. New York: Raven Press, 357–62.
White, J. H., and N. L. Schnaultz. 1977. Successful treatment of anorexia nervosa with imipramine. *Diseases of the Nervous System* 38:567–68. One of the few antidepressant studies in anorexia nervosa that used adequate doses of a tricyclic.
Reilly, P. P. 1977. Anorexia nervosa. *Rhode Island Medical Journal* 60:419–22.

Katz, J. L., and B. T. Walsh. 1978. Depression in anorexia nervosa. *American Journal of Psychiatry* 135:507.

Kendler, K. S. 1978. Amitriptyline-induced obesity in anorexia nervosa: A case report. *American Journal of Psychiatry* 135:1107–08.

Hudson, J. I., H. G. Pope, Jr., J. M. Jonas, et al. 1983, submitted for publication. Treatment of anorexia nervosa with antidepressants.

There are also two studies of shock therapy in anorexia nervosa:

Laboucarié, J., and P. Barres. 1954. Les aspects cliniques et thérapeutiques de l'anorexie mentale. *L'Evolution Psychiatrique* 1:119.

Bernstein, I. C. 1964. Anorexia nervosa treated successfully with electroshock therapy and subsequently followed by pregnancy. *American Journal of Psychiatry* 120:1023–24.

32. Lacey, J. H., and A. H. Crisp. 1980. Hunger, food intake and weight: The impact of clomipramine on a refeeding anorexia nervosa population. *Postgraduate Medical Journal* 56:79–85.

33. Barcai, A. 1977. Lithium in adult anorexia nervosa. *Acta Psychiatrica Scandinavica* 55:97–101.

34. Gross, H. A., M. H. Ebert, V. B. Faden, et al. 1981. A double-blind controlled trial of lithium carbonate in anorexia nervosa. *Journal of Clinical Psychopharmacology* 1:376–81.

35. Cherry Boone O'Neill *Starving for Attention.* © 1982 by the author. Used by permission of The Continuum Publishing Company.

36. For the phenytoin studies, see note 19, Chapter 5.

CHAPTER 8: ANTIDEPRESSANTS: AN EFFECTIVE NEW TREATMENT

1. Moore, D. C. 1977. Amitriptyline therapy in anorexia nervosa. *American Journal of Psychiatry* 134 (11):1303–04. © 1977 American Psychiatric Association.

2. Rich, C. L. 1978. Self-induced vomiting: Psychiatric considerations. *Journal of the American Medical Association* 239:2688–89.

3. Shader, R. I., and D. J. Greenblatt. 1982. The psychiatrist as mind sweeper. *Journal of Clinical Psychopharmacology* 2:233–34.

4. Pope, H. G., Jr., and J. I. Hudson. 1982. Treatment of bulimia with antidepressants. *Psychopharmacology* 78:167–79.

5. Walsh, B. T., J. Stewart, L. Wright, et al. 1982. Treatment of bulimia with monoamine oxidase inhibitors. *American Journal of Psychiatry* 139:1629–30.

6. Glassman, A. H., and B. T. Walsh. 1983. Link between bulimia and depression unclear. *Journal of Clinical Psychopharmacology* 3:203.

7. Walsh, B. T., J. W. Stewart, L. Wright, et al. 2 May 1983. Treatment of bulimia with monoamine oxidase inhibitors. Presented at the Annual Meeting, American Psychiatric Association.

8. Jonas, J. M., H. G. Pope, Jr., and J. I. Hudson. 1983. Treatment of bulimia with MAO inhibitors. *Journal of Clinical Psychopharmacology* 3:59–60.

9. Mendels, J. 1983. Eating disorders and antidepressants. *Journal of Clinical Psychopharmacology* 3:59.

10. Roy-Byrne, P., H. Gwirtsman, C. K. Edelstein, et al. 1983. Eating disorders and antidepressants. *Journal of Clinical Psychopharmacology* 3:60–61.

11. Sabine, E. J., A. Yonace, A. J. Farrington, et al. 1983. Bulimia nervosa: A placebo-controlled therapeutic trial of mianserin. *British Journal of Clinical Pharmacology* 15:195S–202S.

12. McGrath, P. J., F. M. Quitkin, J. W. Stewart, et al. 1981. An open clinical trial of mianserin. *American Journal of Psychiatry* 138:530–32.

13. Pope, H. G., Jr., J. I. Hudson, J. M. Jonas, et al. 1983. Bulimia treated with imipramine: A placebo-controlled double-blind study. *American Journal of Psychiatry* 140:554–58.

14. Pope, H. G. Jr., J. I. Hudson, and J. M. Jonas. 1983. Antidepressant treatment for bulimia: Preliminary experience and practical recommendations. *Journal of Clinical Psychopharmacology* 3:274–81.

CHAPTER 9: HOW TO GET GOOD TREATMENT

1. For information on the drugs used to treat bulimia, see any of the references listed for drug treatment of major affective disorder in the notes for Chapter 6. Particularly useful to the lay reader are the books by Hollister and Baldessarini.

Unless you are well trained in medicine, be very cautious in reading and interpreting the *Physician's Desk Reference* (Oradell, N. J.: Medical Economics, 1983). This volume has legal aspects as well as scientific ones; hence the information it provides about side effects, precautions, and other problems with drugs may not correspond to actual clinical usage of the drug. If in doubt about this, look up any drug you have used recently—antibiotic, sedative, whatever—and you will probably find a long list of all manner of dangerous side effects.

2. For more detailed information and further reference on plasma levels of antidepressants and other practical issues, see the article by Pope et al., Antidepressant treatment of bulimia: Preliminary experience and practical recommendations, cited in note 14, Chapter 8.

CHAPTER 10: THE TWENTY MOST-ASKED QUESTIONS

1. For this study, see reference 11 in Chapter 2.

2. For studies of the compatibility of psychotherapy and pharmacotherapy, see:

Weissman, M. M. 1979. The psychological treatment of depression: Evidence for the efficacy of psychotherapy alone, in comparison with, and in combination with, pharmacotherapy. *Archives of General Psychiatry* 36:1261–1269.

Rounsaville, B. J., G. L. Klerman, and M. M. Weissman. 1981. Do psychotherapy and pharmacotherapy for depression conflict? *Archives of General Psychiatry* 38:24–29.

1985 UPDATES

The controlled study of family members cited in the 1985 update to Chapter 5 is:

Garfinkel, P. E., D. M. Garner, J. Rose, P. L. Darby, O. S. Brandes, J. O'Hanlon, and N. Walsh. 1983. A comparison of characteristics in the families of patients with anorexia nervosa and normal controls. *Psychological Medicine* 13:821–28.

The new controlled study of psychotherapy in anorexia nervosa cited in Chapter 7 is:

Crisp, A. H., and A. Hall. Brief psychotherapy in the treatment of anorexia nervosa: Preliminary findings. In *Anorexia Nervosa: Recent Developments.* Edited by P. L. Darby, P. E. Garfinkel, D. M. Garner, and D. V. Coscina. 1983. New York: Alan R. Liss, Inc., pp. 427–39.

The three new placebo-controlled double-blind studies of antidepressants in bulimia cited in the 1985 update in Chapter 8 are:

Walsh, B. T., J. W. Stewart, S. P. Roose, M. Gladis, and A. M. Glassman. 1984, in press. Treatment of bulimia with phenelzine: A double-blind placebo-controlled study. *Archives of General Psychiatry.*

Hughes, P. L., L. A. Wells, and C. J. Cunningham. 9 May, 1984. Controlled trial using desipramine for bulimia. Presented at the Annual Meeting, American Psychiatric Association, Los Angeles.

Mitchell, J. E., and R. Groat, 1984. A placebo-controlled double-blind trial of amitriptyline in bulimia. *Journal of Clinical Psychopharmacology* 4:186–93.

The summary of group therapy studies described in the update to Chapter 9 is:

Pyle, R. L. 10 May, 1984. Psychotherapy for bulimia: The role of groups. Presented at the Annual Meeting, American Psychiatric Association, Los Angeles.

The uncontrolled Massachusetts General Hospital study is Brotman, A. W., D. B. Herzog, and S. W. Woods. 1984. Antidepressant treatment of bulimia: The relationship between bingeing and depressive symptomatology. *Journal of Clinical Psychiatry* 45:7–9.

Pope, H. G., Jr., J. I. Hudson, J. M. Jonas, D. Yurgelun-Todd. 10 May 1984. Antidepressant treatment of bulimia: A research update, presented at the Annual Meeting, American Psychiatric Association.

SELF-HELP GROUPS FOR EATING DISORDERS

The following list includes both self-help organizations and medical centers that have self-help groups associated with them. We have chosen twelve organizations which we know and can specifically recommend. However, there are many other excellent organizations; a more complete list may be obtained from the National Anorexic Aid Society, P.O. Box 29461, Columbus, OH 43229 (tel.: 614-895-2009). The list is updated every January and July.

These organizations all offer support groups, but usually cannot provide a psychopharmacologist. For details on locating a psychopharmacologist, see Chapter 9.

EAST

Massachusetts
The Anorexia Nervosa Aid Society of Massachusetts, P.O. Box 213, Lincoln Center, MA 01773; contact Patricia Warner at (617) 259-9767.

New York
Group Treatment Program/Center for the Study of Anorexia & Bulimia, 1 West 91st St., New York, NY 10024; contact Dr. William Davis at (212) 595-3449.

New Jersey
American Anorexia/Bulimia Association, Inc., 133 Cedar Lane, Teaneck, NJ 07666; contact Estelle Miller, M.S.W. at (201) 836-1800.

Pennsylvania

American Anorexia Bulimia Association of Philadelphia: Philadelphia Child Guidance Clinic, 34th and Civic Center Blvd., Philadelphia, PA 19104; contact Elizabeth Chace at (215) 387-1919.

Maryland

Maryland Association for Anorexia Nervosa and Bulimia, Inc., 222 Gateswood Road, Lutherville, MD 21093; contact Ann Boyer at (301) 252-7407.

Florida

Mental Health Association of Broward Co., 2312 South Andrews Ave., Fort Lauderdale, FL 33316; contact Barbara Good, executive director at (305) 467-7766.

MIDWEST

Ohio

The Bridge/National Anorexic Aid Society, 4897 Karl Road, Columbus, OH 43229; contact Paula Butterfield, Ph.D. or Leah Melick at (614) 895-2009.

Illinois

National Association of Anorexia Nervosa and Associated Eating Disorders (ANAD), P.O. Box 271, Northfield, IL 60035; contact Vivian Meehan at (312) 831-3438.

Missouri

Bulimia, Anorexia, Self-Help (BASH), Suite 206, 522 N. Ballas Road, St. Louis, MO 63141; contact Felix E. Larocca, M.D., at (314) 567-4080.

WEST

California

UCLA Neuropsychiatric Institute, 760 Westwood Plaza, Los Angeles, CA 90024; contact Karen Lee-Benner, RN, MSN at (213) 825-0173.

Oregon

Anorexia Nervosa and Related Eating Disorders, P.O. Box 5102, Eugene, OR 97405; contact Dr. Jean Rubel at (503) 344-1144.

ENGLAND

The Priory Centre, 11 Priory Road, High Wycombe, Bucks, England; contact Maureen Schiller, Secretary, telephone High Wycombe 21431.

Index

A., Ms., 144
adoptees, manic-depressive illness
    studied in, 94
age, incidence of bulimia and, 34–36,
    75, 191
agoraphobia, 59, 64
    of Nadia, 70
alcohol abuse, 47, 48, 57–58, 64
    as analogous to bulimia, 57–58
alkalosis, 26
American Psychiatric Association:
    bulimia formally recognized by,
        10–11
    group therapy study presented be-
        fore, 132, 184
amitriptyline, 140
ankylosing spondylitis, 39
anorexia nervosa, 48, 49–52, 64
    antidepressants and symptoms of,
        196–197
    bulimic individuals' experience of,
        18
    common progression from depres-
        sion to bulimia and, 51
    in *DMS-III* criteria for bulimia, 11
    ego-syntonic character of, 49
    electrolyte imbalances due to, 26–27
    kleptomania and, 61
    recovery rate for, 36
    see also specific studies and medications
amitriptyline, 161
Anorexia Nervosa Aid Society, 146,
    154–155
anticonvulsants, 86–87, 95–97
antidepressant drugs, 95–97,
    104–106, 133, 134–135, 139–162
    anorexic symptoms and, 196–197
    bulimic patients' response to (chart),
        141
    choice of, for treatment, 165–175
    failure of, 177–178
    misconceptions about, 175–177

Pope and Hudson's first study of,
    140–142
Pope and Hudson's study of im-
    ipramine and, 146–162
as recommended treatment,
    163–164
antipsychotic drugs, 95–97, 106,
    133–134, 195–196
    side effects of, 196
anxiety disorders, 64
    agoraphobia, 59, 64, 70
    grooves in thinking and avoidance
        of, 21
    obsessive-compulsive, 48, 60–61, 64
    panic, 20, 48, 58–59, 82, 84
appetite-stimulating drugs, 133
arrhythmia, 27

Barcai, A., 135
behavioral theories, 75–76, 81–82
    therapy based on, 122–126,
        179–180
Bernard, Claude, 26
binge eating, 2–4
    average calories consumed in, 14
    compulsive, automatic character of,
        14–18
    daily cycles of, 13
    in *DSM-III* criteria for bulimia,
        11–13
    duration of period of, 14
    evening as common time for, 13
    expense of, 14–15
    hunger vs. urge to, 84
    inconspicuous, 11
    medical complications caused by, 25,
        28–29
    normal vs. abnormal, 14
    relapses of, 17
    spontaneous recovery and, 115–116
    termination of, 11, 14, 115–116
    without use of laxatives, 185–186

suicide attempts *(cont.)*
  frequency of, 23–24
  successful but unexplained, 23
Susan, 12–13
Sweden, incidence of bulimia in, 187
sympathomimetic agents, 95

tardive dyskinesia, 133–134
teeth, corrosion of enamel on, 25
temper outbursts, 63–64
tetrahydrocannabinol, 133
theft:
  of food, 14–15
  kleptomania, 61–64
Thorazine (chlorpromazine), 133–134
thyrotropin releasing hormone stimulation test, 90, 103–104
Traité de l'Hystérie (Briquet), 68
tranquilizers, 5, 95–97, 106, 195–196
tranylcypromine, 105–106, 156, 172–175
  side effects of, 174–175
trazodone, 95, 105–106, 165–166
treatment:
  evaluating studies of, 114–119
  of major affective disorder, 95–97
  spontaneous improvement in, 115–116
  see also antidepressant drugs; *specific medications*
tricyclic antidepressants, 95, 134–135, 165–172
  blood levels of, 169–172
  side effects of, 167–168
tyramine, urinary excretion of, 90

University of Minnesota, antidepressants studied at, 161

urinary infections, 26
uterus, theory of wandering, 68

Valium (diazepam), 96
Vernon, Sally, 47
vitamin deficiencies, 28, 188
voluntary control mechanism, breakdown of, 63–64, 65–66
vomiting, self-induced, 4, 25–27
  binge eating without, 185–186
  discovery of usefulness of, 22
  in history, 10, 68
  medical complications caused by, 23, 25–27
  tooth enamel eroded by, 4–5

Waller, John, 76–77
Walsh, Timothy, 53, 142–144, 160
water pills, *see* diuretics, use of
weight fluctuations, 18–19
  DMS-III criteria for bulimia, 11
Weissman, Myrna, 47
West, Ellen, 71–75
  family tree of, 73, 75
  suicide attempts of, 72, 74
White, William, 82–83
  therapy developed by, 126–129
Whytt, Robert, 68
women, bulimic:
  hysteria diagnosed in (pre-1900), 68–69
  prevalence of, 33, 34–36, 38, 192–193
women, physical attractiveness expected of, 75–76, 82–85, 189

Yager, Joel, 79

About the Authors

DR. HARRISON G. POPE, JR., is Assistant Professor of Psychiatry at Harvard Medical School and Assistant Psychiatrist at McLean Hospital in Belmont, Massachusetts. He has written numerous articles on bulimia, anorexia nervosa, and other topics in psychiatry. He is also the author of *Voices from the Drug Culture* and *The Road East*. Dr. Pope was selected for inclusion in the *1984 Esquire Register of Outstanding Americans Under Age 40*.

DR. JAMES HUDSON is instructor in Psychiatry at Harvard Medical School and Assistant Psychiatrist at McLean Hospital. He is currently engaged in full-time research and teaching on the subject of eating disorders, and is the author of numerous publications in this and related fields.